A Place Calle

A Place Called District 12

Appalachian Geography and Music in The Hunger Games

THOMAS W. PARADIS

McFarland & Company, Inc., Publishers

Jefferson, North Carolina

ISBN (print) 978-1-4766-8728-5
ISBN (ebook) 978-1-4766-4573-5

Library of Congress and British Library
cataloguing data are available

Library of Congress Control Number 2021061109

Front cover image © 2022 Panacea Doll/Shutterstock

Printed in the United States of America

*McFarland & Company, Inc., Publishers
Box 611, Jefferson, North Carolina 28640
www.mcfarlandpub.com*

Table of Contents

Acknowledgments

In a similar spirit to Katniss' own debts that she knows can never be repaid, a substantial debt of gratitude is owed to numerous individuals for helping to improve the quality of this manuscript. I particularly wish to give a big "Effie-sized" thank-you to Sally Childs-Helton, Valerie Estelle Frankel, Antwain K. Hunter, Marianne October Nielsen, and Jacki Lynn Wallace-Tatsch for their genuine enthusiasm for this project, and especially for devoting precious time to review earlier drafts. A similar round of appreciation is generally owed to my colleagues at Butler University who endorsed my *Unpacking the Hunger Games* course and collectively provided an appropriate venue for such a thing within Butler's Core Curriculum. And certainly a full-year course devoted to a work of dystopian fiction would not succeed without the curious students who take the plunge to enroll. The only thing more rewarding than watching their academic skills improve is enjoying their ongoing intrigue for Collins' stories and multi-layered meanings. Thank you to all of my students for sharing this ongoing journey with me.

This work is further indebted to the tremendous body of literature that precedes it. Numerous academic scholars, journalists, and local authors have devoted incalculable energy to share their research, knowledge, and perspectives on both Collins' fictitious world and that of our own. Their collective work is thus recognized not only within my own narrative but within the Chapter Notes and Bibliography which can be consulted for further learning opportunities. I am pleased and humbled to showcase their efforts by providing one more outlet to share their knowledge and insights.

I further wish to recognize all the unnamed individuals at McFarland who first expressed enthusiasm for publishing this type of book, and later for their unparalleled editing skills, collaborative spirit, and genuine effort to improve the quality of this work far beyond what I could have delivered on my own.

And my expression of gratitude would be most incomplete without a shout-out to Linda, my wife, partner, and best friend who has remained enthusiastically involved with this project from its inception. Her creative thinking, periodic reviews of earlier drafts, and stimulating conversations around Collins' novels and my own writing have contributed immeasurably to the final creation. With her endless curiosity and desire to learn about our world, I remain convinced that she is the true geographer here.

Preface

My own rewarding journey involving the Hunger Games saga began rather accidentally on an international flight to teach abroad in 2012. I had hesitantly decided to watch "The Hunger Games" while competing with jet engine noise and related onboard distractions. I gleaned enough of the story, however, for the tale to capture my attention. I am a human geographer, and my mind was naturally making connections between my own academic background and the story of an unlikely heroine surviving the 74th Games.

When I discovered the novels later, my continued intrigue with the series led me to collaborate with faculty and staff colleagues on an interdisciplinary student conference at Northern Arizona University in November 2013. This was probably amidst the peak of YA interest in the series, also in the midst of the annual film rollouts. Held strategically around the release of "Catching Fire," student attendance soared well beyond expectations at some 35 concurrent sessions, an all-day poster and video venue dubbed the "Apocalypse Room" by a co-organizer, and various speaker and panel events over two days. We had clearly struck a chord by interpreting a work of popular fiction through a wide array of disciplinary perspectives. I remain convinced that we left no proverbial stone unturned from the breadth of social sciences and humanities disciplines.

It is only now, some eight years later, that I have mustered the self-initiative to write a volume that considers some of the more significant geographic underpinnings of the Hunger Games. My decision to do so came rather effortlessly following the latest surprise from Suzanne Collins during autumn 2019. The unexpected news of a new Hunger Games book in the making simply left my mouth hanging open. Even more shocking, it turns out, was the unforeseen direction of the novel's story line. *The Ballad of Songbirds and Snakes* not only featured the early developmental process of the Games themselves, but essentially invited us to dive back into District 12 and its Appalachian roots. For me, this happily meant even more geographical context to consider and more clues and "breadcrumbs" to decipher.

While many fans and critics alike have dwelt on Collins' choice to feature a younger Coriolanus Snow—with not a little controversy surrounding the book's release—I was admittedly distracted by other matters of the story. For starters, Panem citizens still enjoyed some measure of freedom to move about their country, and no fence had yet been constructed around District 12. Moreover, people still traveled long distance by rather conventional railroad trains! And it became even more evident that the home of Katniss Everdeen and Lucy Gray Baird was not really a "district" at all but was more accurately a small Appalachian mining town complete with a fairly typical American public square. Perhaps most amusing, the Hob had become a hub for local entertainment, featuring the Covey's clear imitation of a traditional bluegrass band. The Covey's repertoire would appropriately provide a veritable highlights reel of Appalachian music from colonial times through the mid-twentieth century. Indeed, white liquor was not the only thing flowing freely within *The Ballad's* story line; so too was Collins' unhindered borrowing of Appalachian culture, music, history, and geographical characteristics. The result was the production of a distinct and recognizable sense of place for a "District 12," the name of which remained paradoxically anonymous. And in any case, just how did Tam Amber get a hold of an A-style mandolin?

This was all too much for me to ignore during the Covid-plagued summer of 2020. It was almost as if Collins' latest prequel was imploring me to finally write my own geographical interpretation of the saga. As presented herein, much of my attention would ultimately focus on a place called District 12, though its spatial connections with the Capitol and within Panem as a whole would come into play as well. What largely informs Collins' own creative if disturbing world of Panem is a solid foundation of actual geography, history, and Appalachian ways of life. I aim to bring at least some of this underlying foundation to light in the chapters that follow.

In addition to Collins' latest prequel, a second factor was equally motivational to undertake this project—that of a university course I now teach at Butler University in Indianapolis. The First-Year Seminar (FYS) is a two-semester course required of all incoming students, aimed at developing foundational skills of academic writing, oral communication, critical thinking, and introductory research methods. This skills-based, experiential learning approach is enveloped within a set of unique themes or topics chosen by the faculty members who teach it. It should come as little surprise, then, that my own FYS course is titled *Unpacking the Hunger Games*.

While this topic continues to attract its share of curious students, this does not necessarily mean they arrive as Hunger Games "super fans." At first I really wasn't sure who would show up, or for what reasons. It turns out that most of my students have not yet read all three of the original novels, and many remember little from the stories. A larger percentage admit to having seen one or more of the films, though they often recall little from those as well. It is the rare incoming student who—during my ice-breaker trivia quiz—recalls how Katniss really acquired her gold mockingjay pin, or knows the English translation of the Latin "Panem." And based on further informal polling, my students generally recall having encountered the trilogy first in middle school—basically half a lifetime ago for them.

Thus, never mind the multi-layered allegorical meanings within the series, or Collins' references to the American Revolution, or its associations with the Roman Empire. These students have rarely formed opinions on the timeless "Team Peeta or Team Gale" question! But that's perfectly fine with me, because it's fun to begin from scratch and to watch them explore this new realm. The reality, however, is that we are now looking to the series almost as historical literature in itself.

During fall semester, my students read all three novels from the original trilogy, with each novel separated by three or four weeks to consider each in turn. I space the books apart to enable a deeper dive, supplemented with additional research and reading assignments on various topics. They also watch and interpret each respective film—now in teams on their own time—prior to moving onward to the next novel (though I tend to relegate "Mockingjay, Part 2" to the holidays if they wish). More humorously, some students express concern with spoilers, not wanting others to divulge the conclusion of *Mockingjay* prior to the end of the semester. I cannot promise this, of course, given that readers or viewers have known for some time how it all ends in the Capitol (and back in District 12). Even so, students seem to remain satisfied with enough surprises that do not manage to leak out in advance. We thus end the first semester quite appropriately with considering various perspectives and personal views on how Collins closes off the series at the end of *Mockingjay*. And yes, we have now come "full circle" to dealing once again with the issue of spoilers!

During spring semester, I now allocate three weeks for *The Ballad of Songbirds and Snakes*, for each of its three parts in turn. This naturally leads into our focus on Appalachian culture, coal mining, music history, and related geographical topics. Students are asked to apply relevant spatial concepts to better understand the geography from which Collins draws— intentionally or otherwise. Namely, we explore concepts of place attachment, culture hearths, migration diffusion, the First Law of Geography, friction of distance, world systems theory, core-periphery relationships, uneven economic development, the boom-bust cycles of extractive industries, and community roles of public and contested spaces (the District 12 square comes to mind).

It follows that one primary goal here is to pull together these and related topics for a broader audience. I have done my utmost best to provide a balanced approach with my writing style, hopefully avoiding too much unwarranted scholarly jargon while still introducing various relevant concepts. I do hope this approach provides for an accessible and engaging book that would be of interest to any readers curious to learn more about this fascinating saga. In that spirit I intend this book to be of value in other courses and classrooms beyond my own.

While this book incorporates and interprets all three productions of the Hunger Games saga—that is, the original trilogy, the four films, and now the recent prequel—this also means that I cannot possibly treat any of them in a comprehensive way. Rather, I highlight specific scenes, dialogue, or plot points from one or more of these productions to demonstrate various real-world or academic connections. I thus offer this material as an invitation for further exploration on any of these introductory topics. This is an approach I regularly take with my own students in the hope of instilling the notion that we are all life-long learners.

Perhaps most important to keep in mind, this is an interpretive and sometimes creative exercise involving a work of fiction. Unless Suzanne Collins has publicly divulged her own intentions, sources, or meanings, it is ultimately left to her readers—scholars or otherwise—to speculate on such matters. On the fun side, there is seemingly endless fodder to decipher from her clues, breadcrumbs, and subtle descriptions of characters and places. For this reason, I clarify when my own interpretation is basically an educated guess, a personal interpretation, or an academic concept supported by previous scholarship.

Other associations or clues from Collins are more reliable, such as the likely geographical inspiration for the Corso, or the music genre represented by the Covey's performance style. For more scholarly information, I have carefully provided notes for every referenced source, also to encourage further exploration of various topics I may have glazed over.

Finally, it is my hope that readers here will take away a stronger appreciation for, and knowledge of, the often-overlooked geographical contexts in which we all live. Through the creation of her own dystopian world of Panem, Collins provides a window through which we might learn more about ourselves, our society, and our collective history and geography. Aside from the endless fun of unpacking Collins' prose, perhaps highlighting some of these less popularized contexts of our own world will prove to be this book's most significant contribution.

Author's Note on Styles

To differentiate film productions from novels or other books, quotations are placed around the names of films (e.g., "The Hunger Games") while book titles are in italics (e.g., *Catching Fire*). Quotations are also used for song titles. Further, the following abbreviations are used to cite specific references to the four Hunger Games novels throughout the narrative:

THG—*The Hunger Games*
CF—*Catching Fire*
MJ—*Mockingjay*
BSS—*The Ballad of Songbirds and Snakes*

Introduction

A Geographer's Eyes

Underlying the dystopian story of Suzanne Collins' *The Hunger Games* is a veritable cornucopia of authentic Appalachian—and American—geography, culture, and history. This book aims to showcase and bring to light some relevant aspects of this real-world context that has so profoundly informed the fictional realms of Panem and District 12. Though easy to overlook within the novels, Katniss provides a continuous litany of subtle commentary about her home, her past, and her observations of District 12 and Panem. Indeed, her sense of identity, attachment to home, and outdoor education through her father's tutelage depend quite heavily upon these largely geographical circumstances.

Now with her more recent prequel, *The Ballad of Songbirds and Snakes*, Collins digs even deeper (pun intended) into Appalachia's authentic cultural heritage to highlight the full gamut of music styles long associated with the mountains. Her intentional—if unspoken—sampling of Appalachian music history only enhances our own sense of place for District 12, along with our appreciation for central Appalachia's extraordinary cultural diversity and natural environments.

Moreover, the novel's very title and story creatively mimic a *ballad* of its own—that is, a song that tells a clear story with distinct characters. This particular ballad features a central protagonist in Lucy Gray Baird, whose extended Covey family lives and performs as an archetypal bluegrass band. With this rather unforeseen turn of events, it is almost as if Collins intended for her focus on young Coriolanus Snow and the chaotic 10th Games to play "second fiddle" to a more nuanced backstory of District 12. Within Part 3 of the prequel, Collins essentially goes "full Appalachia" and takes us back into the intricate community life found within this rural mining town. In this way, her prequel provides a veritable invitation to become more acquainted with the actual historical geography and musical traditions comprising this mountain region.

Despite more than six decades that separate them, Lucy Gray and Katniss share the same antagonist, or foil, in the form of Coriolanus Snow—albeit at opposite ends of his villainous life. Interpreting the story as a ballad of its own, readers find that "songbirds" can directly signify Lucy Gray and the Covey, along with the melodious mockingjay bird itself. As for the "snakes," they make literal appearances as slithering reptiles at key points within the plot, while also connoting the novel's rising villain himself.

It turns out that the prequel provides a variety of subjects—or motifs—that were likewise common to traditional Appalachian ballads. As Elizabeth Hardy explains, Collins embeds topics of "star-crossed love, a mystery ending, rose imagery, whiteness and snow, burning hot weather, furious storms, treachery, hidden murders and secret crimes, and dramatic tragedy," all of which are found within the ballad song tradition identified closely with the central Appalachians.[1]

With these things in mind, the book herein essentially provides a geographical backstory of its own. Now with the recent prequel in hand, it is even more possible to interpret and consider the interplay and connections between this latest novel, the original trilogy, and the trilogy's feature films. In particular, the chapters that follow explore the cultural landscapes and historical contexts of Panem and District 12 through the eyes of a geographer, and more specifically through numerous geographical sub-disciplines.

It is noteworthy that geography constitutes one of the few academic disciplines that straddles both realms of the social and physical sciences. On the one hand, human geographers consider perspectives of urban, cultural, social, economic, demographic, political, and historical patterns and processes of human development. In contrast, physical geographers—or geospatial scientists—tend to focus on aspects related to earth system science, physical landforms, atmospheric sciences, hydrology, and biogeography. Then there are the more integrated realms of environmental geography that seek to understand the relationships between the human world and physical environment. Many geographers are further trained—or specialize in—the computerized mapping and analysis of the planet through Geographic Information Science (GIS). With all of these activities occurring within the geographer's realm, it is sometimes a challenge to pin down exactly what is meant by the discipline of "geography," as any one or more of these areas would certainly qualify.

That said, there is one central aspect that generally unites them all—that of interpreting the earth and its inhabitants through a *spatial* perspective. This necessarily means a focus on geographical patterns, places, and the myriad of connections between those places. In the chapters that follow we will primarily consider relevant examples of these *spatial relationships* that have played out and influenced our own human landscapes. In creating her own fantastical story several hundreds of years into the future, Collins relies heavily upon these actual geographic realities that characterize our own societies. It follows that we can best interpret and understand the spatial and historical contexts of Collins' Panem by bringing to light various aspects of our own world. What follows here is essentially an introduction to—and sampling of—human geography, as it might be interpreted through the world of the Hunger Games.

Plan of the Book

The remainder of this book is organized into two main parts, or themes. The first applies a variety of concepts and perspectives from human geography to better comprehend the functioning of Collins' own imagined world. The first chapter provides an opportunity to revisit the longstanding conversation regarding just where District 12 might be located. Numerous clues and geographical criteria are considered to provide a common locational frame of reference for the remainder of the book. Following a discussion of this "revised" District 12, the chapter proceeds to highlight a few pertinent geographical concepts that will be helpful for future topics. Notably, we will consider how the First Law of Geography can help explain why the Capitol relaxed its draconian oversight of the District 12 fence and various local activities, eventually to the Capitol's ultimate demise.

Following this introductory material, we are off and running, so to speak. Chapters 2 and 3 focus on the roles of local places in shaping our own lives and personal identities, along with those of Katniss Everdeen. We will further consider how we tend to form emotional attachments to our homes and related meaningful places. Chapter 2 is largely devoted to introducing the concept of place attachment, as exemplified by various central Appalachian writers whose experiences can be compared with those of Katniss. This leads into Chapter 3 which focuses principally on Katniss and her own sentiments for District 12, the Seam, and its environs. We explore how Katniss defines "home" in a number of ways, while also considering her own strong attachments to various places that have played meaningful roles in her life. In this respect we cannot ignore the often-understated guidance of Katniss' father in developing her profound ties to home, the woods, and the lake. I argue in this chapter that her father stands as one of the most influential characters within the original series, even without showing up alive for any of it.

We then turn to the historical geography of the central Appalachians in Chapter 4 to highlight the major waves of settlement and population migration into the region. This will provide some insight into the story behind this area's stunning degree of racial and ethnic diversity as exemplified by the mixed-race population of the Seam. While still often considered a homogenous culture region settled primarily by those of Scots-Irish descent, the historical reality of the central Appalachians is more complex. Centuries of racial mixing between peoples of Native American, African, and Western and Eastern European descent produced what scholars describe as one of America's most culturally diverse realms—a veritable melting pot in some ways if not others. It is within this context that we consider Katniss' own mixed-race—or multi-ethnic—background and what Suzanne Collins may have intended. This chapter further provides the historical context necessary for later explorations of various musical instruments, song styles, and music genres that Collins weaves so skillfully throughout her saga.

Our tour of District 12's historical geography continues in Chapter 5, first with a rather detailed interpretation of the public square and surrounding businesses. The central square and street layout of District 12 is less the product of Collins' imagination and more directly reflective of countless smaller towns and cities throughout America. Despite varying images of the square we see portrayed in the films, the actual center of town that Collins describes would be familiar to many of us. The following chapter then moves from the central square to the peripheral community of the Seam. Chapter 6 thus exposes the hard truths of coal-mining practices and the reality of company-controlled towns of the early twentieth century. In some ways, then, Suzanne Collins did not have to stretch the imagination with respect to the hardships and marginalization found within the Seam community. Rather, she simply replaced one source of authoritarian control with another. In a more light-hearted vein, this chapter further includes a discussion of the filming location utilized to depict the Everdeen home and the Seam that viewers see within "The Hunger Games."

We then turn to the urban and economic geography of the Capitol within the final two chapters of Part I to consider some aspects of architecture and urban design. Not unlike the public square of District 12, the portrayal of the City Circle within the films diverges in significant ways from that which Collins had envisioned for her novels. Chapter 7 therefore flushes out the urban design of the Capitol's city center and considers possible European and American urban precedents. We also spend some time along the Corso, the grand avenue introduced within the prequel as the home of the Snow's family apartment. The source of inspiration for the Corso is further identified, along with the related role of Renaissance and more recent modernist architecture as it appears within the novels and the films.

We then close out Part I with a more global perspective in Chapter

8. Here we interpret the nation of Panem as a world system in miniature, with the Capitol and districts organized around a wealthy, urban core, and a marginalized, largely impoverished periphery. Adapted from various efforts to explain the planet's uneven economic geography, the world system framework will help us comprehend the vast socioeconomic disparity and underdevelopment that occurs between those who live within the Capitol as opposed to those in the districts. This is followed by a discussion of the stark contrast in authoritarian oversight that we witness in the original series as compared with that of the prequel, six decades earlier. At some point between these two stories, a significant transition must occur as a more capitalist, free-market Panem gives way to a despotic police state. As a tangible case in point, the infamous District 12 fence does not yet exist within the prequel, though by Katniss' time it certainly does.

The geographical context from Part I lays the groundwork to explore the origins and development of Appalachian music traditions in Part II. We begin Chapter 9 with the ballad song style itself, including its historical roots and geographical source regions. And, of course, we focus on the backstories of certain representative ballads that Collins integrates within the original series, the prequel, or both. The multi-layered meanings of "The Hanging Tree" come to mind, which can be interpreted as a quintessential Appalachian murder ballad. We further look at Collins' incorporation of "Oh My Darling Clementine" and the rather curious and ongoing appearance of gold throughout the saga. A discussion of similar scope is further provided to consider the poetry of William Wordsworth and how his work inspires the identity and life path for the prequel's own Lucy Gray Baird.

Chapter 10 then leaps ahead from the colonial and early American Appalachians to the later nineteenth century. The origins and instrumental composition of the mountain string band are considered here, along with the string band's multi-cultural roots and performance styles. The diffusion of various string instruments into the central mountains is explored here as well, including the fiddle, guitar, and banjo, along with their multi-racial contexts and pasts. While this musical era was still too early to best represent the Covey's own performance style, the string band phase served as a significant forerunner to later country and bluegrass music.

The origins of early country music thus provide the topic for Chapter 11, coupled with the parallel roles of the early recording and radio broadcasting industries. These emerging mass-media technologies of the early twentieth century coincided with the rise of so-called hillbilly music, the precursor to the genre known today as country—or Country & Western. This discussion provides the perfect place to highlight key songs within the Hunger Games saga that represent this historical era. For that purpose we must explore the rise of the Carter Family and Jimmie Rodgers, and the ways their work came to inspire Suzanne Collins' latest prequel. The actual songs "Keep on the Sunny Side" and "Down in the Valley" figure prominently here. Of additional relevance is the emergence of the hillbilly stereotype, early hillbilly music, and the persistence of both positive and negative stereotypes oriented toward Appalachian people.

And while the members of the Covey—most notably Lucy Gray herself—demonstrate a varied repertoire of Appalachian-style ballads and early country tunes, it is argued here that the Covey does not reflect a bona-fide country band as some observers have considered. Rather, their performance style and instrumentation are the product of more recent developments. What the Covey best represents is a quintessential bluegrass outfit from the World War II era. It is this topic to which Chapter 12 is devoted—perhaps appropriately, considering the Covey's current home district. We specifically examine the musical and stylistic traits of real-life bluegrass bands and match them with the vivid descriptions provided by the Covey's own performances.

After making the case for the Covey and its own bluegrass roots, Chapter 13 provides additional context that allows us to place this District 12 band within the historical timeline of mountain (and southern) music. We consider America's first bluegrass ensemble, namely Bill Monroe and the Blue Grass Boys and how this pioneering bluegrass band provides the most reasonable model for the Covey. This further provides one possible explanation for the ongoing puzzlement as to why the Covey does not include a banjo player.

And for those interested in exploring the more recent evolution of bluegrass music heritage beyond the 1940s, Chapter 14 provides an overview of more recent bluegrass happenings. While little is discussed here with respect to Collins' own stories, this material is included nonetheless for those curious about the progression of bluegrass music and the generational handoff of the style to more recent musicians.

This volume concludes with a fun and admittedly more fan-based, interpretive chapter focused on the youngest member of the Covey, Maude Ivory. Chapter 15 exposes a number of strangely coincidental scenarios and character descriptions that essentially speak to one another between Collins' original series and the new prequel. Is Katniss related by blood to someone within the Covey? Beyond this interpretive analysis, readers are left to decide for themselves how the currently missing history between the times of Lucy Gray Baird and Katniss Everdeen will ultimately play out should Collins decide to continue her saga. For now, let's begin our tour by considering the most likely Appalachian backdrop for a place called District 12.

1

District 12 of Central Appalachia

This first chapter encourages you to start thinking like a geographer, by interpreting Katniss' home through more of a spatial perspective. To launch us in this direction, what better place to begin than to reconsider the possible range of geographical locations where District 12 would most likely be found? Generally, its setting within the Appalachian Mountains has been common knowledge for quite some time. But to what extent might District 12's likely geographical range be narrowed down? This regional puzzle has provided years of ongoing fun and not a little debate among fans and scholars alike.

While Collins does not answer this ongoing question directly, she provides plenty of cultural and environmental clues—or breadcrumbs—scattered throughout the original series and now within her recent prequel. Thoughtful readers have produced numerous interpretive maps of Panem since the initial release of *The Hunger Games* in 2008, many of which can still be found online. Their creative and multi-colored maps provide imagined locations of the Capitol and Districts as they may have been overlaid across a reconfigured North American continent. As with other parts of Panem, these maps locate District 12 in a variety of creative regional configurations, both within and around the actual mountains.

How might we refine this District 12 realm even further? The highland region is unequivocally vast, with its unparalleled diversity of physical landscapes, ecosystems, and climate zones between its northern and southern extremes. The Appalachians as defined by one pair of geographers encompasses a full six percent of the land area of the United States.[1] Likewise, the Appalachian Regional Commission (ARC) defines the mountainous region as including 420 counties sprawled across portions of 13 states. Such a broad swath of territory provides an immense realm of possible locations for an isolated community of some 8,000 people, as Katniss described the population there (*THG* 17).

It follows that District 12 is much less a sprawling region than it is a quintessential small town. Such communities would normally be symbolized as a simple dot on a U.S. state map, as opposed to an extensive area encompassing thousands of square miles. Yet this latter scenario is how most imagined maps of Panem portray it. While other unknown communities may be lurking beyond the District 12 fence line, Collins provides no apparent indication this is the case. In her world of Panem, District 12 is surrounded by hundreds of miles of vast wilderness—and teaming wildlife—in all directions. This scenario is very different from the hundreds of networked towns and cities we find scattered throughout the actual Appalachians. Imagine if all but one of these places simply vanished. Add to that an absolute ban on communication with anyone outside the District and restrictions on any type of travel for non-authorized purposes. Such extreme isolation is precisely the geographic situation in which the population of District 12 finds itself. For many of us, this would make for a foreboding, lonely experience indeed.

The important point to make here is that District 12 is more characteristic of an American small town than it is a multi-state region. Consequently, whenever attempting to map the location of District 12, we are actually delimiting the area within which this small town could possibly exist. Numerous cultural criteria and other clues from the original series already point us to the central Appalachians, somewhere south of Pennsylvania and north of Georgia—criteria including forest vegetation, seasonal weather and climate (from winter snowstorms to scorching, humid summers), and aspects of regional culture and history, economics, and agricultural approaches. All of these criteria are considered in more depth throughout this book, and many have already been considered by previous authors as well.

Perhaps the most definitive clue, of course, stares us in the face—that of coal. District 12 is primarily based on a coal mining town, the likes of which were found in the central Appalachians of the early twentieth century. Numerous fans and authors have, to their credit, wisely considered the general location of coal deposits—or *coal seams* embedded within sedimentary rock strata—to inform their own interpretations of District 12. We can therefore narrow down the possible location of District 12 even further by considering where actual coal mining activities have historically occurred. To do so requires us to dig further—pun intended—into maps of coal mining production and employment.

Despite significant changes to the scope and technology of mining operations throughout the twentieth century, the geography of Appalachian coal mining has remained remarkably consistent. For purposes here I rely upon a coal mining report generated for the Appalachian Regional Commission in 2016.[2] This extensive economic overview provides numerous detailed maps of coal mining activities and employment trends for every Appalachian county.

Through a comparison between this report's 2016 maps with similar patterns of the mid-twentieth century, we can generally conclude that coal mining has historically occurred—and continues to occur—in rather discrete, concentrated sub-regions of the mountains. Like other kinds of rocks and minerals that humans extract from the earth, coal is a *place-based* natural resource. These deposits of mostly bituminous, or lower-quality coal that formed millions of years ago are, quite logically, stuck in place. Because these earth-bound resources are not simply found everywhere humans settle, this geographic dilemma necessitates a massive investment in mining infrastructure, railroad networks, and new settlements placed adjacent to the resource itself. This is not an insignificant task, nor an inexpensive one. The human settlements, urban patterns, and local economies of entire regions are sometimes defined primarily by the location of such natural resources.

The Appalachian coalfields are no different. In the rather unique case of Panem, Suzanne Collins decided that her dystopian nation would depend heavily upon this carbon-based fuel to support the Capitol's own urban development. Whether or not it was a particularly wise choice to depend on far-off Appalachia for its coal supply is another matter. Regardless, this is the economic geography of Panem that Collins provides.

It stands to reason that should a particular Appalachian county not produce some minimal amount of coal, then it should probably be omitted from District 12 contention. Call me a realist. Maps within the ARC report provide county-level data such as coal production in 2016, coal mining employment in 2015, and the change in coal mining employment between 2011 and 2015. All of these maps largely reinforce one another, revealing specific areas of coal-mining activity within the Appalachians. By superimposing these maps onto the cultural descriptions provided by Suzanne Collins, we can determine more specifically the likely location of District 12. Cutting to the chase, this exercise yields a more concise region comprising portions of eastern Kentucky, southern West Virginia, extreme southwestern Virginia, and a smidge of northern Tennessee, just to be fair. This revised area of possible District 12 locations is thus proposed in the map below.

I will sometimes refer to this area as the "District 12 core." The District's somewhat fuzzy boundary coincides with the concentration of coal mining activities in the central Appalachians, while it also overlaps with other cultural indicators discussed later. The "core" label leaves room for interpretation and acknowledges that others may "place" District 12 elsewhere. After all, we are interpreting a work of fiction here, making this more of an exercise in geographic thought. If someone insists that Katniss

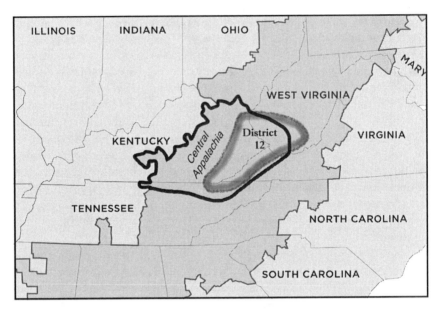

grew up in western Pennsylvania or North Carolina, so be it. Still, the array of data considered here indicates otherwise. No coal? No District 12.

One could argue for the existence of a possible "secondary" District 12, consisting of northern West Virginia or western Pennsylvania. Substantial coal mining activities occur within this region as well. For purposes here, however, these areas are found too far north to reasonably correspond with various cultural and environmental traits more associated with the central or southern Appalachians. This interpretation is only reinforced within Collins' more recent prequel. The origins and proliferation of folk ballads, early country music, sweltering summers, and bluegrass musicians all point to a District 12 within central Appalachia. This will become more evident as we move into Part II later.

This brings us to the concept of "central Appalachia" for its own part. Some might describe this area as part of "southern Appalachia," meaning the southern half of the extensive Appalachian mountain chain. Still, it will be useful to retain some consistency with our geographic descriptors for purposes of this book. To that end, the ARC provides an accepted definition of mountain sub-regions. The area identified as central Appalachia in the map above coincides closely with the ARC region of the same name. I will therefore refer to the general location of District 12 within its larger central Appalachian context. Various local media outlets and community organizations likewise describe these portions of Kentucky, West Virginia, and Virginia as being a part of central Appalachia.

Reactions from Real Appalachians

The intimate connections between Katniss and her Appalachian home did not go unnoticed by actual mountain residents and writers. Jim Poe noted in a piece for the *Times West Virginian* in 2015 that many fans "in West Virginia and elsewhere in the Appalachian region have taken particular interest in 'The Hunger Games' and its tenacious teenaged heroine."[3] He goes on to explain that—despite the fantastical, dystopian story line— the setting for District 12 is "marked by a heartfelt depiction of Appalachian people and traditions." Although clues to local culture are even more pronounced within the prequel, the central Appalachians had already been easily recognized from Collins' first novel as the home of Katniss Everdeen.

Likewise, Rachel Parsons, a West Virginia resident and writer, had written in a review of *The Hunger Games* that she had recognized her own coal-town home of southern West Virginia. "More than that," Parsons continued, "I was also presented with the heroine I'd been looking for since I was a small child. Katniss Everdeen is everything a girl from Appalachia hopes and has to be. She is strong, she is smart, and she has pushed aside her own needs for the good of her family." Thus, Katniss gained Parson's immediate attention because "I knew her—I was her, and I am her."[4] If such accolades are any indicator, it appears Suzanne Collins deserves credit for infusing a realistic Appalachian sense of place into her saga.

Others reacted similarly. According to Tina Hanlon, Suzanne Collins "really nailed it with regard to the first half of the 20th century in the coal towns."[5] Even the coal dust mentioned by Katniss was realistic for the actual mining towns of central Appalachia. And while many fans might view the impoverished and derelict conditions of District 12 as exaggerated for the story, the reality for such places could be shockingly similar. In place of the Capitol and its Peacekeepers were the omnipresent mining companies that exerted various degrees of control over local populations. Such corporate authority only aggravated existing hardships for miners and their families. As Elizabeth Hardy explains, "[h]istorical miners often suffered the same punishments as the District 12 rebels: lack of work, food shortages, physical punishment and humiliation in the guise of justice."[6]

Moreover, Katniss and her peers in the Seam exhibit personality traits commonly associated with rural Appalachians, including cynical attitudes, terse speech ways, and a bleak sense of humor. For instance, a rather grim Haymitch Abernathy tells Katniss, "Here's some advice: Stay alive" (*THG* 56). According to Hardy, this is typical Appalachian deadpan humor that comes with rather pessimistic outlooks on life, and a tendency to not trust people.[7] Katniss expresses such humor when speaking of fellow residents who cautiously gather apples in the woods, but always within safe reach of the Meadow. To this she mutters, "District 12. Where you can starve to death in safety" (*THG* 6). Readers will find plenty of similar instances peppered throughout the original series, if one knows what to look for. Such use of deadpan humor provides for some welcome—if dark—levity, along with the occasional chuckle.

Katniss demonstrates a variety of additional traits of mountain people as well—namely, her self-sufficiency, acts of boldness, loyalty to kin, and determination to feed her family.[8] Beyond these aspects, various medicinal herbs and practices of folk medicine are quintessentially Appalachian. And as we will explore in more detail in Part II, Appalachian folk songs and more recent music genres play a crucial and unifying role throughout the Hunger Games saga. It is no wonder that numerous observers from central Appalachia easily recognize Katniss as one of their own.

Appalachian Stereotypes

Until recently the national image of Appalachia was ceaselessly portrayed as poor, backward, and white.[9] The persistent "hillbilly" stereotype has survived intact for more than 150 years, aimed primarily at rural white families of Scots-Irish descent. At the same time, the Appalachian Mountains have also been romanticized as a repository of simpler lifestyles and folk traditions not entirely overcome by industrial and urban growth.

Just the term "Appalachia" conjures a wide array of conflicting ideas, including a long list of stereotypes involving "feuds, individualism, moonshine, subsistence farming, quilting bees, illiteracy, dueling banjos, and many other things," as described by David Hsiung.[10] Some are complimentary and desirable qualities of family life, while others persist as derogatory put-downs and persistent prejudices. These latter types are demonstrated emphatically by Capitol citizens throughout the Hunger Games saga. By the late nineteenth century when much of urban America was industrializing with railroads, factories and manufacturing plants, Appalachia came to be viewed as even further removed from the national mainstream.

The perceived isolation of Appalachian communities provided its own stereotype. Henry Shapiro noted that such isolation referred to a "state of mind, an undesirable provincialism resulting from the lack of contact between the mountaineers and outsiders."[11] Such stereotypes have led to the "othering" of Appalachian people since the late nineteenth century. This practice of portraying an entire rural population as the undesirable "Other" is precisely how the Capitol's citizens view the outlying districts of Panem.

Such "othering" sets up an oversimplified "us versus them" dichotomy, the likes of which are easily promoted through cultural stereotypes.

Collins purposely brings attention to the negative stereotypes endured by Appalachian people. For instance, Katniss and Peeta are perceived by Effie Trinket and many Capitol residents (except Cinna) as backward, barbaric, and generally uncivilized. These "othered" folks are therefore perceived as unworthy of the lifestyles afforded to those of the more desirable, urban, high-tech Capitol. Elizabeth Hardy claims that "the stereotypes of District 12 vary little from those slapped onto Appalachian people in the past and even today."[12]

Hardy further commended Collins for creatively intermixing both positive and negative stereotypes—namely the "thrifty, wholesome, clean-living mountain person" as contrasted with "the filthy, drunken, violent brute."[13] If such stereotyping was more subtle in the original series, it practically jumps out at us from the prequel. Perhaps the most blatant diatribes against district people come from Coriolanus' Grandma'am. In one memorable exchange, she chastises Coriolanus for having a picnic with Lucy Gray at the Zoo. The mere idea of dining with her, says Grandma'am, suggests that Lucy Gray and Coriolanus represent a similar social status. She then describes the districts generally as "barbaric" (*BSS* 77). This is her way of stereotyping district populations as brutish, violent, and uncivilized. In a similar vein, a young Coriolanus tries incessantly to mask the fact that his family "was as poor as district scum" (*BSS* 3). Collins' choice of such language to emphasize Capitol perceptions of the districts is arguably jaw-dropping for those unused to being on the receiving end of such contempt. Perhaps Collins felt the need to emphasize this blatant "othering" of all things District within the prequel. If so, her inclusion of Grandma'am's character succeeds quite handily.

The Grandma'am's reference to barbarism is a curious if instructive choice as well. The term "barbarian" historically referred to groups of people perceived as uncivilized or primitive. While numerous countries and empires throughout history have identified their own "barbarian" populations, perhaps the case of the Roman Empire is most notable here. Like the privileged population of the Capitol, the ancient Romans used variations of the term to describe tribal non–Romans located along the Empire's vast periphery. These "barbarian" tribes included no less than the Celts, Gauls, Germanics, and Iberians—the very barbarians who eventually developed into the modern-era nations of Western Europe. *Oops.*

Once again, then, Collins weaves the geography of the ancient Roman Empire into her saga, perhaps hoping her readers will confront similar stereotypes. Just as European tribes found themselves on the periphery of ancient Rome, the outlying district populations of Panem occupy a similar relative position in the social hierarchy. It is no accident that Collins employs characters such as Grandma'am to reference the "barbarians" on the rural periphery, compared to their more civilized, urban counterparts of the Capitol. In this way, geographical distance plays a fundamental role in the persistence of these socioeconomic and cultural stereotypes.

Of course, the historical realities of Appalachian communities are more complex than simple stereotypes would have us believe. As Aaron Thompson summarized in a story for National Public Radio, "There's no one story of Appalachia, no one voice. It's time for everyone to feel like they can speak up, like their story is important."[14] The truth is that Appalachia is defined as much by its ethnic mixing and multiracial history than by any popular stereotype would have us believe. As National Public Radio writer Sarah Baird declares, Appalachia can be defined as a "mountainous melting pot" of successive waves of settlers and immigrant groups.[15] We will further explore the characteristics and origins of this cultural melting pot in Chapter 4.

The First Law of Geography

With her decision to set District 12 within the central Appalachians, Collins highlights a significant silver lining to the region's rural isolation. That is, Katniss and her peers find ways to take advantage of the Capitol's lackluster oversight of the area. Most notably, Peacekeepers fail to maintain that pesky electric fence, allowing Katniss and Gale to practice their life-saving skills of hunting and gathering. Their regular trade and bartering activities go overlooked as well, to the point where Peacekeepers become some of their best customers. From a geographic perspective, Katniss and Gale have essentially established an Appalachian-type subsistence lifestyle that likely would not have been tolerated elsewhere in Panem.

One could argue—as I often do in my own teaching—that a principle called the *First Law of Geography* applies to this curious situation quite well. This seminal concept was first presented in 1969 by Waldo Tobler and was published a year later. The notion is deceptively simple. His First Law states quite elegantly that "everything is related to everything else, but near things are more related than distant things."[16] The impact of distance allowed District 12 to retain some of its cultural distinctiveness, most notably various aspects of food, music, celebration, schooling, and local trade routines that had not yet been stifled or diluted by the Capitol. This separation by geographic distance provides one fundamental explanation for how Katniss defies the Capitol's control and evolves into the healthy and skilled individual she herself describes. Everything she accomplishes on both sides of the fence is dependent upon her ability to operate unhindered. She effectively remains under the radar of the Capitol's gaze—at least until she garners too much attention following the 74th Games.

By inadvertently loosening its control over District 12, the Capitol essentially sealed its own fate. For one thing, Katniss and Gale could take good advantage of that poorly maintained district fence. In turn, the local Peacekeepers not only ignored the black market occurring under their noses, but actively participated in it. Given their own hunger for fresh meat, the Peacekeepers simply turn a blind eye to hunting taking place beyond the fence. And this situation had not changed measurably since Lucy Gray's time in District 12. As a clear nod by Suzanne Collins to her original series, Lucy Gray admits to Coriolanus that the Peacekeepers are likewise some of the Covey's best customers, but in this case with respect to their paying for musical entertainment.

This is not the first time an authoritarian regime has let down its guard along a vast frontier. Even the formidable Roman Empire could not control all activities within its distant borderlands. For instance, the ancient ancestors of the British Isles and northern Europe found themselves on the uncontrollable periphery of that same empire. Katniss Everdeen—as a self-confident hunter and survivor—would simply not have existed were it not for the Capitol's relaxed oversight and, well, for its subpar fence maintenance. Just as the evolution of the hybrid mockingjay bird was unpredicted by the Capitol, the rise of Katniss was likewise unpredicted. As Collins herself explained during a 2010 interview, neither one of them should have logically existed.[17] Both Katniss and the mockingjay have thus been allowed to survive and prosper within the Capitol's isolated periphery, due largely to the First Law of Geography.

As such, the mockingjay became a fitting metaphor for Katniss' own life. And quite creatively, both of these symbols of rebellion—Katniss and the mockingjay—effectively become one. This is perhaps most poignantly manifested through the transformation of her wedding dress into a veritable mockingjay in *Catching Fire*—care of Cinna's fashion skills and some well-placed political expression of his own.

Cultural Diffusion in District 12

If Collins grounded her story within the distinctive cultural traits of the central Appalachians, where did those cultural precedents originate prior to their arrival into the mountains? The story of how diverse peoples settled the central Appalachians is largely a geographical one. The region's cultural traits have been shaped by the actions of Indigenous peoples and immigrant groups alike, hailing primarily from three continents—Europe, Africa, and North America. From all of these territories, various ethnic groups found their way into the mountains, along with the cultural "luggage" they carried with them.

For our purpose here, we can define *culture* as the total combination of customary beliefs, values, social forms, language, and material traits that reflect a population's traditions and ways of life, including the things they produce and build. For instance, the notion of reciprocation in the Seam is highly valued.[18] Katniss struggles internally throughout the series with her feeling of "owing" Peeta and numerous others who have assisted her in some way. A high value is also placed on nature and the physical environment, most notably the "woods" where Katniss and Gale hunt, gather, and collect edible and medicinal plants. Of course, one of the more iconic cultural traits of District 12 is the now-famous three-finger funerary salute which residents use as a sign of mutual respect.

It should be noted that the concept of culture differs somewhat from those of race and ethnicity, the meanings of which have evolved through time. Social scientists now generally perceive *race* as a specific aspect that contributes to one's *ethnicity*—which, for its part, can be described as a "colorless, catch-all term."[19] *Ethnicity* can refer to groups of people who have shared a common history, whether real or perceived, and a sense of a common geographic place of origin. Further, ethnicity also includes the concept of a shared culture which can be described as "a broad term that can include within it traditions, folkways, values, symbols, language, and religion."[20] While we will occasionally consider specific racial or ethnic differences between various populations—whether within District 12 or our own society—I will tend to focus on the broader aspects of *culture* for our ongoing discussions that follow.

The predecessors of today's Appalachian people had arrived carrying a diverse collection of cultural values, beliefs, and practices from their original homes. Suzanne Collins highlights a particular collection of these traits with which to create her fictitious world of District 12 and its endearing characters. It follows that if we are going to best understand how—for instance—the prequel's Lucy Gray was able to sing and compose so many ballads, how Katniss and her father learned to sing "mountain airs" and the "valley song," or how the mandolin becomes a featured instrument within the Covey band, it will be helpful to consider how such cultural practices came to the mountains in the first place.

When large population groups migrate from one place to another, they naturally bring along familiar ways of life. It is instructive to keep in mind that we as humans only know how to behave and interact within our existing set of knowledge. Of course, as necessity would have it, we will adapt creatively over time to new environments or circumstances (or maybe not). But until then, humans can only practice what they have previously learned. Familiar examples include intangible (immaterial) traits such as religious beliefs, language and music traditions, and moral values, along with more tangible (material) cultural practices such as farming techniques, architectural styles, food and diet preferences, street patterns, place names, and economic activities—to name but a few. Collins adroitly pulls from a variety of these traits to create a realistic sense of place for District 12.

The process of transferring a distinct set of cultural traits or ideas from one place to another is known as *cultural diffusion*. Cultural geographers generally agree that specific customs and ways of life have to originate somewhere—that is, within a *culture hearth*. This is where ideas and belief systems can bloom and influence the cultural patterns of an entire population.

With respect to the mountainous home of one Katniss Everdeen, geographers have identified several culture hearths in the eastern United States that are largely responsible for engendering American settlement patterns. Residents of the thirteen British colonies once referred to the mysterious mountains of Appalachia as the "backcountry," then located on their vast western periphery. The culture hearths that contributed most to populating the mountains with those of European descent were those of southern New England (primarily Massachusetts and Connecticut, focused on Boston), southeastern Pennsylvania (focused on and around Philadelphia), and tidewater Virginia (the Chesapeake Bay area).

How do cultural patterns and social activities spread, or diffuse outward from a hearth? There are two principal ways in which this happens. The first is through *migration diffusion*, or the physical movement of people from a core population area to elsewhere on the planet. When people move around, their familiar cultural traits naturally come along for the ride. Should enough people with similar traditions migrate together or to the same new place, their collective cultural and social practices will likewise be transplanted to their new location.

This is why—for starters—massive German-style barns and agricultural practices are found throughout Pennsylvania and as far west as Indiana; New England village landscapes can be found as far west as Michigan and southern Wisconsin; French place names and architecture are found in Missouri and Louisiana; and Spanish Baroque–style churches are found in central New Mexico. All of these cultural traits had to come from somewhere. They did so through the movement of people from one place to another, quite regardless of any Indigenous peoples who might have gotten in their way. One might further note that District 12 residents generally speak English—a seemingly obvious fact often taken for granted. Had the Spanish, French, or Dutch imperial powers more successfully claimed the eastern seaboard, any hopeful English settlers might have been chased out long ago. In which case, Katniss and her counterparts would not likely be found dancing to Scots-Irish jigs and reels.

The diffusion of cultural traits can also occur through direct communication from one person to another. This process of *imitation diffusion* is how we learn new information and skills—by imitating them, or learning from others. Individuals will naturally observe and copy the practices of their neighbors. This is more instantly accomplished nowadays with the proliferation of smartphones, telecommunication systems, and social media outlets.

Sometimes this process is also referred to as *contagious diffusion*, in that cultural traits are spread from person to person as they teach one another—not unlike the more insidious spread of a contagious virus. The notion of "going viral" through "viral videos" on social media speaks to a contemporary version of contagious diffusion. Today, the standard teenager can share the latest video game, group photos, or favorite hangout places rather instantly, just as neighbors can share their experiences with new recipes, clothing styles, or newfangled lawn equipment. Such diffusion of ideas and cultural practices occurred much more slowly centuries ago, when the fastest way to travel was by foot or horse.

It turns out that both processes of diffusion—through migration and imitation—greatly influenced Appalachian cultural practices. Given that Collins chose to set much of her story here, it follows that these very same cultural patterns describe a place called District 12 as well. The remainder of this book will focus quite extensively on the origins and characteristics of these culture ways, and how they ultimately came to shape the lives of Katniss, Lucy Gray, and their contemporaries.

A Geographical Paradox

The Hunger Games saga comes with a number of curious geographical paradoxes, though one in particular stands out. That is, despite the highly anonymous names provided for Districts One through Thirteen, Collins provides a distinctive—and identifiably Appalachian—sense of place for her District 12. She further imbues various geographical traits to describe other districts as well—not the least being their specialized economic activities. Should one simply consider their place names alone, however, the districts lack any sense of identity beyond their respective numbers.

For its part, the Capitol does not fare much better. Collins dubbed this glamorous and sparkling urban center simply as, well, the Capitol. This does allow for a colorful play on words. In this context, a "capital" is a place, as with a capital city, whereas "the Capitol" serves as the political and urban hub of Panem. Beyond these meanings, "the Capitol" often refers specifically to the American seat of government in Washington, D.C., namely the Capitol building, located prominently on "Capitol Hill." One might be curious as to why Panem's primary city was not awarded with a more meaningful name harkening back to ancient Rome or, in the least, the American West. No matter; instead we have the Capitol. As with the districts, Collins clearly intended their locations to remain ambiguous and largely unattached from recognizable place names.

As for the generic districts, their numbering system does provide a sense of diminishing importance—a social hierarchy, that is—with the Capitol at the "top" and lower-numbered districts signifying a greater importance within the economic and social structures of Panem. Such naming hierarchies—Capitol and District, First and Third World—imply a hierarchy from better to worse, or from more to least desirable. This is likely one of the countless veiled messages Collins hoped readers would uncover. Her generic place names provide no identifiable sense of place in their own right, to geographically distinguish one place from another. Much like the anonymous and silent Avoxes—who may represent the unheard, or voiceless segments of society—so too are the people of Panem's districts rendered anonymous, lacking their own unique identities.

By contrast, then, Collins provides a delightfully rich sense of place for District 12 in its central Appalachian setting, despite its otherwise placeless identity. Underlying Collins' overtly dystopian story of inequality and revolution is a tale of a small Appalachian community. It is for this fundamental reason that the book herein has been written. The protagonists of both the original series and the more recent prequel are set and staged within a realistic setting rooted in Appalachian history and culture. In this way the nameless District 12 transforms into a distinctive and recognizable place. The next chapter explores this elusive concept of *place* and how the culture ways of central Appalachia come to life within the otherwise anonymous District 12.

2

Places and Spaces of District 12

A few words should be said here about the concept of place. What is "place" as compared with "space"? For purposes here, it might help to think of "space" more generically. We use variations of this term all the time, quite often without much thought as to why. We exist in *space*; we need more *space* for this furniture; public versus private *spaces*; this classroom *space* is devoted to group activities. You get the idea. What these all have in common is that there is no specific meaning attached to *space*. It's just there, for us to occupy (or to remain distant from).

Place, on the other hand, is a space with meaning imparted upon it by humans. Put simply, places hold specific meanings for us as individuals. Every place—whether at the scale of house or home, neighborhood, city, or region—maintains unique characteristics and nuances that can be deemed as special, or distinct from places elsewhere. As one writer claims, "Where you live is what you are."[1] As a whole, we live our lives in specific places, each with distinct cultural and social norms, geographical qualities, and local histories. These unique characteristics can also give rise to a distinctive *sense of place*, allowing us to distinguish one interesting place from another—such as a local downtown, public square, urban neighborhood, mountain village, or local coffee shop.

Spaces therefore can become places through human intervention, such as through intentional design, physical construction, or designation for a particular function. Places will typically be defined by borders, occupy a specified area, and be locatable within a larger area or region. This is very different from more generic spaces that might be perceived as open, undesignated, and undifferentiated from other spaces around it.[2] As humans we can physically intervene and alter a space, the very act of which converts that space into a now-recognizable place. Of course, that same space could also become a place with nary a trace of human activity, perhaps through one's imagination or a work of fiction.

As one instance of how a space can be transformed into a place, take the case of an unnamed grassy field. This geographical shift could occur through any number of approaches. We could surround it with storefronts and anoint it as a public square—as a central place for local community engagement. Or we could construct a fence around the field and thereby designate it a district of some kind. The field could also be "developed" to create a mixed-use housing subdivision named Primrose Place. If converted into a baseball field, the space suddenly becomes known as a community landmark for competitive sports. In all cases, human meaning has been generated from either personal or group interactions, or through the social processes of community decision making.[3]

Within the Hunger Games, consider the Meadow in District 12. Throughout most of the series, this more-or-less natural space just inside the fence line is altered little by humans—aside from occasional dandelion harvesting by Katniss and Prim to keep their family alive. It also provides a peaceful respite for Katniss and—some six decades earlier—for Lucy Gray, to sit, reflect, or to practice the guitar. For these reasons alone, this natural greenspace becomes a meaningful place for Katniss (and Prim), or in earlier times for Lucy Gray. We can imagine that the Meadow represents not only a place of sustenance, but also one of natural tranquility where Katniss and others can feel at home. Beyond these meanings, we learn early within the third novel, *Mockingjay*, that the Meadow comes to serve as a sanctuary. It becomes a safe refuge for some 800 District 12 residents who—thanks to Gale's quick thinking—escape the Capitol's firebombing. It is further instructive that Collins capitalizes "Meadow," both in the original series and in the prequel. This subtle decision instantly provides for it a firm status as a recognized place, now also designated as a proper noun.

The song "Deep in the Meadow," sometimes referred to as "Rue's Lullaby," is a mountain air sung by both Katniss and the Covey in different generations. The song serves to enhance the significance of this place—for readers and characters alike. For readers, the Meadow becomes a firm place within our own minds. We can imagine the type of meadow that Katniss or Lucy Gray describes, and how the place influences their lives. Then in the Epilogue of *Mockingjay*, Katniss returns to find much of her beloved greenspace converted into a mass grave, a fact which goes unnoticed by her unsuspecting children who happily frolic above it. The Meadow's meaning as a place has to some extent shifted for Katniss. It now serves as a silent memorial to the many lives lost from the bombing of District 12. Through natural processes, however, the Meadow has transitioned back to a peaceful, therapeutic place for Katniss and her family. It is perhaps fitting that Katniss' emotional bond to this piece of geography is unwavering, sustained from the beginning of the series to its very end.

As another familiar instance, the lake where Katniss spends time with her father is, from a human perspective, simply a natural lake—we presume—unless it was actually an artificial reservoir at one time. Either way, Collins takes this otherwise unspecified lake and describes it as a particular place which becomes a focus of interaction for her characters. As we learn through both the original series and the prequel, a variety of meaningful and memorable human activities occur there. The lake becomes significant to Katniss due to fond memories of times spent there with her father. And of fundamental importance to the story line, this is where Katniss learns to swim, and it serves as an important setting for various interactions with Gale.

Within the prequel, similar types of activities—and ensuing drama—occur at what is presumably the same lake. The Covey members relax there, and it serves as the setting for Lucy Gray's dramatic attempts to outwit an impulsive Coriolanus. For these reasons, even though "the lake" remains unnamed, human interaction and social activity have imbued it with meaning and memories for those who spent time there. The geography of the lake plays a fundamental role in the personal histories of Collins' characters. Further, readers are provided with enough descriptive detail for us to imagine this specific place within our minds. Although each reader will envision the lake somewhat differently, it becomes for all of us a distinctly recognizable place.

Suzanne Collins clearly understands how to organize her characters and their interactions within key spaces and places. In one respect, Katniss particularly understands her environment in terms of distinctly separated spaces in general. She views the Seam, for instance, as a recognizable and defined place, as "our part of District 12" (*THG* 4). We can further imagine the Seam based on Katniss' vivid descriptions, such as the coal miners heading out for the morning shift. On another level, her descriptions indicate that "District 12 is divided between Katniss' 'us' and a so-far unseen 'them.'"[4] Invoking the "us versus them" dichotomy, the "them" comprises the population of District 12 outside the Seam, namely the merchant class.

After Katniss introduces the Seam as her home place, she zooms out to reveal more about District 12 in general. This larger place, she tells us, is physically defined by an imposing though rather derelict electric fence, capped by loops of barbed wire. Beyond the fence is another place eventually defined by Collins as "the woods," representing a nearly endless expanse of natural forest. To venture beyond the fence is considered trespassing and therefore illegal, which helps readers initially imagine and define the space as distinctly separate from District 12. For her part, Katniss provides a bridge, or connection between the woods and her district, through her cunning ability to pass unseen from one side of the fence to the other.[5]

Losing Our Sense of Place

The local qualities that make places unique are sometimes in opposition to more globalizing forces of standardization. Geographers thus sometimes recognize a binary "local versus global" contradiction, or tension. Global processes tend to reduce, or dilute, the distinctiveness of places or regions over time. We are all familiar with the proliferation of—to name a few mere examples—national (and global) fast-food chains, modernist glass and concrete architecture, suburban "sprawl" and big-box, discount retail stores like Walmart and Target which can be found in any city. In our society's constant push for more convenience, some lament the resulting loss of local "flavor" or "character." Even when a local sense of place might be particularly strong, it is still quite fragile and easily lost.[6] With this ongoing march of globalization, Wilfred McClay posits that "we stand powerfully in need of such stable and coherent places in our lives—to ground us and orient us, and mark off a finite area, rich with memory, for our activity as parents and children, as friends and neighbors, and as free and productive citizens."[7] When familiar and comfortable places disappear or are somehow diluted, we can feel strong emotions of loss and regret.

A similar sentiment of loss was famously recorded by the words of American author and playwright Gertrude Stein (1874–1946). Upon her return to the city of Oakland, California, where she was raised, she declared that there was no "there" there. Although this famous statement has been mistaken as a derogatory judgment against the city, the intent of those words—written within her autobiography—was entirely different. She had felt a strong attachment to Oakland when she lived there as a child, essentially a stable, precious place in an otherwise unstable upbringing. Much to her dismay, she returned later in life to find her childhood home had been razed. There was little if anything familiar upon her return, and thus Oakland had lost a lot of its former meaning. That is, the "blooming, buzzing confusion of the city no longer had a nucleus around which she could orient it."[8] By saying there was no "there" there, Stein was lamenting the loss of a place once considered familiar and comforting.

We might compare Stein's experience with that of our heroine, Katniss Everdeen. Just as Stein lost her sense of place for Oakland, Katniss experiences profound shock and loss upon her return to a devastated District 12 in *Mockingjay*. She, too, ultimately loses the place that helped define her personal identity from the time she was born. The nearly complete annihilation of her hometown shakes her to the core. First and foremost, she feels responsible for causing the deaths of thousands of people. On top of this incomparable burden, she walks through the rubble of her hometown to find anything familiar, to ground her in a place she once knew. Likewise, the opening scene of *Mockingjay* finds Katniss desperately trying to make sense of what remains of her demolished house within the Seam. She manages to identify where her bed once stood. Likewise, the collapsed chimney provides "a point of reference" to help orient herself within the home's remains (*MJ* 3). She is considerably desperate to identify any shred of familiarity within the place she once held dear.

The places most cherished by Katniss are consequently used as pawns by President Snow as weapons of psychological torment. He knows precisely how to destabilize Katniss and keep her mentally off balance, first by playing to her instincts of kindness and compassion. He arguably orders the firebombing of her hometown because he knows District 12 is her most cherished place. He likewise understands that torturing poor Peeta in *Mockingjay* will hold precisely the same effect.

Continuing her morbid tour in town, Katniss further recognizes the paving stones under a layer of ash, and where the shops once stood. Once again she tries to orient herself to places that had been familiar and comforting, serving as important markers of place identity. The Justice Building has also been reduced to a pile of rubble. She further assesses the condition of other local landmarks once meaningful as geographic cues: Peeta's bakery and its oven, the mayor's house, and the houses of the Victor's Village. Incidentally, unlike the damage to the Victors Village we see in the film "Mockingjay Part 1," the Village and all of its houses remain unscathed in the novel. She thus takes a moment during her tour to gather her thoughts inside the house where she has lived since winning the 74th Games.

Firebombings notwithstanding, the disappearance of one's childhood home, neighborhood or entire community can trigger a deep sense of loss. Residents of once-vibrant mining towns have often lamented the abandonment and dereliction of places they depended upon for their physical and emotional well-being. In the typical boom-bust economic cycle of one-industry towns, the mining or logging companies simply move elsewhere when a particular natural resource is depleted or becomes too expensive to extract. The railroads stop running, local businesses falter, and people move on to find employment elsewhere. Like their counterparts across the United States, family farms, small towns, and rural communities throughout Appalachia have succumbed to such global economic forces since the 1950s. As a result, countless Appalachian residents lost the sense of place they once felt for their homes. Thus, while the dramatic firebombing of an entire town may—quite thankfully—only be the stuff of dystopian novels, the ultimate loss of meaningful places in our lives is all too common.

The fact that Collins chose to end *Catching Fire* with the firebombing of District 12 is especially telling of the place's influence on Katniss' own identity. The main cliffhanger at the end of the novel occurs with Gale's dramatic, somber declaration that District 12 no longer exists. The message we might take from this is threefold. First, District 12 was important enough for Collins to conclude her second novel with its nearly complete obliteration. Second, President Snow decides to destroy the very place that Katniss loves the most, and third, Katniss unwaveringly keeps her hometown at the forefront of her mind throughout the series. Her life, values, and very identity are indelibly tied to this important mountain community. Just before Gale drops his final bombshell (pun intended) about the fate of District 12, Katniss can already imagine the worst-case scenario—that of firebombs obliterating the Seam. By destroying these places, President Snow is quite aware that he will simultaneously destroy a large piece of Katniss herself.

Becoming Attached to Place

What roles do meaningful places play in our own lives, and within the lives of our esteemed Hunger Games characters? We often come to feel specific sentiments and emotions for the places where we grew up, work, play, and socialize. This can often occur quite unconsciously and with nary a thought about the places we cherish. Geographers, environmental psychologists and other social scientists refer to such sentiments as *place attachment* or, to say it another way, demonstrating an *attachment to place*. According to Maria Giuliani, there is perhaps no type of human relationship, feelings of mutual affinity, social activity, or even feelings of bitterness and hostility that is not somehow rooted in place, or more specifically in one's attachment to places.[9]

In short, places matter. We live our lives and interact daily in places that are meaningful to us. They further contribute to our own cultural and personal identities, helping to determine something about who we are as individuals. Just as humans can affect places, these same places affect us in profound and often unconscious ways. It turns out that one particularly illuminating case in point is found within our unlikely heroine herself, Katniss Everdeen. Perhaps more than any other character, her personal identity is inextricably tied to District 12 as a distinctly special place. Her everyday behaviors and decisions are thereby shaped by her strong roots within her Appalachian home.

Research on the phenomenon of place attachment has revealed that entire groups of people, such as families, communities, or cultures, can collectively share emotional attachments to places. One prominent instance is found in the Seam of District 12, where its downtrodden if determined families share a common set of local cultural and ethnic backgrounds, ways of life, and socio-economic challenges.

Whether or not we are consciously aware, we all feel a complex range of emotional bonds—positive or negative—with certain places. These bonds can occur from current or past experiences within a place, such as those generated by fond or troublesome childhood memories. Such sentiments can apply to places of any geographic scale, including a specific residence or room, a local business, a neighborhood, town, city, or entire region like that of the central Appalachians. Our varied attachments to the "home place" is often nurtured by experiences with family, friends, and various personal relationships. Attachments to the workplace often occur due to favorable interactions and friendships with colleagues. Then there are the *third places*, or the places where we socialize outside of work and home. This concept was dubbed by sociologist Ray Oldenburg, who documented the importance of social relationships forged at community hangouts such as coffee shops, local restaurants, and other inexpensive venues.[10]

One way to consider your own place attachment is to ask yourself two successive questions: "Where do you feel most at home?" and "For what reasons do you feel at home there?" A sense of "at home-ness" is a fairly good indicator of attachment to a particularly meaningful place. When I pose these questions to my students, their responses consistently focus on a few central themes, namely childhood memories, recollections of important life events such as birthdays or graduations, regular social interactions with friends and family, quality time spent within nature or some version of a natural environment, and familiarity or comfort within the places they know well. As mentioned earlier, how and why people feel attached to various places in their lives will be unique from one person to another. This is because our feelings, experiences, imaginations, and interpretations are necessarily subjective and deeply personal.

This is why the observation of one's attachment to place has always been a challenge for researchers to pin down. It constitutes a subjective and complex set of feelings or emotions that is difficult to expose. While this situation is not likely to change much, certain themes have emerged from such research. Robert Riley confirms that attachment to places may be stimulated through social interactions and relationships with other people—family, friends, community, and even entire cultural groups.[11] Such feelings of place attachment may not be based primarily on the physical landscape of the place itself, but on the social meanings and experiences associated with that place. This might seem familiar with respect to Katniss' own consistent sentiments for home. Her primary concern from day one of the original series centers on feeding and protecting her immediate family.

She secondarily hopes to maintain important relationships with meaningful friends throughout the Seam and District 12 overall.

What role does place attachment actually play in our own lives? On one level, our affections and sentiments for various chunks of geography can provide a sense of daily security and personal comfort. Our favored places and the objects within them can provide predictable and familiar settings. Places also allow us to unleash our creativity and to feel that we maintain control over aspects of our lives. Consider, for instance, Katniss' development of confidence with hunting and gathering in the woods, and later her mastering of trading at the Hob and elsewhere. The woods, as a special place in its own right, provides physical sustenance, coupled with an opportunity to develop creative and necessary survival skills. In the woods she learns to think and act on her own, to make her own choices. Her personal agency is thus enabled here. For these reasons, the woods become a meaningful place where she feels at home. In this sense, places within and outside District 12 contribute directly to Katniss' development into a capable and skilled young woman who has a fighting chance to win two annual Games and a revolution to boot.

This is why the geographical paradox discussed in the previous chapter is pivotal for interpreting the Hunger Games saga. In the otherwise anonymous place called District 12, we find a distinctive and recognizable community and region. To convey her story and embedded messaging, Collins relies heavily on the historical, cultural, and environmental characteristics unique to the central Appalachians. And Katniss provides us with nothing less than a textbook case of how we can all form strong personal bonds with meaningful places.

Katniss' attachment to her mountain home is reminiscent of that felt by real Appalachians. The case of one accomplished writer with central Appalachian roots is particularly instructive. As a widely published black American author, professor, and social activist, Gloria Jean Watkins has considered her own sense of place and attachment to two homes in Kentucky. Readers may better recognize Watkins' pen name, bell hooks, which she prefers for her authored publications. In honor of her great-grandmother, Bell Blair Hooks, Watkins' pen name remains in all lower-case letters, she explains, to focus readers on the substance of her books rather than on her own self.

In a deeply personal reflection on how certain places have shaped her own identity, hooks considers her decision to move from New York City back to her former Appalachian home in Kentucky. Her personal relationship with the Blue Grass State, she realized, was primarily due to her parents, who were now aging in Hopkinsville where she was raised. "In my mind, Kentucky meant my parents," she explains. One could thus interpret her own attachment to Kentucky as arising from her own child-hood memories.[12]

The story does not end there but rather becomes more complicated. Hooks ultimately made a conscious decision to not move back to Hopkins-ville, as not all of her memories of the place were positive or happy. "I never felt that Hopkinsville was a place for me—the severe racial apartheid I'd grown up in, all those things...."[13] She had discovered early in life that, from her perspective, everything in Hopkinsville had become "deeply raced and deeply gendered."[14] In particular, the outward aggression of white commu-nity members toward people of color including herself thus engendered a deeply negative sense of place. These experiences, she reflects, "created in me, even as a child, a bitterness toward Kentucky and toward the land."[15] Intermixed with fond memories of her parents and the home place, there-fore, were troubling recollections of racial tension and mistreatment expe-rienced within the larger community.

She consequently decided to move to Berea Kentucky, where she had once given a lecture at the college there. Upon visiting, she "felt immedi-ately that Berea was a place for me that I could come and abide in."[16] In her case, the influence of place attachment—engendered through a mix of positive and negative sentiments—directly influenced her decision to move away from New York City. It further affected her ultimate decision of where to move and where not to move. Perhaps we can all conjure instances of how specific places and memories have influenced our own directions in life.

Bell hooks continues to discuss her conflicted sentiments for Ken-tucky in the Foreword to her book of poetry, *Appalachian Elegy*. In this piece, she discusses her belief that her soul was "imprinted with the hills of Kentucky" by age five or six.[17] The only time in her life when she remained racially unaware was as a girl in the Kentucky hills. There were no close neighbors, and her most "profound relationship" at that time was with the natural environment. Much like Katniss, the woods was where she could be herself. Hooks reflects further on her personal relationship with nature:

> It was "not the world of white people, white supremacy, but it was the world of nature, snakes, and other animals that could possibly attack you.... We were always there in this natural environment that was both for us and at times against us, and you had to respect it."[18]

Katniss understood the woods in a similar, contradictory light. At once the woods provided sustenance and comfort while also providing the threat of danger and harm. Like Katniss in certain ways, hooks came to feel a positive affinity—and a personal respect—for the woods and its sense of unhindered wilderness. And like Katniss, such potent childhood memories of nature and home engendered a considerable attachment to the place of her upbringing.

Black Lung

The life story of another remarkable individual intersects with all of these aspects: place attachment for home and family, Appalachian culture, coal mining and company towns, and Katniss' own sense of place for District 12. In the case of singer-songwriter and bluegrass musician Hazel Dickins, it is hard not to recognize numerous parallels between her own life experiences and that of our District 12 heroine. Hazel was born in Mercer County, West Virginia, in 1935 as the eighth of 11 children (including six boys, and five girls). The family home was located in the heart of our presumed District 12 core area in the extreme southern portion of the state, just to the northeast of the now-famed coal seams of Harlan County, Kentucky.

Like Katniss, Hazel and her family were brought up amidst the coal dust of surrounding mining camps. As Hazel's biographer Bill Malone states, Mercer County embodied a continued paradox of Appalachian coal country. That is, embedded within a breathtaking mountain region of stunning natural beauty is found some of America's most impoverished local communities dependent upon vast environmental degradation. The lives of the people living there have thus been "sacrificed on the altar of corporate greed."[19] During the early twentieth century at the peak of employment in the mines, this region held massive quantities of bituminous coal ready for the taking. It is this timeframe on which Suzanne Collins largely bases her own story of Katniss and the coal mining scene of District 12.

Hazel's father had been employed to cut and sell timber for mine roofing, while her brothers, brother-in-law, and cousins all labored in the mines. Their lives and sense of place were therefore all tied directly to the mining industry and its central role in community life. Eerily reminiscent of Katniss' own description of life in the Seam, Hazel grew up "seeing her brothers march off to the mines each morning and return in the evening with their faces and clothes covered with coal dust."[20] Hazel's sense of poor, working-class life was thus significantly shaped by the cultural experience of her youth, not unlike Katniss' own experiences within the Seam.

Eventually Hazel's family and lifestyle were permanently disrupted due to the intrusion of global influences from outside the community. In particular, more advanced mining technologies and approaches took their toll on the local economy and employment. As a trend that affected all of Appalachian coal country, these changes led to the region's great outmigration of the 1950s, a demographic transition that continued apace throughout the late twentieth century. The mechanization of coal mining progressed relentlessly, with innovations such as the "continuous miner" and the wholesale process of strip mining and mountain-top removal. The need for labor spiraled downward as large machinery replaced human workers. The population of Hazel's own county likewise declined steadily. Following the migration pattern of countless Appalachian families looking for work, Hazel eventually relocated to a working-class neighborhood in Baltimore. It was there where she ultimately nurtured her budding music career.

By the time she left home in 1954 for the big city, Hazel had come to understand a more troubling truth. The coal dust that had accompanied her family's livelihood in Mercer County had mercilessly seeped into the lungs of her brothers and cousins. This only cemented her realization that hard-working men like those of her family were being exploited for their labor. They were decidedly undervalued as human beings by the corporations that employed them. Much like the coal miners and Avox characters of the Hunger Games saga, working-class families like that of Hazel enjoyed little collective voice or self-determination within society.

Members of her own beloved family were exhibiting the persistent symptoms of what is known medically as coal workers' pneumoconiosis (CWP)—or, by its more familiar name, *black lung disease*. Although symptoms may not become serious for years or decades, it is decidedly a coal miner's infliction. As coal dust is continuously breathed in, particles settle in the airways and lungs. The body's natural response is to fight and remove the particles, though this continuous effort leads to inflammation. The extent of the disease is primarily based on how much dust someone has breathed in, and for how long. Typical symptoms may not surface until retirement and may include severe coughing, tightening of the chest, and shortness of breath—all of which can of course trigger additional ailments.

Readers might recall the subtle mention of black lung within the prequel, as Lucy Gray recalls some recent family history. An older man had agreed to take in all six Covey kids, for which Lucy Gray was grateful. She continued to explain that he had died a year earlier from the "black lung," though fortunately some of the Covey were able to take over his household duties (*BSS* 87).

While Suzanne Collins does not belabor the point, she makes it clear that the lives of Lucy Gray and the Covey have been directly affected by the disease. The coal miner who had taken in the clan following the death of Lucy Gray's parents had finally succumbed to black lung disease at an older age, as often occurs. They were consequently left to fend for themselves, with the older children—especially Lucy Gray—forced to grow up quickly.

Like any disease, this one does not only affect the life of the person afflicted, but of family members as well.

During the peak of her career many years later, Hazel rose to fame as a nationally renowned protest singer and advocate for the rights of working people. Her aim was particularly focused on improving the working conditions for Appalachian coal miners. Her own composition titled "Black Lung" became one of numerous "protest songs" sung by Hazel to raise awareness of corporate injustice. Written in 1969, the poignant elegy was inspired by the death of her own brother, Thurman, along with many other coal miners inflicted with the disease.[21] She had endured the trauma of watching Thurman die a horrible death from the affliction, with no means to pay for medical expenses or—later—for a funeral.

Hazel first introduced her song during the Smithsonian Folklife Festival, which served as a turning point in her own life. It was at this event where she became more widely known to others already passionate about similar causes. And, as is often the case, one opportunity can open doors to another. A year later she sang "Black Lung" at an event in Clay County, Kentucky, which was sponsored by Mountain People's Rights. This was a grassroots organization which aimed to raise awareness of coal companies refusing to pay benefits to victims of black lung disease. Hazel's performance of the song was covered in a *New York Times* article and was featured on the *CBS Evening News* with Walter Cronkite.[22]

With this exposure, opportunities snowballed quickly. She soon received a litany of invitations to perform "Black Lung" at union meetings and similar political events. She was further inspired to write additional songs with similar messaging, including a sub-style known as political ballads. One ballad she penned was "Clay County Miner." By 1972 she was participating in a series of Appalachian music workshops that concentrated on topics specifically geared to coal mining. She had been invited to the series by singer-activist Guy Carawan, just one of many influential voices who had learned of Hazel's work. In turn, these workshops increased her visibility among other well-known activists and musicians fighting for working-class justice. She later participated in the recording of a full LP album, *Come All You Coal Miners*.

Aside from these accomplishments—or because of them—Hazel's work went truly national with her singing role in the 1976 Academy Award–winning documentary film, *Harlan County, USA*. The film told the story of the prolonged strike in the coal fields of eastern Kentucky. Later in her lengthy and active music career she became a symbol for women's rights and the ongoing feminist movement, ushering in new roles for women in a world of country and bluegrass music dominated by men.

It is safe to conclude that Hazel's championing of workers' rights and her parallel singing career were profoundly influenced by a passionate, persistent attachment to the mountain home of her upbringing. Still, her sentiments for Appalachian coal country were highly conflicted. Hazel's biographer described her as having "mixed feelings" about leaving home to relocate to Baltimore in 1954, not unlike countless other families that risked everything to find work in larger cities. In the dead of night, Hazel later recalled her own poignant memories, "summoning up those ancient, dark mountains and the sight of her mother waving good-bye from the doorway" as she left their house for the last time.[23] "Adorned in a new dress that her brother Dan bought for her at the company store, Hazel 'said goodbye to that plain little mining town' and caught a Greyhound bus to Baltimore."[24] She chose this city at the behest of her sister, Velvie, who had already been living and working there. This was a common pattern known as *chain migration*, whereby rural migrants follow on the heels of family members who had already established themselves in a new city.

Like many immigrant groups who move to strange new places, Hazel and her family found comfort in living among people like themselves. Communities like "Little Appalachia"—as their neighborhood in Baltimore's Lower Charles Village was dubbed—allowed them to live amongst people with familiar dialects, customs, and even musical interests. Still, living in Baltimore proved to be an intensely lonely, hostile, and unforgiving place for Hazel. She recalled becoming self-conscious about the way she dressed in public, not to mention her accent and mannerisms. She was an outsider, having moved away from a familiar place that she had called home.

Katniss, Coal, and the Seam

Hazel's experience may be reminiscent of Katniss' own emotional departure from District 12, as she is summarily ripped from her home and thrown on a train to the Capitol. Hazel's situation was more a voluntary one, of course. She had been lured to some extent by her own sister, who gushed about the amazing "creature comforts that were available in the city."[25] Such a sense of wonder about urban life reminds one of Katniss and Peeta's own culture shock upon their arrival in the Capitol for the first time.

For Katniss, coal dust and the mines were integral to her upbringing in the Seam. Like Hazel, Katniss' identity and sense of self were immeasurably shaped by the coalfields and the kind of life they provided. She clarifies this with various statements that would normally go unnoticed, such as her description of Prim polishing their father's shaving mirror every night to rid it of accumulated coal dust (*THG* 27). Coal also literally seeps in and around the Hob, perhaps the most important local place for fostering a sense of community. The Hob, Katniss explains, is the marketplace—albeit officially illegal—which makes use of an abandoned coal warehouse. She also describes technological improvements for coal extraction and conveyance, adding that the Hob took over the space when a more efficient means of transporting coal to the trains was developed (*THG* 11).

Katniss' descriptions of life in coal country could easily have been written by her authentic Appalachian counterparts. One case in point is that of Shirley Glass, a lifetime resident of Dante, Virginia. Located in the extreme southwestern part of the state, this mountain mining town is found at the heart of our aforementioned District 12 core area. Nearly all facets of the town and its community were controlled by the Clinchfield Coal Corporation until it closed its mines permanently. Glass recounts her own life and times within the now-struggling town:

> I've lived here all my life. I was born and raised in the house—it just recently was tore down—here in Dante. My father worked for Clinchfield; well, he retired, or really he got disabled, from Clinchfield. He had black lung. And he worked for them like thirty, forty years, up into the '80s. It used to be, above where I lived was the tipple [structure where coal is screened and loaded into trucks or railway cars]. And they would wash the coal, and the creek would be black as coal. And we'd be playing, and sometimes we'd fall in the creek and get black as coal.[26]

Shirley's story and recollections are representative of people's experiences within coal mining towns and the companies that owned them. No doubt, Katniss would have felt at home in Dante. It follows that Katniss' own challenging life within the Seam, surrounded by all things coal, was not merely an exaggerated dystopian scenario. Rather, Suzanne Collins created a believable character imbued with a realistic perspective on coal-town life.

The realistic impressions of life in the Seam went even further. Katniss comments on the accidents and injuries commonly associated with coal mining in District 12. While inspecting her own severe burns during her first Games, Katniss reflects on the place she knows best, that of home. She tries to recall what she knows about treating burns. Such injuries are common, she explains, due to the community's dependence on cooking and heating with coal. Then she further recalls the mine accidents with far worse implications than daily coal burns (*THG* 178). In this way, Katniss recognizes the paradox of coal in their own lives and community. The black rock is at once a household necessity and a constant threat of danger, death, and local tragedy.

Such dangers were all too real, especially prior to greater mechanization after the 1960s. As Peter Crow explains,

Before unions and mechanization, a miner got paid only for the coal he hand-loaded, not for setting safety timbers or for traveling sometimes miles to the coalface. If the company inspector found too much shale in a load of coal, he dumped it out, and the miner got nothing. Before mid–1900s federal safety regulations, a miner's safety was almost exclusively in his own hands and those of his buddies. A less-than-vigilant miner was not only a walking dead man; he was a liability to his entire crew.[27]

Of course, Katniss is forever changed by her father's death from just such a tragedy—in his case, a coal mine explosion of mysterious origin. For Katniss, coal and its integral roles in the local community and family life are inseparable; her sense of place for District 12 is largely shaped by this valuable—and flammable—black rock. Nor can Katniss escape coal at school. Early in *The Hunger Games*, she describes her education to date: "Somehow it all comes back to coal at school. Besides basic reading and math most of our instruction is coal-related" (*THG* 41–42). She then dismissively comments on other lessons primarily centered around how much the districts owe the Capitol.

Coal is thus an omnipresent—if sometimes annoying—part of Katniss' life experience. But the main point here is unavoidable: District 12 and the Seam, as distinct places, are largely defined by coal and their collective role in serving the Capitol. Whether dominated by an authoritarian regime or an impersonal corporation, the effect is essentially the same. Not only is pro-industrial propaganda infused into the school curriculum, but Katniss further recognizes on some level that the relative benefit to her community is minuscule. Her dismissive tone essentially asks why they need to learn so much about coal when its benefits are largely going to a faraway place.

Despite living with the hardships levied by an oppressive organization (whether a mining company or the Capitol), these coal-seam communities were considered home by both Katniss Everdeen and Hazel Dickens. Both women had generated a strong, emotional attachment to their home places which influenced decisions and directions later in life. Indeed, their personal identities and the very causes they fought for were inextricably shaped by these fundamental aspects of home.

3

Katniss at Home

Why is home so important to Katniss? From a light-hearted perspective, Katniss may be one of the few fictional characters who can rival *E.T.—the Extra Terrestrial* in her desire for going home. This is because Katniss' own identity, sense of self, and cultural traits are all significantly shaped by her upbringing within central Appalachia, and within District 12 in particular. Collins' original series is much more than a story of rebellion and the rise of an unlikely heroine. It is also a story of one's cultural and emotional connections with home, and how our home places ultimately influence our own individual senses of self. This is the topic to which we turn here, to consider the ways in which meaningful places help to shape our personal identities and even our future paths in life. In Katniss' case, her own identity and sense of self are rooted in the places she interprets collectively as "home." For these reasons, it will be instructive to examine a bit of how Katniss defines home and how she expresses her attachment to home throughout the series. Her own fictional case might ultimately resonate with a lot of us.

In one respect, Katniss Everdeen is central Appalachia personified. As we saw in previous chapters, Suzanne Collins decided to locate Katniss and her personal identity within this mountainous region, and more specifically within a marginalized coal-mining community. Whatever motives drove her to do so, she could not have designed a more genuine, convincing case of how we can all identify with, and be defined by, the places we call home. The very geography that underlies Katniss' formative years arguably played a fundamental role in molding her own sense of self and her emotional ties to family, friends, and community.

How Katniss Defines Home

Katniss' identity with the Seam and District 12 is magnified even more so by her limited travel opportunities. The Capitol simply forbids such individual freedom of movement—at least by the time Katniss is born and raised. The furthest she ventures is apparently out to the lake—quite a hike, but within a two-hour walk we are told. It is therefore not hard to imagine that she was experiencing a particularly acute sense of homesickness after being summarily ripped away from her home of sixteen years. And her narrative throughout the series is replete with statements making that case.

Let's look first at how Katniss defines home and how, for her, the idea of home represents a variety of related meanings. While being whisked toward the Capitol after her first reaping, for instance, Katniss reflects on what—and whom—she is leaving behind: "Imagining my home makes me ache with loneliness. This day has been endless. Could Gale and I have been eating blackberries only this morning?" She continues to ponder the notion that if she goes back to sleep, she will happily end up back in District 12, where she "belongs" (*THG* 54).

This brief passage is packed with clues as to how Katniss perceives her home place and what it means to her. When imagining home, she aches with loneliness, a typical indicator of homesickness and how she profoundly misses the place. Further, she immediately thinks of Gale and their shared, symbiotic relationship with the natural environment—represented in this case by their mutual enjoyment of wild blackberries. This version of home is therefore synonymous with the woods, a distinct though unbounded place she associates with meaningful memories of her times with Gale. But she then hopes to wake up "back in District 12" where she "belongs." Her conception of place, and her attachment to home, are thus broadened to include all of District 12 as a bounded, designated place. She therefore feels at home—and defines home—as those familiar places existing on both sides of the District 12 fence. Home is not just a house or a site for Katniss. It is a multi-faceted, rather ambiguous mix of places or imaginations, depending upon which memory or story she is recalling.

In terms of the physical sites or locations to which Katniss feels attached, there are many. Her notion of "home" may connote her original house located in the Seam, or—perhaps less so—her later house in the Victor's Village. But home might also include places where she interacts regularly with her mother, Prim, and Gale. In this case her "home" is identified with her close bonds to family or friends, even after being relocated to District 13. Home can also encompass broader realms of her community, including the Seam, the town square, District 12 as a whole, and beyond the fence to the woods and lake. As we will consider more below, Katniss associates her meaning of home with all of these places at various points throughout the series.

As is true for many of us, Katniss often associates feeling at home with her close proximity to immediate family members—notably Prim, her mother, and deceased father. Such associations and memories appear often as she navigates her way through the 74th Games. On one level she remains emotionally distant from her mother for reasons she does not yet understand. Her feelings are conflicted, however, given that her entire family still provides her with the most fundamental connections to home.

During her first full morning on the train following the reaping, Katniss is disturbingly awoken by Effie promising a big, big day. While getting dressed, Katniss contemplates the gold mockingjay pin that Madge had given her. "My fingers trace the circle around the little gold mockingjay and I think of the woods, and of my father, and of my mother and Prim waking up, having to get on with things" (*THG* 54). This is a powerful admission of how the pin comes to represent home, and Katniss' personal attachment to place. Touching the pin triggers memories of home and its varied meanings, including the woods, her father, mother, and Prim, along with their familiar, daily routine. Sure, the little pin and its inclusive bird would grow to symbolize nothing less than a full-blown rebellion for the districts. It would even spark a fashion craze in the Capitol. But for Katniss its meaning is a simple one; it signifies the home place and her attachment to it.

At one point after arriving in the Capitol, thoughts of home become unbearable, giving rise to a lingering if tenuous bond with her mother. While stroking the "silky braids" her mother "so carefully arranged," this experience triggers deeper thoughts of family and home. For one thing, Katniss expresses regret for having left her blue dress and shoes on the floor of the train. In this bout of remorse, she wishes that she would have tried to "hold on to a piece of her, of home." In this case, her mother and her home place are conceived essentially as one and the same (*THG* 63).

These varied definitions of home would likely be familiar to geographers Alison Blunt and Robyn Dowling.[1] Their own preferred definition of home, from a humanistic geography perspective, involves two key elements. First, a home can be conceptualized as an actual *place*, a specific site in which we live. This place or site could be at the scale of an apartment or house (or other physical dwelling), street or neighborhood, or community or city. The second element of home is more imaginary, one that is imbued with feelings. Such feelings are not necessarily simple nor one-dimensional. One might report feelings of belonging, comfort, desire, or safety, for instance, while simultaneously countered by feelings of fear, alienation, or discomfort. That said, these feelings are still spatially defined and tied to place. As such, home is a "complex and multi-layered geographical concept," as Blunt and Dowling summarize.

It follows that home can be conceived as "a place/site, a set of feelings/cultural meanings, and the relations between the two."[2] It is normal for us to accumulate a set of sentiments and emotions associated with our own homes. These places become meaningful through time and are full of personal significance. The main point, perhaps, is that the concept of "home" for Katniss is at once a physical location and an emotional space to which she feels a sense of belonging—or a sense of feeling "at home."

We learn more about Katniss' attachment to both of her home residences at the beginning of *Catching Fire*. With Gale in the mines now, Katniss is on her own in the woods to continue their necessary and familiar routine of hunting and gathering. Following an impressively productive hunting foray, she clarifies to which home she is returning—that is, to her old residence near the Meadow. She explains that while Prim and her mother are now "happily installed" in their new house within the Victor's Village, she still makes use of their older home in various ways. She is the only one who continues to use the "squat, little place," she explains, telling us emphatically that this place is where she was raised and is therefore her real home (*CF* 6).

This is a significant indication of her relative level of attachment to both dwellings. Her strongest bond is with the original house. This does not come as a surprise given her wealth of accumulated memories there. The vast majority of her fond—or at least familiar and comfortable—recollections are associated with that particular house, and with being raised by her parents. While visiting her original house after the hunt, she changes clothes and reminisces about those very experiences. She gives herself a few minutes to sit in the kitchen and mourn for her old life there. This is followed by another telling admission: "We barely scraped by, but I knew where I fit in, I knew what my place was in the tightly interwoven fabric that was our life" (*CF* 7). She further considers that this life she once knew was actually more secure and safe compared to her current life as a Victor, even now that she is showered with the riches of the Capitol.

She therefore knew her "place," which in this case refers to her role within the family unit and its "interwoven fabric." A geographer could not have stated this more eloquently. This previous life had afforded Katniss with a sense of security and comfort—and also predictability—to which she would ideally like to return. Such a strong attachment to place is therefore not predicated on one's overall physical comforts or socioeconomic status. She had arguably lost a piece of her identity with her removal from "her place" within the family unit.

On the second day following the reaping, Katniss' mind wanders back to her mother and Prim. She imagines their morning routine and that they must be out of bed by now. Her mother would be preparing a breakfast of mush, and Prim would be milking her goat before school. She further notes that she was still at home only two mornings earlier (*THG* 87). In this case, house and home are one and the same. The house serves as a meaningful container of memories and shared experiences. The place literally houses her family's otherwise mundane habits and behaviors that now hold more meaning than ever. A full-blown case of homesickness has now set in.

Katniss' sentiments for Prim and her mother become even more evident during time spent with Rue. One might even argue that her strong attachment to home is what led—albeit unwittingly—to her first act of defiance following Rue's death. Had Rue not reminded Katniss so much of Prim and—by association—of home, she may not have erupted so emotionally upon Rue's death, thereby causing some raised eyebrows in the Capitol.

We first meet Rue when she meekly encounters Katniss and Peeta in the Training Center. Katniss tells us that Rue is the twelve year old who reminded her so much of Prim, though up close she appears to be only ten (*THG* 98). At this point Katniss bites her lip as memories of home come roaring back. She quickly makes a meaningful association between Rue and a small, yellow flower of the same name that adorns the Meadow back in District 12. She further compares Rue with her sister Prim, noting that neither of them could be heavier than 70 pounds soaking wet (*THG* 99).

The little girl from District 11 thus becomes a signifier, or symbol of home, and more specifically a reminder of the Meadow. As discussed in Chapter 2, the Meadow is identified as one of Katniss' most meaningful places. Later during the Games, Katniss admits what we likely already suspected, that Rue unwittingly becomes a surrogate for Prim. While sharing a meal with Rue during some rare downtime, Rue asks if Katniss was joking about wanting her for an ally. Although Katniss imagines Haymitch's displeasure with this decision, she quickly justifies it for us: "Because she's a survivor, and I trust her, and why not admit it? She reminds me of Prim" (*THG* 201). Then a bit later Katniss makes the connection between Rue, Prim, and home. The "brief sense of home" she had enjoyed during her night with Rue had already vanished (*THG* 238). Consequently, Prim likely serves as Katniss' most important association with home throughout the series. And Rue temporarily elevates that association to the surface of Katniss' conscience.

Running Away

Katniss' resilient, unwavering bond with her family is clearly the fundamental reason for her attachment to District 12. Such intertwined connections between family, friends, and the places we live can provide a powerful rationale for staying rooted in place. We are inextricably tied to the social bonds of geography. Following an uncomfortable discussion and some pangs of reality, Katniss and Gale realize the extent to which they remain attached—physically and emotionally—to District 12 and the Seam. Both of them seriously contemplate escaping District 12 for the wilderness, not once but twice within the original series. Confident as they are with their survival and teamwork skills, they conclude quite reasonably that they could make a run for it and escape, perhaps forever.

Except for the rather limiting fact that they are literally stuck in place. Early in the first novel they are perched in the woods and contemplating a run for freedom. Gale suggests to Katniss that they run off and live in the woods. He convinces her that they could make it on their own (*THG* 9). They ultimately dismiss the idea outright, however, recognizing that their fantasy escape can never happen. They consider that their combined families have too many kids between them, and that they all can't possibly tromp through the wilderness together. Further, Katniss reveals her devotion to her sister, asking herself how she could leave Prim when she is the only person on the planet who she is certain of loving (*THG* 10).

Like many humans, then, Katniss and Gale recognize they are tied to place, tied to home, and are at least partly responsible for the well-being of their respective families. Thus, while one's local geographic setting can provide various opportunities, geography can also be constraining. Many of us cannot simply uproot ourselves and move elsewhere on a whim. Few humans are truly footloose. There are jobs, families, responsibilities—not to mention the people we desire to have around us to make our lives more meaningful. It is this realization to which Katniss and Gale eventually concede.

The pair makes a second, futile attempt to escape within *Catching Fire*. While sitting inside the cabin by the lake, Katniss mentions to Gale that she has a plan, the highlight of which involves running away. For the moment, they are both keen on the idea. Katniss further presumes this time that they will indeed bring their families. They actually make plans to convince numerous others to escape with them. The presumed escape party thus continues to grow in number—now including their own siblings, Haymitch, Peeta, Peeta's family (though Katniss presumes they will decline), and Hazelle Hawthorne.

Then Katniss accidentally foils the plan altogether by mentioning the uprising in District Eight. With that news, Gale's focus shifts, and he begins to envision a larger rebellion. He wants to join the fight. Katniss is still intent on escaping, but Gale retorts that he would never leave in a million years. He then asks Katniss about the other families of District 12 who do not enjoy the wherewithal to run away. Now that the rebellion has started, Gale begins to think more globally about assisting the cause (*CF* 96–100). Gale has verbalized what Katniss likely knows internally, that they now have a greater responsibility to see the rebellion through and—more directly—to defend the place they call home.

At Home in the Woods

Katniss' longing for home makes a surprising appearance in the first film, "The Hunger Games." In this scene, Katniss (played by Jennifer Lawrence) is acclimating to the spacious accommodations of the Training Center's penthouse suite. No dialogue is spoken, though her body language speaks volumes. Left to her own devices—quite literally—Katniss finds a remote control and starts pushing buttons. Anyone who enjoys exploring new electronic gadgets could certainly relate to her fascination, and the scene is certainly worth a chuckle. With the remote control in hand, she faces a massive window that provides real-time video of various urban and natural settings.

While changing the scenes with each click, Katniss is simply transfixed with the technology and the images presented. She first views an urban street scene, followed by—for some unfathomable reason—a desert landscape filled with Joshua Trees. It is the next view, however, that gives her pause as she is visibly taken aback. A tranquil scene of a lush, forested environment envelops her view. Considering this for a moment, she slowly moves toward the window as if falling into some sort of trance. She is visually flustered, most definitely because the image serves as a powerful reminder of home, and more specifically, of the woods where she hunts. She is thereby reminded of her recent and traumatic departure from District 12—a place to which she is unlikely to return. Becoming visibly disturbed, she turns off the device completely. Though not a particularly memorable action scene, viewers obtain a sense of what she left behind, along with her poignant memories of home.

Perhaps more than any other place, Katniss' own personal identity and sense of self are tied to the woods. This otherwise ambiguous stretch of nature holds various levels of meaning. Like the Meadow, the woods can be defined as a distinct place, albeit with fuzzy boundaries. As discussed earlier, such a natural space becomes a distinctive place for Katniss—and for her readers—based on the human interaction that occurs there.

On an emotional level, the woods provide Katniss with a litany of positive, soothing memories of past experiences. Perhaps most prominently, Katniss' early life was shaped by the precious times she spent with her father, always under his tutelage. Later she is forced to apply and improve upon her skills while teaming up with Gale to feed their families. As the pair's friendship continues to grow, the woods provide a rare outlet for social interaction in a place where they both feel relatively comfortable.

Katniss' attachment to the woods is expressed on numerous occasions throughout the series. At one point in the first novel, Katniss is recovering from the tracker-jacker venom during the 74th Games. She manages to drag herself to a honeysuckle bush and pluck a flower, setting a drop of its nectar on her tongue. This in turn triggers a pleasant memory of home, "warming my veins with memories of summer, and my home woods and Gale's presence beside me" (*THG* 196). In this case, her imagination of home involves being in the woods with Gale, particularly during the summer.

One night in the arena Katniss enjoys the site of a full moon, though she wonders whether it is real or manufactured by the Gamemakers. Just prior to leaving District 12, she had observed the full moon while hunting into the late hours with Gale. She uses this fond memory to estimate her time away from home, thinking the moon may have now completed its cycle. This triggers additional introspection. She tells us how badly she wants it to be her own moon, meaning the same one she enjoys from the woods around District 12. While the authenticity of everything within the arena can and should be questioned, the image of the moon provides her with a tangible connection to the home place—and more specifically, to the woods.

The woods further serve as a sanctuary where Katniss feels most comfortable being herself, presumably without surveillance. Following her father's death, she had formed a second meaningful relationship with her hunting partner, Gale. This friendship provided an additional layer of meaning to the place they called the woods. Early in *The Hunger Games* Katniss tells us that she is only comfortable being herself when Gale is present. She climbs the hill to "our place," consisting of a rocky ledge protected from surveillance by a thicket of berry bushes. She further tells us that Gale claims she never smiles unless she is in the woods (*THG* 6).

Katniss thus recognizes that only in this place, and with Gale, is she able to relax her guard and enjoy displaying her authentic self. She further claims to have "our place," consisting of a specific rock ledge, conveniently obscured by berry bushes. If we take Gale's observation on face value that she never smiles except in the woods, this seems to indicate that it is out here beyond the District 12 fence where she is the most genuinely happy. Gale's presence as a trusted friend only strengthens her bond with the woods and the meanings associated with it.

Of course, President Snow is well aware of Katniss' close identity with the woods, and thus he cannot resist turning this otherwise soothing tract of nature against her. To Katniss' horror near the beginning of *Catching Fire*, Snow essentially invades her house in the Victor's Village. During this uncomfortable exchange she learns that even her exploits in the woods have been recorded. She is clearly distraught and puzzled when Snow reveals his knowledge of her forays with Gale each Sunday. Being watched in the woods had never crossed her mind until that moment, she tells us, adding that the woods always represented a safe place beyond the gaze of the Capitol (*CF* 24). With this revelation, Snow has already begun to torment Katniss by ripping away a piece of her own authentic self. And now even that emotional sanctuary has been taken from her.

The place known generally as the woods has clearly become an integral part of Katniss' life and identity. It is hard to imagine how Katniss would have developed her survival skills and personal confidence without access to this wilderness beyond the fence. Without the woods and the determined teachings of her father, we would not be talking about Katniss Everdeen, the Girl on Fire. It is to the sizable influence of her father's teachings that we now turn.

An Influential Father

In one respect the skilled, capable girl we know as Katniss Everdeen was raised in the woods—at least from the earliest years she can remember. Her identity is largely a product of the experiential education she obtained there. And the story of the woods is the story of her father—at least while he was alive. Her father is—as I tell my students—perhaps the most influential character in the trilogy despite having died before the story begins. As Tina Hanlon claims, her father's death is most certainly the defining event of Katniss' life prior to the 74th Games.[3] We have her father to thank for virtually all of Katniss' knowledge learned within the woods, not to mention her growing confidence to venture beyond the fence. In this way her father represents the Appalachian cultural practice of living off the land.[4] Following his untimely death, she eventually returns to the woods to hone the skills handed down from her father, with the singular aim of sustaining her family.

Although her father remains nameless, we learn that he was an avid and capable hunter. Moreover, he had clearly gained his own skill set well prior to his daughter's birth. As Katniss reflects prior to the 74th Games, she calculates that she had been feeding her family for four years—taking her back to probably age 12. With this thought she awards herself a rare compliment, believing that feeding her family since that age was "no small task." She then humbly admits that she still does not live up to the skills mastered by her late father, because he "had more practice" at hunting with his bow and arrows (*THG* 89). Given his experience and ability to craft exquisite bows of his own, the man had likely learned his wilderness skills as a youth himself. Recent readers of the prequel have appropriately considered her father's possible origin, perhaps having garnered his wilderness skills from someone connected to Lucy Gray and the Covey.

Throughout much of *The Hunger Games*, Collins provides only occasional bits of information about Katniss' father, somewhat in the manner of a dripping faucet. This is likely why his character receives relatively scant attention from scholars and fans alike. We learn that Katniss has several bows she uses for hunting, all crafted by her father before he died in the mine explosion. He had also met Katniss' future mother for the first time due specifically to his forest gathering skills. Although her mother was from District 12's merchant class, her father had collected medicinal herbs and sold them at her mother's apothecary in town.

In one sense, then, it was the woods that ultimately brought Katniss' parents together. While her mother had already assembled a book of plant knowledge for purposes of treating ailments, her father provided additional entries of his own. Katniss paid more attention to this book while coping with her father's death. Expressing her personal awe, she notes that the book is filled with valuable information about plants that could be eaten, including dandelions, pokeweed, wild onions, and pines. She and Prim spend much of one night absorbing its knowledge (*THG* 50).

Perhaps most famously, it is Katniss' father who shares with us the origin of her very identity, the katniss plant. Prior to the 74th Games, Katniss tells us about the time in late summer when she noticed a special type of tuber plant growing near a pond, with tall, arrowhead-shaped leaves. She then recalls her father joking that as long as she can "find herself," she will never starve (*THG* 52). One can interpret this statement in the literal sense—that of finding the plant which can put food on the table. Or his statement can further be viewed as a metaphor for Katniss recognizing her own sense of self while maturing into adulthood. Alternatively, this could serve as yet another example of that characteristic Appalachian dead-pan humor. In any case, Katniss' identity is clearly tied to nature and specifically to the wilderness of the woods. Indeed, she is actually named for the very plant that would help sustain her and her family. If there is a more effective approach to symbolically tying a character with a specific place, I cannot fathom what it would be.

Following her father's death, Katniss gains the courage—not to mention a personal determination—to venture into the woods on her own. "The woods became our savior, and each day I went a bit farther into its arms" (*THG* 51). She found eggs, caught fish, shot the occasional squirrel or rabbit, and gathered recognizable plants. She then once again acknowledges her father's posthumous role in their very survival, explaining that she double-checked her harvested plants with the photos he had taken. In this way, she kept her and her family alive.

It is reasonable to conclude that she would not have garnered the courage or incentive to venture beyond the fence without her father by her side. At one point in *The Hunger Games*, Katniss mentally compares herself with other tributes and reflects on various advantages she had gained back in District 12 (*THG* 94). She explains that her family's resourcefulness has provided her with certain advantages, notably her strength and ability to stand up straight. A combination of her hunting activities and the resulting dependable food supply had consequently improved her overall health as compared to much of the Seam's population.

Katniss may have admirably taken on the challenge of feeding her family, but it was her father who was responsible for forging her bonds with the woods as a distinct place. Beyond the immediate sustenance of the Everdeen family, Katniss' skills proved absolutely necessary for surviving both Games, and throughout the rebellion as well. Do we not have her father to thank, therefore, for indirectly bringing down the Capitol? For all of these reasons, Katniss' father can easily be considered one of the most influential characters of the entire series—even without showing up alive.

At the Lake

About a two-hour hike from District 12 is "the lake," which in itself becomes a special place for Katniss. The water and its environs serve as a repository for pleasant memories, particularly related to times spent with her father. Although Collins does not award the lake with a capitalized, proper name like the Meadow, it nonetheless becomes a meaningful place unto itself. Together, the woods and the lake provide a familiar and comfortable outdoor environment which is woven throughout the story line of the original series as well as the more recent prequel.

And while some 64 years separate the original series from the prequel, it is clear that three successive generations have considered this nameless lake as part of their collective homes. In chronological order, we first learn that the Covey kids and young Coriolanus enjoy time around the lake following the tenth Games. It is this setting that serves as a veritable stage for the drama playing out between Coriolanus and Lucy Gray near the conclusion of the prequel. It follows, then, that the generational link between the prequel and the original series is found in Katniss' father. He represents the next successive generation beyond the Covey. And there is no doubt that he becomes fully familiar with the lake and the woods surrounding it during his younger years. Of course, whether a direct familial link exists between

him and the Covey remains to be seen. What is certain is that three generations of Hunger Games characters have perceived the lake and its environs
as a special place in their lives.

Representing the third generation of this chain, Katniss benefits
grandly from her father's wealth of knowledge as well as from his intentional nurturing. In one of numerous enjoyable recollections, Katniss
relates how her father would hunt around the lake's margins for waterfowl
while she searched for eggs hidden in the grasses. They would both dig
for katniss roots, which, as she recalls, once led to an "amazing" dinner of
roasted duck and baked tubers upon their return home (*CF* 34). As we have
seen, it is precisely this type of social interaction among family or friends
that can engender strong emotional attachments to important places in our
lives.

One focus of human activity at the lake is found in a small, single-room
cabin. This refuge is described in some detail by Katniss within *Catching
Fire*. After walking for approximately two hours through the woods, she
arrives at a one-room, concrete building that she hesitates to call a "house"
due to its small size. She then notices the fireplace that still remains from
years ago when she and her father had collected wood. The same wood pile
is still there, providing a physical connection between their prior shared
experiences and her current visit. She had also "played house" here with a
twig broom made by her father when she was approximately eight years old.
Her father had also suspected, she tells us, that many such cabins existed
here in the distant past. This is likely a tip from Suzanne Collins that these
derelict properties once likely served as a mountain resort for lakeside rec-
reation during the American era.

We learn further from the prequel that the Covey and even Coriolanus had plied these very same environs more than six decades earlier. Likewise, the concrete cabin is likely the very same one Katniss recalls in her
own time. In these ways, Collins has taken a once-remote, uninhabited site
in the wilderness and converted it into a meaningful place for her main
characters. And due to her father's own strong connection to the lake, Katniss comes to feel at home there, demonstrating a substantial attachment to
place.

Learning to Swim, to Trade, and to Survive

For those who have not read (or do not remember) the novels, one may
ponder in the second film, "Catching Fire," just how Katniss had become
so comfortable around water. At the launch of the 75th Games, she simply dives in like a professional swimmer. As with other subtle pieces of the

story line, only the novels can provide the meticulous background to such mysteries. It turns out that Katniss learned to swim at the infamous lake in the woods, once again through her father's initiative. This topic arises at one point while Katniss is in the bathtub calming herself prior to kicking off the Victory Tour. In a rare moment of escape, she sinks below the water and reflects on fond memories with her father. She focuses particularly on the hot summer Sundays when her father would lead her to a small lake in the woods that he had discovered while hunting. She further tells us that she does not recall learning to swim because she was so young (*CF* 34).

Aside from her invaluable hunting and gathering acumen, her ability to swim becomes an indispensable—if rather convenient—skill with the opening of the 75th Games in *Catching Fire*. After comfortably diving into the water around the Cornucopia, she even compares the tropical-like water to the lake of her youth. Granted, she does admit the need to contend with a longer distance and larger waves than found within her "quiet lake at home," though she quickly finds her body cutting effortlessly through the water (due to—it turns out—a unique floatation device).

Her ability to swim thus provides quite an advantage as the 75th Games begin. Even Finnick is impressed with her water skills, asking where she might have learned to swim in the vast interior of District 12. She deflects this question with a joke about having learned in the bathtub. Focused less on her own advantage, she realizes with a touch of bitterness that this particular arena holds an "enormous advantage" for District 4 tributes like Finnick and Mags. At the start of the Games she bets that most of the victors cannot swim, noting correctly that there was no swimming pool provided at the Training Center. Her deadpan humor surfaces as she quips in the arena, "Either you came in here a swimmer or you'd better be a really fast learner" (*CF* 270). In fact, following some initial skirmishes at the Cornucopia, Katniss surveys the arena to discover that many of the tributes still remained stuck on their starting plates, having not yet even ventured into the water. Once again, her father's prophetic planning had awarded Katniss with a decided advantage during the 75th Games.

One persistent curiosity remains about her father. For what reasons was he so intent on teaching Katniss this litany of wilderness skills beginning at such a young age? During the bathtub scene, we learn that Katniss was very young when her father taught her to swim; she cannot even recall when she learned to do so. This points directly to her father's early and persistent determination to train Katniss to fend for herself should the need arise. And, of course, the need does arise grandly. Certainly, learning to swim at an early age is not uncommon; many of us were swimming at the behest of determined adults before we could speak full sentences. What is more remarkable is the full package of outdoor training that Katniss' father intentionally—and illegally—delivered right up through his untimely death. It is apparent that he was on a serious personal mission to transform his oldest daughter into a survivor. And job well done!

Katniss' father was driven by a unique and unwavering determination, one likely rooted in his own discontent with the Capitol's oppressive hand. He suspected that his family may not be able to survive the impoverished conditions of the Seam without developing some kind of advantage. He may have also considered the distinct possibility of his own premature death. The risk of mining accidents—for one thing—was very real, as discussed previously. There was a fair chance that he would not be able to provide for his family or watch his daughters grow up.

But was he primarily concerned with potential mining accidents, or more so with being punished for his own rebellious activities? He had already demonstrated such behaviors simply by singing and teaching "The Hanging Tree" to his daughters before their horrified mother put a stop to it (*MJ* 124). And, to what extent did both fathers of Katniss and Gale know each other? They were both miners from the Seam, of course, and Gale had somehow learned his own survival skills in the woods. There is seemingly more of this larger story lurking beneath the surface of Katniss' own training at the hands of her skillful father.

Either way, it is safe to presume that very few fathers—whether living within the fictitious world of District 12 or within our own—would aspire to teach and train their children in such a determined, strategic manner. Most children with access to some vestige of a forest would be content to have their fathers help build a simple treehouse or play the occasional game of hide-and-seek. The main takeaway here is that what Katniss' father successfully accomplished—both through his own wilderness skills and his methodical training regimen for Katniss—is not just uncommon, it is remarkable. Whatever his inner motive may have been, Katniss was clearly being groomed for a future life without him, and as someone who could confidently care for their family.

Katniss' training continued inside the District 12 fence as well. Notably, she had accompanied her father to learn how to navigate the local black market centered on the Hob. In what social scientists refer to as an *informal economy*, Katniss learned how to barter and trade under the radar of the watchful eyes of the Capitol. Her experiential education involved finding buyers for game and other forest products useful for various household needs. Following her father's death, Katniss recalled that it had been a "frightening" experience to enter the Hob alone the first time. In this way we learn that her father had allowed—or outright encouraged—Katniss to join him on his trading expeditions through town. She recalls fondly that "people respected him," and so by association they became more comfortable with Katniss as well. Not only had her father become an avid wilderness expert, but he had successfully assembled a local community network. Upon his death, therefore, Katniss was well poised to take the proverbial baton to carry on that role. She would not be just another stranger wading into an unfamiliar local community.

Perhaps the most significant outcome from all of Katniss' training comes at the conclusion of her first Games. Beyond all of her father's contributions, the ability to discern between nutritious and poisonous forest foods comes into play. Late within the 74th Games, Katniss carefully considers a suspicious berry she encounters in the forested arena. At this point, she recalls one of her father's vital lessons: "Not these, Katniss. Never these. They're nightlock. You'll be dead before they reach your stomach" (*THG* 318).

This knowledge, of course, ultimately saves her life—while likely ending that of Foxface. But it also provides Katniss and Peeta with a strategic way out of the 74th Games. And, of course, we know the chain reaction of events that follows this episode. It is a bunch of berries—in one sense or another—that does indeed bring down the Capitol. Katniss may have pulled off this "stunt" through her own guile and creativity. But it was arguably her father who laid the groundwork for Katniss' unique set of wilderness skills and knowledge that allowed her to succeed when confronted with such challenging scenarios.

Coming Home

As Katniss' first Games are wrapping up, she allows herself to contemplate what her life will now become. She even considers her own identity while in the cave with Peeta, imagining a life beyond the Games. At first she is excited about the prospects. She would enjoy a certain level of fame and wealth, she first ponders, combined with a much grander house within the Victor's Village. She would further enjoy more freedom from hunger and the pressing need to feed her family. But then she returns to reality as she considers how her life would change on a daily basis. Without the need to acquire food, what would she do with herself? She contemplates: "Take that away and I'm not really sure who I am, what my identity is. The idea scares me some" (*THG* 311). She proceeds to think about Haymitch and his own challenges in life which were not solved by riches, food, or even a new house within District 12's first suburb. No, Haymitch did not provide an admirable model for success, she notes.

Then on the train headed home, Katniss begins to transform back into her authentic self. She is essentially detoxifying from all things Capitol.

Despite all the ways the Capitol had tried to change her, she manages to recognize—and reclaim—her own sense of identity. She thinks specifically of home, which includes Prim, her mother, and Gale—that is, the three individuals who matter most in her life. She changes out of her dress, returning to a more familiar plain shirt and pair of pants. Her physical transformation continues apace as she washes away the Capitol makeup and she returns her hair to its distinctive braid. She tells us, "I begin transforming back into myself. Katniss Everdeen. A girl who lives in the Seam. Hunts in the woods. Trades in the Hob. I stare in the mirror as I try to remember who I am and who I am not" (*THG* 370). These are all significant markers of place attachment and personal identity.

Perhaps fittingly, the original series concludes in the same place it began, at home. In one respect the entire Hunger Games series can be viewed as a testament to the fundamental importance of home and how it shapes our very identity. For her part, Katniss' sense of place and attachment to home are unwavering. Physically damaged and emotionally scarred after the revolution, she finds enough of the home she once knew to provide a sense of comfort, familiarity, and belonging. Thoughts of home—in all of its varied meanings—had never entirely vanished. Her cherished memories may have even steadied and comforted her throughout the entire series and its tragic sequence of events.

Just as the series begins with her familiar home routine, the trilogy circles back to a place called District 12. In the final chapter of *Mockingjay*, Katniss describes the gradual makeover of the place she once knew. The Meadow has been converted into a mass grave, and the "reaping of the dead" continues unabated, spearheaded by steadfast community members like Thom. She takes stock of what is left of her home, even while other friends and family have moved elsewhere within postwar Panem. Gale has moved to District 2, and even Katniss' mother has relocated to District 4 to help found a new hospital. With such news it is tempting for readers to believe that Katniss has chosen an isolated existence away from the hubbub of rebuilding a democratic nation. Not just a few fans have expressed serious issues with such a conclusion.

But Katniss is not alone back in 12. Rather, she initially has Greasy Sae and Haymitch to keep her company, and she eventually recognizes Thom as a District 12 acquaintance. Thom unfortunately announces that Madge and her family had not escaped the firebombing alive. Of course, Peeta returns in time as well. To her surprise, Buttercup returns—as always; Katniss spends some emotional moments with the mangy cat to mourn the loss of Prim. They ultimately form some semblance of a truce and learn to comfort one another. Providing Katniss with further comfort is her father's old hunting jacket, her family's plant book, and her renewed interest in heading into the woods to hunt upon the grandmotherly prodding of Greasy Sae.

While Appalachian people certainly do not hold a monopoly on cherishing the values of home, explains Tina Hanlon, "they have an exceptionally strong tradition of devotion to home and returning home for those who are inspired or compelled to spend parts of their lives elsewhere."[5] For Katniss to return to the home she always knew, therefore, makes perfect sense within the cultural context of her central Appalachian roots.

Beyond her immediate home, there are additional signs that the District 12 community is in the early stages of rebuilding and reinventing itself. Katniss describes her new scenario near the conclusion of *Mockingjay*, telling us that they are learning how to keep busy again, particularly through Peeta's baking and her hunting activities. Haymitch drinks and raises geese. Importantly, she declares that they are not alone. In fact, she claims that a few hundred other people have also returned to District 12 because, regardless of what has happened there, "this is our home" (*MJ* 388).

She continues to tell us how the mines have been closed and the ashes are being cycled back as nutrients for new agricultural fields. And machines are breaking ground for a new factory to produce medicines, thereby acknowledging a fitting amalgam of regional folk healing remedies with more modern medical practices previously only available to privileged Capitol citizens.[6] Katniss further notes that the Meadow has grown green again, as nature is revitalizing the place and is beginning life anew. And once more, Katniss is at home. Attachment to place can be a powerful influence indeed.

4

An Appalachian Melting Pot

If the previous chapters have revealed anything, it is the extent to which Suzanne Collins relied upon central Appalachia's cultural and historical legacies to frame her story and main characters. On one level, District 12 is the epitome of early twentieth-century Appalachian coal towns. This brings us to the question of the region's settlement history. In this chapter we take a tour back in time, to explore the diverse geographic origins and cultural roots of the people who settled this mountain realm.

The story of how this region was populated, and by whom, is largely based on the diffusion of cultural traditions brought to the mountains by successive waves of settlers. We already know that Appalachian music plays a fundamental role within the story lines of both the original series and the prequel. To understand the origins of the region's folk music and ballads, for instance, we cannot ignore the in-migration of Scots-Irish and English settlers who entered the United States largely through the port of Philadelphia during the eighteenth century. Their story provides much of the cultural foundation for the musical heritage of the mountains that Collins daftly weaves throughout her dystopian saga.

Of course, the early Europeans trickling into the mountains, sometimes with their slaves or servants, arrived to find various Indigenous peoples already well established there. From their earliest interactions, the Europeans and Indigenous populations—most notably the Cherokee—educated one another and unwittingly participated in a complex process of cultural exchange. Indigenous cultural practices intermixed with those of the newcomers in profound ways, including everything from growing crops and identifying healing remedies to clearing forest land for farmsteads. We will explore this cross-cultural exchange more thoroughly below to better comprehend Katniss' own complex racial and cultural identity.

Adding further to the array of diverse cultures influencing the central mountains were the largely involuntary newcomers from the African continent. Their own cultural imprint began with the first European forays into the highlands. The earliest expeditions consisted of Spanish explorers, particularly as far back as 1540 and 1567. Both expeditions included African slaves among their numbers, which led to a continuous trend of racial mixing within the mountains.[1] Though such early escapades were temporary and made little impact on the land, these excursions represented the vanguard of a relentless push of European and African traders, hunters, and permanent settlers into the Appalachian backcountry.

On top of all of this racial and ethnic diversity came a later wave of immigrants hailing primarily from Eastern Europe and Italy. Displaced by the Industrial Revolution, their own cultural legacies remain fully identifiable throughout the communities and human landscapes of central Appalachia today. Most notably, the extractive industries of mining and logging attracted a wide array of Eastern European and Italian immigrants by the late nineteenth century. While it would be highly naïve to suggest that everybody got along well or was treated fairly, scholars of the region have described central Appalachia as a multi-cultural melting pot to an extent that eclipsed most if not all other American regions. It is from this intricate set of mixed-race traditions that Suzanne Collins purposely molded her heroine, Katniss Everdeen, and many others within her local community.

Pennsylvanians in District 12

In stark contrast to the Cherokee and other Indigenous peoples who had claimed the mountains as home for centuries, early European colonists viewed this rugged territory as a foreboding western frontier. For them the north-south oriented Appalachians presented an ominous and challenging physical barrier that would stymie westward settlement for generations. Finding ways across this heavily wooded terrain was no easy feat in the days when inland transportation relied on foot, horse, or—well, that's about it. As geographers might say, the *friction of distance*—that is, the resistance to the movement of people and ideas—was all but insurmountable in the days before railroads and decent overland wagon roads. If a location was not immediately accessible by a navigable waterway, it was immensely difficult to reach. The progress of European and African settlement of the interior Appalachians, therefore, remained sluggish and required numerous generations to effectively accomplish.

What might surprise more is the source region from which a large proportion of mountain settlers originated during the eighteenth century (1700s). And it was not tidewater Virginia or elsewhere in the South. Rather, many of the Appalachian's initial waves of English, German, and Scots-Irish migrants came southward from Pennsylvania, and more specifically, through the port city of Philadelphia. William Penn's 1682 founding of that colony and its principal city ultimately provided the primary gateway to the Appalachian backcountry during the colonial period. This was owed mainly to the city's economic prominence on the East Coast, as an attractive magnet for European immigrants. And, as the principle of cultural diffusion would have it, these immigrants brought their ways of life with them, not the least being their musical instruments, songs, dances—and ballads. While southern Atlantic ports such as Wilmington, Charleston, and Savannah each provided a small share of migrants into the backcountry, their combined contribution was "nowhere near the numbers as Philadelphia."[2]

Let's back up, then, to understand how the carriers of the ballad tradition moved through Philadelphia and southward into the mountains. After all, Suzanne Collins relies heavily on the traditions of Appalachian music. While all three eastern cultural hearths were primarily English in their ethnic background, William Penn's Philadelphia attracted an array of additional nationalities from elsewhere in Europe. This was no accident. By the time Penn and his band of Quakers had arrived to settle their new colony, new opportunities were arising for political and social experimentation. Recognizing these changing times, Penn set out to prove that one could follow one's own religious belief system while simultaneously recognizing the religious views of others. In theory, such religious tolerance would lead to economic benefits for everyone. Penn thus launched his "Holy Experiment" and promoted Pennsylvania as a haven of religious—and thus ethnic—diversity.[3]

Most notable for our ongoing story, successive waves of German and Scots-Irish settlers found this newfound social experiment as highly attractive. They consequently came in veritable waves of migration to the colony's gateway city of Philadelphia largely after the 1720s. They were hardly alone, however, as they were often joined by a smattering of Welsh, French Huguenots, Irish, Swiss, and others of Northern European descent.[4]

This migration trend during the 1700s led to a ring-shaped pattern of ethnic influence within and around Philadelphia, depending upon the arrival timeframe of each group. The earliest settlers were the English and Quaker immigrants who favored the city's original city grid plan. The farmland just outside the city proper came to be occupied primarily by German-speaking communities who would collectively become known as the *Pennsylvania Deutsch* (Americanized to "Pennsylvania Dutch," although most had no connection to the Netherlands). These Pennsylvania Germans transferred their familiar agricultural patterns to the rolling hills of southeastern Pennsylvania, characterized by individual family farms, massive German "bank" barns (one side built into the bank of a hill), and formal, Georgian-style farm houses borrowed from the English.

With the Germans now toiling the land around Philadelphia, a sizeable wave of immigrants arrived from the Northern Ireland province of Ulster. Known by Americans as the Scots-Irish (or sometimes as the Scotch-Irish), these immigrants were primarily Presbyterians. Their own ancestors had migrated to Ulster from northern England or the lowlands of Scotland. During the eighteenth century—primarily between the 1720s and 1770s—an estimated 200,000 Scots-Irish people migrated to America. The vast majority of them ultimately landed in Philadelphia. They were soon dismayed to discover that the Germans had already taken all the good farmland and, in any case, it was already too expensive. Being of sound, logical minds, they consequently settled the next ring of land beyond the Germans. This took many of them into the interior of southeastern Pennsylvania, essentially backing them up against the eastern ridges of the Appalachians. For this reason, the Scots-Irish immigrants unwittingly became the first European settlers to venture westward into the mountainous frontier.

With them came their traditional agricultural techniques, including the Celtic dispersed farm, complete with grazing land for cattle and kitchen gardens. All of this had been standard practice in Ireland and Scotland. To this day, Scots-Irish place names abound through central and southern Pennsylvania, marking the first wave of their settlement efforts. Their core settlement area became the Pennsylvania counties of Chester, Lancaster, and Dauphin, and their early towns are still recognizable today, including the likes of York, Carlisle, Gettysburg, and Chambersburg. Their next generation moved further into western Pennsylvania and into the Ridge-and-Valley region of the Appalachians. Upon establishing themselves within the parallel valleys of southern Pennsylvania, they nostalgically named their new townships for places they had known back home in Ulster: Antrim, Armagh, Derry, Fermanagh, and Tyrone—to name a few.[5]

By 1800, approximately one in six European immigrants to America was Scots-Irish. They even outnumbered the Germans by some 50,000.[6] Along with smatterings of other nationalities, it was these Scots-Irish families who for several generations utilized the natural "highway" of the Appalachian chain—the expansive Shenandoah Valley (also known as the Great Valley) hidden on the western side of the foreboding Blue Ridge. Throughout much of the eighteenth century, the Scots-Irish expanded southwestward along this natural path into the central Appalachians and to the future realm of District 12.

Somewhat amusingly, their migration was so successful that Augusta and Rockbridge counties in the Shenandoah Valley of Virginia actually laid claim to being the most Scots-Irish places in America, despite the group's Pennsylvania ancestry.[7] And through the process of cultural diffusion they brought their folk songs, agricultural practices, and building styles with them wherever they happened to settle.

In contrast, the tidewater Virginia area contributed only minimally to the growing population of mountain settlers. Among other reasons, the Virginia plantation system that had developed as a large-scale farming practice was not practical in the mountainous environment. The so-called planter class and its operations tended to remain east of the mountains on the more hospitable Piedmont and coastal plain. Succeeding generations then carried the plantation system deeper into the South, skirting the Appalachians entirely. This is one reason why—although immigrants of African ancestry continuously entered the mountains—slavery in the Appalachians never reached the proportion or levels of that on the southern Piedmont. Rather, the vast majority of slaves were needed for hard labor and were thus put to work in coastal plantation societies.

By 1860 on the eve of the Civil War, Blacks in Appalachia made up approximately ten percent of the population. Many were slaves, though a portion of them were free.[8] This led to the development of a multicultural, "tri-racial society" in the central and southern Appalachians. For more than a century the Indigenous Peoples, Europeans, and Africans managed to create for themselves a surprisingly intercultural settlement system. As for the Europeans, their own eclectic combination of national origins only enhanced the diversity of this racial mix. As mentioned earlier, the region became as much a true "melting pot" as might have been possible during colonial times. We turn now to the Indigenous people themselves—or America's First Nations—to consider their own contributions to mountain culture and possible inspirational roles for the future District 12.

Katniss and the Cherokee

It is important to keep in mind that before any significant intrusion of Europeans settled the central Appalachians, it was the Indigenous, Native American peoples who inhabited the mountains. It is likely that Suzanne Collins borrowed at least indirectly from Indigenous cultural patterns to shape the personality of Katniss Everdeen and the mountain setting of District 12. The most influential population of Native Americans during the early colonial period consisted of some 20,000 Cherokee.[9] They typically occupied the fertile river valleys, and the Cherokee way of life was generally similar across all five of their core village settlements. Each village was politically independent, so the Cherokee maintained no centralized, unified government until much later in their history. Their most fundamental cultural bond involved a shared clan system and body of religious beliefs. Each Cherokee was a member of one of seven distinct clans, which essentially functioned as large, extended families. Marriage within the same clan was not allowed, and clans were *matrilineal*—that is, each person identified as a member of the mother's clan. In addition, each village included members of all seven clans, which allowed for travel, communication, and familiarity of people moving from one settlement to another.

The religious belief system practiced by the Cherokee was polytheistic, known more specifically as *animism*. Basically, this was a belief that natural objects including rivers, plants, and rocks were all imbued with spirits or souls.[10] One of the Cherokee's most important annual ceremonies was the Green Corn Feast—or Busk—to celebrate the corn harvest in late September and to purify their communities for the upcoming year. In terms of the gender division of labor and food production, the women typically managed the agricultural fields and gardens while the men hunted game such as white-tailed deer, typically during autumn months.

It is certainly plausible that Katniss and her various hunting and gathering skills reflect certain Cherokee traditions, though the connections are ambiguous. First, dependence on the bow and arrow for hunting large game and for warfare was ubiquitous in virtually all Native American communities. The weapon was therefore not solely a specialty of the Cherokee or other Appalachian peoples. Further, given that the bow and arrow play one of the most prominent roles throughout the original Hunger Games series, the weapon could easily be perceived as stereotypical of Native American cultural practices, a risk that Suzanne Collins was not likely to take.[11] Rather, Katniss' personal identity was tied more directly to the nutritious tuber plant for which she was named—which, by the way, happens to feature arrow-shaped leaves! As Elizabeth Hardy points out, the plant is thus commonly referred to as *arrowhead*, a name derived from its Latin moniker, Sagittaria, or "belonging to an arrow." It follows logically that the constellation Sagittarius is an archer.[12] For these reasons it seems that the bow and arrow is a perfectly appropriate weapon for a young heroine whose identity is tied so intimately with the earth and nature.

Moreover, the Cherokee utilized weapons beyond the bow and arrow, especially blow guns to capture smaller game such as squirrels and birds. This is in stark contrast to Katniss' dependence on the bow and arrow to obtain much of her game, no matter the size of the animal. Somehow, Katniss became so skilled with hunting even small game that she had already earned the attention of Peeta and his father prior to being reaped for the Games. During a strategy breakfast in the Capitol, Peeta describes to Haymitch how his father—the Baker—buys her squirrels. Peeta continues to praise Katniss' acumen with a bow, in that her arrows never pierce the body because she manages to hit every one of them in the eye (*THG* 89). And, well, Katniss verifies this claim with her successful kill of the ill-fated apple while demonstrating her chosen skill for the Gamemakers.

Another ambiguous connection between Katniss, District 12, and the Cherokee might be found in the Harvest Festival which Katniss references in passing several times. This is seemingly at odds with the crippling hunger that characterizes the Seam. Exactly where and how District 12 manages to grow its own food crops remains a mystery, let alone the puzzling dilemma of why a harvest festival occurs at all. Regardless, this too may owe its roots to the Cherokee's Green Corn Feast, or Busk, as mentioned above.

The District 12 event is first brought to our attention late in The Hunger Games, when Katniss and Peeta are clawing their way to the top of the Cornucopia to escape the mutts. During this desperately intense moment, she somehow musters the wherewithal to describe the Cornucopia's golden surface which resembles the "woven horn that we fill at harvest" (*THG* 331). She later mentions the festival not once, but twice in the second novel, *Catching Fire*. While describing the homes within the Victors' Village, she notes the home-like feel of the three inhabited dwellings with their glowing windows, chimney smoke and—most important for purposes here—"bunches of brightly colored corn affixed to the front doors as decorations for the upcoming Harvest Festival" (*CF* 13). She mentions later in the story that the victory rally held to officially congratulate Katniss and Peeta will conveniently align with the very same event, in that the Harvest Festival celebration always coincides with the final day of the Victory Tour (*CF* 86).

Notably, harvest festivals are not unique to the Cherokee, nor to the Appalachians. Rather, they are common to agricultural communities worldwide. Collins nevertheless carries the harvest theme into the reaping. At its most superficial meaning, the reaping represents a celebration of the harvest, when workers can finally enjoy the fruits of their labor. Of course, as Jill Olthouse explains, the Capitol twists this meaning to represent a celebration of victory over the district populations, evoking images of the Grim Reaper. The term "reaping," therefore, is appropriated to make the murder of young people seem as natural as a fall harvest.[13] Whether this imagery surrounding the reaping and its double meaning reflect a distant association with the Cherokee remains unclear.

Use of cornucopia imagery throughout the series may lend more credence to a possible Indigenous connection. Originally tied to Greek creation myths, the modern-day cornucopia typically takes on the appearance of a horn-shaped wicker basket filled with an abundance of fruit and vegetables, supplemented with various combinations of leaves, acorns, gourds, and cranberries.[14] It is meant to symbolize abundance—a veritable "horn of plenty"—and is now associated with America's Thanksgiving tradition.

The first Thanksgiving, as it is dubbed quite erroneously, was represented by a historical event described as a celebration of the fall harvest. It involved three days of festivities between the Puritan Pilgrims of Plymouth Colony and the remaining Native Americans who had not yet perished from European diseases. Unlike what many Americans were taught to believe, however, this seminal, multi-cultural event was not considered "Thanksgiving" at the time. Rather, America's first true Thanksgiving did not become a recognized national holiday until 1863 under President Abraham Lincoln. Much later in 1941 Congress permanently established that the holiday would thereafter occur on the fourth Thursday of November.

The general theme of a fall harvest is therefore woven throughout the original series, consisting of the following four intersecting elements: (1) Collins' use of the cornucopia as a symbolic device, (2) the cornucopia's association with the American Thanksgiving tradition, (3) the enigmatic Harvest Festival of District 12, and (4) the reaping as a celebration—in this case representing the Capitol's victory. It is difficult to conclude outright that all of these elements intersect by mere coincidence. Still, any reference to the Cherokee Green Corn Feast remains vague, and perhaps Collins intended it that way.

Katniss and the Columbian Exchange

While Katniss' character may not directly reflect specific Indigenous cultures, a more indirect, multicultural influence is certainly plausible. In one sense, Katniss and her family are a continued, if much later, product of what scholars refer to as the *Columbian* (or *Cultural*) *Exchange*, a term that refers to the trans-Atlantic diffusion of food ways, people, disease, and related cultural traits that began with the voyages of Christopher Columbus. American historian Alfred W. Crosby coined the term in 1972 to describe the global diffusion of agricultural crops and cultural practices between the so-called New and Old Worlds. Crosby and his successors have demonstrated that such cultural patterns had been transferred in both directions across the Atlantic Ocean—not just into the Americas as had previously been taught. The concept gained wide acceptance thereafter, and it can help us better understand the mixing of cultural practices that occurred through centuries of contact between Europeans, Africans, and Native Americans.

Colonial settlers and Indigenous peoples—particularly the Cherokee, in this case—had initially learned to rely upon one another for mutual survival within the Appalachians. Through the process of the cultural exchange, the people from New and Old World cultures continued to mix and learn from one another. As a result, a synthesis or "shared core" of cultural traits emerged for Appalachians of all ethnic backgrounds, focusing on the practices of herding, farming, hunting, and fishing.[15]

This cultural exchange drew upon numerous Indigenous culture ways. European newcomers quickly and wisely learned to adopt Indigenous farming approaches and crops, especially several strains of corn, beans, squash, and tobacco.[16] Settlers further learned the Indigenous practice of *slash and burn*—that of clearing a forested track of land by girdling trees to kill them, followed by their burning to release nutrients into the soils. The Indigenous people further diversified their diets through centuries-old skills of hunting, fishing, and gathering. It was not uncommon for newcomers from both Europe and Africa to acquire the same agricultural plots previously used by their Indigenous predecessors.

In turn, Europeans contributed their own traditional food ways through the introduction of various grains once foreign to the Appalachians, including wheat, rye, barley, oats, and peas. Likewise, the raising of livestock involved the domesticated animals of cattle, sheep, and hogs. Appalachian agricultural diversity was further augmented through African contributions, particularly edible plants such as watermelons, okra, groundnuts (peanuts), millet, and yams. Settlers of African origin further contributed dozens of domesticated plants grown for medicinal purposes.[17] This all speaks to the reality of a multicultural frontier that existed for nearly two centuries, roughly from the mid–1600s through the mid–1800s.

Hunting practices also reflected this ongoing cultural exchange. Europeans contributed to earlier Indigenous practices with the introduction of gunpowder technology to increase the killing efficiency of the hunt. In turn, Indigenous people taught both European and African settlers how to live off the land, and how to prepare and preserve game following the kill. Curiously, outside observers often reported their own confusion, sometimes scratching their heads over whether various hunters they encountered were of Indigenous or European descent. Their outward physical appearance and approaches were remarkably similar.

The cultural sharing thus went both ways and gave rise to some entirely blended cultural practices. By the 1740s the Cherokees had become ever more dependent on English and European manufactured items, such as firearms, metal tools, and glass beads. They typically traded deerskin to the European settlers in exchange for these goods.[18] Ultimately, the Cherokee and other tribes became less self-sufficient and more caught up in the cash-based economy of the new settlers. This trend only encouraged further dependence upon the Europeans, thereby diluting Indigenous culture ways and self-sufficient means of survival they had practiced for untold generations.

Readers may recognize these activities as similar to those which occurred at the Hob and, more generally under lackluster Capitol oversight within District 12. Katniss and Gale traded game for manufactured and other food goods not unlike the Cherokee—exemplifying what is known as a *barter economy*. At one point while dining on Capitol food prior to the 74th Games, Katniss provides examples of bartering while trying to imagine assembling a similar meal back home. She first claims that the chickens would be too expensive, necessitating the substitution of a wild turkey. She could trade a second turkey for a precious orange. Goat's milk could substitute for cream, and peas would come from their home garden. Acquiring the fancy Capitol rolls would require another trade with the baker, probably requiring two or three squirrels (*THG* 65).

The team of Katniss and Gale likewise sold game to Peacekeepers, in return for small amounts of cash. This practice closely mirrors how Indigenous people had been pulled into the cash economy of the European colonists. In District 12, of course, this creative trading scheme was necessary to keep them and their families alive under otherwise oppressive conditions. Their goal was to become more self-sufficient, even while under the Capitol's gaze.

Indigenous people borrowed additional behaviors from both Europeans and Africans, including the adoption of new crops and the raising of livestock. They eventually came to protect their own land holdings with European-style fences.[19] Even traditional gender roles were turned on end, as Cherokee men increasingly tended agricultural fields in place of the women. Eventually a shared cultural pattern emerged in the form of the Appalachian family farm, characterized by the staple crop of corn on roughly cleared forest land, with supplemental crops including wheat and oats. Smaller "kitchen gardens" supplemented the staple crops with daily and healthy goodies such as potatoes, onions, peas, squash, and cabbages—not unlike the garden Katniss describes. Livestock and other barnyard animals were similarly diversified—populated most often by combinations of hogs, cattle, sheep, horses, and mules.

Forest products rounded out the diets and production of Appalachian farmsteads, providing everything from small and large game, fish, fruits, and nuts, to natural sweeteners including maple tree sap and honey. In sum, these self-sufficient family operations were characterized as small-scale, *subsistence agriculture*—that is, producing assorted food products primarily for their own consumption. If the farm happened to produce a surplus during a bountiful season, these products could be sold or traded at local markets, often located on or near the town square like that of District 12.

It is therefore most likely that Suzanne Collins intended for Katniss, her father, and—within the prequel—members of the Covey, to vaguely represent this type of multicultural subsistence farming pattern. By the 1820s—when any vestiges of traditional Cherokee livelihood would take a sharp turn for the worse—the standard Appalachian family farm had become well established. Such farmsteads could easily have served as models for both the Everdeen and Covey families. Though probably not directly pointing to specific Cherokee practices, the persistent efforts of our Hunger Games characters certainly mirrored Indigenous approaches toward sustainable self-sufficiency.

Although largely blended with European and African culture ways, the legacy of the Cherokees and their Indigenous counterparts was immense. Their contributions to the Columbian Exchange during the colonial era provided for one of America's most diverse, multi-ethnic populations found anywhere. Such diversity became—to use Stevan Jackson's words—the "unheralded hallmark of Appalachia."[20] The combined folk ways, music, lifestyles, and agricultural practices of the central Appalachians all provided a stage for the future community of District 12, for the Covey, and for one emerging heroine named Katniss Everdeen.

The Melungeons

One additional, mixed-race population has inhabited central Appalachia since early colonial times, that of the Melungeons. Their ancestry and racial origins have remained rather mysterious for centuries, though it is quite possible—and I would argue probable—that Suzanne Collins intended this distinct ethnic population to inspire her characters from the Seam.

Researchers have found trace evidence of the Melungeons all the way back to the first eastern settlements in America, originating sometime between 1492 and the founding of Jamestown in 1607. Evidence suggests the Melungeons are descended from a blend of dark-skinned peoples of Mediterranean origin, including Turks, Berbers, Moors, Jews, Portuguese, Spanish, and likely others as well.[21] Their original Mediterranean blood has mingled over the centuries with more regional, mixed-race people of African, Indigenous, and Northern European descent, the likes of whom were described earlier. As early as 1690, it is reported that French settlers moving into the mountains of North Carolina had encountered a mysterious population already living there, who identified themselves as "Portyghee," or Portuguese.[22] The Scots-Irish later found them already living in secluded alcoves of southwestern Virginia and northeastern Tennessee by the 1750s—essentially within the accepted District 12 core area.

Today's largest Melungeon communities are found within these same parts of Virginia and Tennessee, as well as in northwestern North Carolina where the French had purportedly first encountered them. Beyond this core area, its members can be found throughout the Appalachians and elsewhere.[23] None of the numerous theories as to their origins have been proven conclusively. More recent if circumstantial evidence collected since the 1990s points to a Mediterranean source region. However, competing theories suggest an earlier tri-racial population consisting of a mixture of Black, White, and Indigenous blood.

What has raised eyebrows among some Hunger Games enthusiasts—including this one—is how the common physical descriptions of Melungeon people compare with those of Katniss and Gale in the original series. Early in The Hunger Games, Katniss watches Gale slice their bread, contemplating that he could easily be her brother. They both exhibit "straight, black hair, olive skin, and gray eyes." Katniss further claims that most of the families in the Seam resemble one another in these ways (*THG* 8).

This otherwise vague description has raised the question of whether Suzanne Collins purposely intended for Katniss and "most of the families" of the Seam to be Melungeon. Various scholars and mountain residents alike have provided uncanny physical descriptions of Melungeons that closely resemble that of Katniss, with her straight, black hair, olive skin, and gray eyes. Of course, Suzanne Collins does not inform readers outright of her characters' racial or ethnic identities, though she certainly provides these clues—or breadcrumbs—for us to consider.

Perhaps most notable, the Appalachian scholar Stevan Jackson describes the typical Melungeon person as exhibiting "Mediterranean complexions, blue eyes, high cheek bones, and straight, black hair."[24] Another recent writer describes the "mysterious Melungeons, with their dark, Mediterranean skin setting off startling blue eyes; fine, European features; their high cheekbones and straight, black hair."[25] Similar descriptions were noted some sixty years earlier by geographer Edward Price in 1951. He described Melungeons in eastern Tennessee and neighboring states as a "dark-skinned mixed-blood group of uncertain origin," occasionally displaying an "Oriental appearance" and "most commonly thought to be at least partly of Portuguese descent."[26] Price further identified one regional group of Melungeons as exhibiting a "distinctly brown complexion and straight black hair … whose ancestry might be [Native American]."[27] While Price's terminology with respect to people of color is admittedly out of date, the similarities of his descriptions with those mentioned above are not likely coincidental.

It is entirely conceivable that Suzanne Collins intentionally shifted Katniss' and Gale's eye color to gray rather than blue, simply to throw readers off the trail a bit. This is standard practice for Collins, especially with respect to naming her characters. She admits for the record that Katniss

Everdeen's last name was derived from another favorite character of hers, Bathsheba Everdene, the lead character in *Far from the Madding Crowd*.[28] It is further conceivable that her "olive skin" description is code for suggesting a Mediterranean connection, which would be consistent with the historical descriptions above.

Further, it is not likely that Katniss' darker skin represents someone specifically of African descent. We can infer this based on Collins' description of Rue, who is intended to be at least part African American. Rue is described as exhibiting "bright, dark eyes and satiny brown skin" (*THG* 98). This is not consistent with Collins' use of the "olive skin" description for people of the Seam. Had she intended Katniss and Rue to represent the same race, she would have likely continued her practice of using similar descriptors—such as that of Katniss and Gale. To posit an educated guess, I would suggest the distinct possibility that Collins discovered one or more of these scholarly accounts—perhaps specifically that of Stevan Jackson mentioned above. Then she simply altered the description to provide clues, leaving it to the rest of us to contemplate. Challenge accepted!

As for today's Melungeon population, its community members often live in relatively rural, isolated places while working in occupations similar to those of other Appalachian residents. Stevan Jackson provides typical examples of favored occupations: "farmers owning their own land, farmers working for others, and laborers working in urban industrial plants or coal mines."[29] Similarly, Edward Price had specifically noted that mid-century Melungeons were identified in a half dozen counties of southwestern Virginia—also District 12 country—and that their "trail leads on into the coal-mining camps of Kentucky."[30]

If all of these parallels were not enough, Melungeon families often adopted Euro-American surnames. Given their mixed-race, darker appearance, the Melungeons of the nineteenth century were listed in early U.S. Census reports as "free persons of color" or "mulatto." Unfortunately for them, this meant they were summarily discriminated against and were denied the right to vote.[31] To call someone "Melungeon" in central Appalachia was considered an insult, as the label had become a derogatory term. They consequently remained within their own isolated communities and adopted English and Scots-Irish surnames including Collins, Kennedy, Campbell, and Adams. Price had identified similar names in his 1951 article, including the most "prominent" examples of Collins, Mullins, Gibson, Goins, Freeman, and Sexton.[32] It is not unreasonable to presume that Suzanne Collins was quite aware that her own surname is consistently found at the top of such lists.

In one insightful discussion surrounding the possible racial origins of Seam residents, author V. Arrow explains that the "question of race in the

Seam is the subject of a long, bitter, multifold debate within the Hunger Games fandom."[33] Arrow further clarifies that Suzanne Collins purposely left Katniss and her fellow Seam residents racially ambiguous, aside from her nebulous description of olive skin, straight, black hair, and gray eyes. Such ambiguity has predictably led to an array of reactions from readers who claim that Katniss looks like them.

To paraphrase Young-Adult author Shannon Riffe, we may not know what Katniss' racial background is, but we do know what she is not—that is, a White, Anglo-American female with fair skin and blue eyes like her sister.[34] Rather, she is dark-skinned like Gale, similar to earlier Seam residents, notably including Lil within the prequel. It is no coincidence that Collins described Lil in nearly the same way as Katniss—as a young woman with "olive skin and long black hair" (*BSS* 350). Those are the two key descriptors. We meet Lil quite tragically for the first time during the hanging of the condemned Arlo Chance on the edge of District 12. Arlo sees Lil in the crowd from the makeshift gallows and yells at her to "Run, Lil! Ru—!"

Readers then learn of the stunning connection between this scene and "The Hanging Tree" ballad. Despite the myriad of efforts to interpret the ballad's meaning prior to the release of the prequel, its lyrics were actually written by Lucy Gray Baird in her attempt to tell the story of this very incident. More important for purposes here, Collins codes Lil directly as a resident of the Seam, not unlike Katniss and her future Seam counterparts. As V. Arrow supposes, Collins introduces us to Gale in part to define a specific Seam identity that is not white and is "uniquely 'Seam' in the world of Panem."[35] Katniss explains through her own narrative that Gale could be her brother because the two of them look similar. Moreover, they are purposely set apart ethnically and racially from those of District 12's merchant class, from residents of the Capitol, and from the tributes of District Eleven like Rue.

It is noteworthy that scholars and writers from the Appalachian region have provided similar interpretations of Katniss' racial background. In Jim Poe's (2015) article for the *Times West Virginian* cited earlier, he considers that various regional characteristics further point to Katniss' racial background, reflecting the region's "complex racial heritage."[36] He notes correctly that Katniss, Gale, and their fellow mining families exhibit straight, black hair, olive skin, and gray eyes. He then offers that "these traits are typical of the Melungeon, a marginalized mixed-race Appalachian community." He cites recent DNA evidence indicating that the Melungeons are at least in part descended from escaped African American slaves.

But then Poe also mentions a possible Italian connection, suggesting that "Katniss' complexion could also symbolize the importance of Italian migrant workers to the region's history and culture." Given the prominence of Italian coal miners in southern West Virginia, it would make sense that an article for the *Times West Virginian* would at least consider this possibility. Let's look at the Italians more closely.

Empty Promises and Corporate Control

One should not be faulted for thinking, *Italians? In the central Appalachians? No way.* Way. For their part, the vast majority of Italian immigrants preferred to settle in larger urban areas. Although now considered part of America's white population of European descent, the Italians and the Eastern Europeans who immigrated with them likewise experienced racial prejudice from the dominantly white, Anglo-American society. Theirs is a larger story, tied to waves of immigrant workers coming to America around the peak of the Industrial Revolution. A sizeable portion of them were people of Italian and Eastern European origins, many of whom found their way to the Appalachians in search of employment. Their arrivals only added to the existing ethnic diversity of the highlands.

Even more surprising is the extent to which the Italians helped populate the mining camps and towns up through the early twentieth century. Of the numerous immigrant populations relocating to Appalachia in search of work and a better life, the largest ethnic group by far was the Italians.[37] In 1910 there were some 7,600 Italian miners in West Virginia alone, one of the accepted core areas of District 12. Whether or not their ethnic contributions were meant to influence the Seam's cultural diversity remains uncertain. Regardless, it is still instructive to note how those of Italian and Eastern European descent contributed their own cultural and ethnic qualities to the already diverse "melting pot" of central Appalachia.

What might not be as well-known is the story of how coal mining companies actually sent recruiting agents to Italy and elsewhere in Europe to attract workers with the false promise of a better life. Such practices became illegal by the late nineteenth century, but the mining companies simply shifted their recruiting efforts to Ellis Island where the bulk of immigrants arrived later from Europe.[38] In this way, large numbers of Italians and other immigrants were lured—often with fabricated promises—to the Appalachian mines. Many came unwillingly, and others had been clearly misled by their recruiters. Like black miners before them, many Italians found themselves unhappy with their new lives amidst deplorable working conditions.

Kathy Shearer speaks to the type of deception and mistreatment experienced by immigrants who came to the mining camps. For her part, Shearer had come to the mining town of Dante, Virginia, as a social service agent in the 1990s and became involved in a book project about the town, along with ensuing grassroots efforts to keep the town alive post-coal. She explains the situation that many immigrants faced: "Italians, Hungarians, Poles—they were flooding in from Europe. The war was heating up over there. They were coming here for, they thought, a safe place to work, where they were promised a decent place to live and work. And many of them just died."[39] She further explains that immigrants and their families typically did not own property or have other means to protect themselves from corporate excesses. The companies were desperate to secure a stable, year-round workforce, and they found such individuals in the ongoing pool of immigrants who had no other land or home to return to. She continues,

> And it was a lot easier if you had foreigners who didn't own anything. And it was a whole lot easier to control people who didn't own anything. Because you had total control over them. If a miner died in that household, they were in a company house with no miner in it, they could be put out on the street. And they were. You had to have a miner in the home.... [P]eople could not make their own decisions here. The coal company made every decision for everybody in the town.[40]

This lack of ability for families to fend for themselves upon the death of a coal miner closely parallels the families of Katniss and Gale. Both of their fathers had been killed in the coal mine explosion, which had nearly led to their families' own deaths by starvation. That is, until Katniss was thrown those infamous loaves of bread behind the bakery. Recalling her father's training, she and Gale became self-sufficient and, of course, the rest of their story is history. What might be eye-opening for some readers is that their fictional scenario was not merely concocted as some extreme, dystopian tale that grossly exaggerates reality. Instead, such cases actually occurred in real mining towns. In places controlled by the corporation, local families enjoyed no social safety net should they suddenly lose their income from coal mining.

Frank Kilgore, an attorney in St. Paul, Virginia, likewise recalled the lies and false promises made to immigrants by the mining companies. Kilgore's family history in that area went back generations, and he had been centrally involved in strip-mine legislation, the Pittston strike, and various regional development efforts. Here he recalls the stories of his grandfather:

> I think a lot of coal operators would go recruit these workers down south or at Ellis Island and lie to them. Basically, my grandfather's recollection was they would tell the black workers, who were tenant farmers down south, that the coal was laying in piles here, and all you had to do was shovel it in the coal cars, and that was it. He said that he had actually witnessed several occasions where these black plantation workers would be brought up here, and when they started taking them into the mines, they would become claustrophobic and bolt and run, and try to find their way back home.[41]

The black miners who managed to stay, Kilgore added—and there were many who did—ended up becoming some of the most effective coal miners in the region. They raised families and contributed significantly to the multicultural qualities of coal-town communities through present day.

Consequently, black coal miners had been similarly deceived along with their immigrant counterparts. The coalfields of central Appalachia attracted black men in numbers only matched by the Italians and Eastern Europeans. Between 1880 and 1900 the black population of the region more than doubled and continued to grow steadily throughout the next several decades. Southern West Virginia was particularly attractive, as that area lured black men in sizable numbers to the mines and their communities. Between the conclusion of the Civil War and 1910 the area's black population became home to some 42,000 miners and their families.[42] Ten years later, 96 percent of blacks in all of central Appalachia were concentrated in only sixteen coal-producing counties. Despite the hardships many faced, their growing communities eventually translated to increased political clout. They established black schools, churches, and fraternal organizations.

One of the better-known historical figures to emerge during this community-building era was none other than Booker T. Washington. Following his education at the Hampton Institute, he returned to the Kanawha Valley of West Virginia in 1875 not long after the Civil War. There he taught school and served as a Sunday school teacher and clerk for the black Baptist church. From this experience he became involved in local and state politics and successfully mobilized black voters to support the Kanawha Republicans, thereby helping to make that party highly influential in the southern Appalachians.[43]

As for their European counterparts, Stevan Jackson explains that Italian and other immigrant miners "often lived under armed guards until they worked off the cost of their transportation, much like indentured servants of past centuries."[44] It is difficult for Hunger Games readers to not notice a distinct parallel here with the surveillance role of Peacekeepers and the inhumane conditions of mining life in District 12.

In a similar vein, Kilgore had been told that the central Appalachian mining region had become the second largest "melting pot" in the nation, surpassed only by New York City itself. Some 32 nationalities were identified within Virginia's Wise County alone during the 1920s and 1930s. The cultural landscape of Pocahontas reflects this multi-ethnic heritage, a mining community located on the West Virginia border. Kilgore describes the place as he recalls it:

> You go up there, and they have a Hungarian Catholic Church in the middle of their town. They have a big mountainside graveyard where you find Hungarians, Poles, Italians. When you see these rock walls around St. Paul and Lebanon, and

these hand-hewn rock basements in Wise and all these other places, those were Italian rock masons. Entire families of rock masons would come over from Italy and Sicily, and they would do rock work for the coal companies and the town, and you still see that everywhere around here.[45]

It follows that Katniss could theoretically claim some percentage of an Italian or Eastern European blood line, just as she may very well represent a Melungeon heritage. Either or both of these scenarios would be realistic options for Katniss, given her mixed-race origins within a central Appalachian mining town.

Regardless, this may not be the message Collins intended with her ongoing saga. In an interview for *Entertainment Weekly*, she claimed that Katniss and Gale "were not particularly intended to be biracial." Given that hundreds of years have passed between our present day and the era of the 74th Games, she adds that there has "been a lot of ethnic mixing."[46] Appalachian history informs us that the mountains had already witnessed centuries of similar "ethnic mixing" since colonial times. Even more racial blending would have therefore occurred by the time of District 12 and Panem. Given her own choice of language above, it may be more accurate to describe Katniss as multi-ethnic rather than mixed-race.

Although often tempting to stereotype and place people into neat, tidy racial boxes, it is much more common for humans to represent complex racial makeups from centuries of ethnic blending. It would therefore be a challenge—even with modern-day DNA testing—to definitively determine Katniss' racial background or that of other members of the Seam community. Rather, Collins intended for us to continue our discussions surrounding differences in race, ethnic identity, stereotyping, and the ways we treat and view each other.

In setting up a story about a multi-ethnic teenage heroine, Collins could hardly have done better than to land her in the culturally diverse realm of the central Appalachians—Melungeon or otherwise. This persistent theme of "ethnic mixing" will reappear in future chapters as we uncover the complicated origins of folk music and later genres largely identified with this mountain realm.

5

Small Town in Panem

What was the District 12 of the novels designed to look like? Many of us likely retain vivid mental images of scenes from the feature films, most notably the original Everdeen household, portions of the Seam, the public square and its surroundings, and later activity within the Victor's Village. While the chosen filming locations were—for me—appropriate on their own merit to effectively ground the story, the various scenes featuring District 12 present a stark contrast from their intended appearance within the novels. In some ways the films and novels portray two very different types of places. Indeed, the public square and its surroundings as interpreted in the films would likely be nearly unrecognizable to our young heroine.

Key descriptions of District 12's human landscapes are peppered generously throughout the original trilogy and—even more prominently—within the recent prequel. Unlike other aspects of the story line, there is little need to guess or hypothesize what Collins intended for the physical layout of this isolated Appalachian community. With this in mind, let's take a virtual tour of the real stomping grounds of Katniss Everdeen and Lucy Gray Baird.

Around the Square

As she and her family prepare for the reaping in *The Hunger Games*, Katniss introduces us to one of the more iconic features of her hometown, referred to generically as "the square." We learn that this public space serves as a focus for the community, and fittingly as a central place for District 12 activities—whether desired or not. The space is "quite large," she describes, though not large enough to comfortably hold all of its eight thousand some-odd residents. These descriptors alone provide important geographic information. First, we have a District 12 that can be interpreted more as an isolated small town with less than 10,000 people. This is a sizable distinction from a more expansive "district" that might include numerous urban centers and rural communities networked together.

Despite what the films may have us believe, the square is neither separated from the town center, nor is it randomly placed among industrial buildings. Rather, Collins repeatedly clarifies that the square occupies a prime location within the town's central street grid. An outdoor market is held there periodically, which in real life typically translates to "weekly." Temporary markets like this are held within public places and squares the world over. We know that Katniss can find inexpensive clothing there and—if true to its real-life counterparts—probably an array of household goods as well. The market therefore contributes favorably to Katniss' sense of place and attachment for District 12, and for her sense of community as a whole.

Katniss recalls, in one instance, that she and Gale had shopped at the "market on the square" to purchase dress materials. If true to the common layout of markets elsewhere, we might imagine an ad-hoc collection of tables protected by tarps or tents assembled for one day each week. They would either be perched somewhere near the square's center or off to one side to likewise benefit patronage at established local businesses.

The square's paved surface is also notable. It consists of either "cobblestones" as described within the prequel, or "paving stones" as Katniss notices more grimly while sifting under a layer of ash early in *Mockingjay* (8). The cobblestones of Lucy Gray's time would be more irregularly shaped. As cobbles typically appear, these likely consist of individual, rounded stones cemented together in a pattern. Such a surface provides a rougher texture, the likes of which can still be found in older European public spaces or American colonial-era neighborhoods. Though sometimes presenting a challenge to one's feet for those not properly shoed, such cobblestone patterns can elicit a comforting sense of place, and a sense of local history as well.

Consequently, by the time Katniss volunteers for her sister at the reaping, the original cobblestones have been replaced with flatter paving stones. In real public squares, however, even these simpler brick-type pavers can be laid in patterns signifying an important community gathering place. Either way, the District 12 square maintains a textured surface, reminiscent of renowned public spaces elsewhere around the world. This design alone differs from the square(s) portrayed within the films. Particularly in "The Hunger Games," people appear to be wading across a mucky open space of dirt or clay, rather than enjoying their time spent atop a patterned stone surface.

Katniss further notes that on public market days the place can have a "holiday feel to it" (*THG* 16). She even laments that the reapings have to be held in the square, as it is one of the few places that can actually be pleasant. The square in normal times of the year is thus compared with the "air of grimness" that descends during the reaping—despite the colorful banners hung by the Capitol. Bright colors or not, such banners symbolize oppression and the loss of individual agency and freedom. Everyone is required to be there, so this is no voluntary outing for community members. Katniss further notes that the camera crews resemble buzzards, perched on surrounding rooftops. From her perspective, the place has been transformed from an important and comfortable community hub into one that is dictated by an oppressive regime. The square can thus be interpreted as a *contested space*—one in which local activities valued by the community are occasionally replaced by the propaganda and order imposed by an authoritarian state.

Capitol presence or not, the town's public space is physically and spatially defined by rows of storefront buildings around its perimeter. As Katniss notes, the "square is surrounded by shops" (*THG* 16). As for these more permanent storefronts, Coriolanus and Sejanus confirm this spatial layout within the prequel, even some 64 years earlier. Soon after Coriolanus arrives at the Peacekeepers' base in District 12, his new friend Smiley reviews the highlights of their new home. While the market and various entertainments at the Hob continue into the night, Smiley also mentions the town square, "with its smattering of small shops and tradespeople." The shops and their operators alike, he adds, are only more active during the day as one might expect (*BSS* 335). As with typical small-town business districts, most shops on the square likely coordinate for mutual interest and keep similar daytime business hours.

The Mellark bakery is clearly part of the business mix around the square. As narrated in Part 3 of the prequel, one evening after the mines have shut down for the day, "[o]nly a small bakery stood open in the town square." Though its specific placement is not specified, it is most certainly adjacent to other shops. On that same evening, a spatially confused Coriolanus and Sejanus make a desperate stop for directions at the bakery. If Suzanne Collins is true to her ways, this is likely the very same bakery featured in the original series—one of her many *Easter eggs* readers are meant to uncover. Even the "beet-faced woman" who runs it is not particularly friendly. True to form, she refuses to provide directions—and to Peacekeepers no less! *What's up with that?* Being the young men they are, Sejanus begrudgingly trades his prized chewing gum for a loaf of bread, to which she finally relents. From her shop, she notably takes them "out on the square" and points to the street they should follow to the Seam (*BSS* 376). The bakery is therefore located flush against the square and is clearly one of the numerous storefronts that line it.

As further confirmation of the bakery's true location, Peeta attempts at one point to explain his cake decorating habits to Katniss. She then recalls the cakes that appear temptingly in the storefront window display, telling us that they are meant primarily for birthdays and New Year's Day. Although unable to afford them, Katniss notes how Prim would always drag her over to admire the beautifully decorated cakes, to which Katniss acquiesces because there is otherwise such little beauty to be found in District 12 (*THG* 96).

The bakery's location on the square is contrary to the image of a separate, free-standing storefront along a narrow road, as portrayed in "The Hunger Games." Moreover, the flashback scenes in the film have Peeta exiting the front door to eventually throw a loaf of bread to Katniss in the rain. The pig sty is set to the structure's side, a scene more akin to a farmstead than a downtown business block. In the novel, this scene actually occurs at the rear of the shops in the alley. More about this later.

The prequel provides additional clues regarding the scale and layout of the town beyond the square and its storefronts. As Coriolanus and his peers escort the mayor's daughter, Mayfair, back home following some mayhem at the Hob, we learn that "a few short blocks" of residential streets extend outward from the town center (*BSS* 372). Then later, when Coriolanus and Sejanus make their stop at the bakery for directions, they head for the Seam to find that the "regular streets" around the square quickly dissolve into a "web of smaller, unmarked lanes" that emerge and disappear with no discernable pattern (*BSS* 376). This irregular pattern describes the Seam on the periphery of town which, according to the narrator, stretches out for miles. Some lanes are lined with rows of identical houses while other streets reveal "makeshift structures it would be generous to call shacks." Some are abandoned, while others are temporarily patched up. What the duo finds, therefore, is a desperately impoverished and derelict residential area, the basic needs of which have been long ignored by mainstream society and its government.

Though easy to overlook as mundane prose, this descriptive text provides some vital imagery. It becomes evident that Collins has modeled District 12 as a quintessential small-town landscape, the likes of which many Americans would recognize: a comfortably-sized public square downtown, surrounded by two- or three-story commercial buildings with shops on the ground floor and apartments or offices above. The next blocks beyond the businesses are devoted to the more lavish homes of the merchant class, bank owners, industrialists, and community leaders. Middle-class or working-class homes fill in the remainder of the planned residential street grid.

The location of the mayor's house in District 12 exemplifies this typical residential pattern close to downtown. Although Katniss does not indicate its precise location within the original series, we learn more from the prequel. As our youthful Peacekeepers, Coriolanus and Sejanus, accompany Mayfair home following the Hob concert, the narrator reveals their path, crossing the square diagonally to a newly paved road one block over. It is further noted that the mayor's house "might count for a mansion in District 12 but would be unremarkable in the Capitol" (*BSS* 372).

Prior to automobile suburbia, the center of a community and its business and retail trade were still focused downtown, largely up through the mid-twentieth century. Many of the wealthier and politically connected citizens—the vast majority of them being of the male gender—would typically live with their families in more upscale, expensive homes closest to the center. These people often included the more successful merchants, bankers, lawyers or other businesspeople with close financial ties to downtown. In larger cities, entire streets were claimed by extravagant, multi-floor Victorian-era mansions with gables, dormers, and wrap-around porches aimed every which way. These homes were clear markers of family wealth generated through America's industrial revolution during the late nineteenth and early twentieth centuries. Of course, such streets were also home to various political leaders, such as the mayor of District 12.

It stands to reason that the upper-scale homes of smaller towns would be proportionally less extravagant than those found in larger urban and metropolitan places. This is because the overall scale of capital accumulation in smaller places did not come close to matching the wealth of larger urban industrialists. Thus, Collins was certainly channeling her inner geographer by recognizing this difference between places like District 12 and the metropolis of the Capitol. The narrator's observation that the mayor's house would be rather "unremarkable" in the Capitol is right on point. Relative to the typical residential neighborhoods in District 12, the mayor's house clearly stands out as stylish and perhaps somewhat extravagant. The same residence placed in the wealthier neighborhoods of Chicago, Cincinnati, Pittsburgh, or Boston, however, would pale in comparison to its more lavish and spacious counterparts.

District 12 in the Films

The setting for the public square in the first film, "The Hunger Games," could not have diverged much further from that of the novel. For the reaping scenes, the film crews made use of a private collection of warehouses in Shelby, North Carolina. The setting for the Hob was filmed here as well. The industrial area of District 12 was filmed nearby, comprising a collection of commercial buildings adjacent to the railroad along Shelby's South Morgan Street. These are all private properties and are therefore not accessible to the public.[1] Without the novel as a guide, one could certainly defend the use of such derelict places to represent a gritty, impoverished industrial community like that of District 12. From a visual standpoint it all works just fine. The place's geographic accuracy, however, leaves much to be desired. For one thing, the tall, brick nineteenth-century manufacturing buildings portrayed in the film have little to do with the extraction of coal. There is really nothing substantial to manufacture in District 12. Rather, the mining company and its employees simply extract the coal, dump it into standardized railroad cars, and ship it out to the wealthier Capitol in the nation's urban core.

As for the public square during the first reaping, its spatial layout in the film contrasts markedly with that of the novel. In place of modest, brick or wood-framed storefronts, the public square of the film is surrounded on two sides by unremarkable corrugated metal sheds or warehouses. The back side of the square, opposite the Justice Building, is occupied by a conventional railroad siding with two standard coal hopper cars providing for an admittedly impressive backdrop. As a marker of central authority, the railroad cars are labeled appropriately for "Capitol Coal" in place of otherwise typical names of corporate railroad owners. And as noted earlier, the square's more picturesque paving stones are summarily replaced with a gray, mucky mess.

In the second film, "Catching Fire," the center of District 12 receives yet another makeover. This is because the film's producers relied on a completely different set of filming locations. For instance, the Justice Building, where Katniss and Haymitch (then Peeta) are reaped for the 75th Games, was filmed within a collection of former manufacturing buildings on the west side of Atlanta, Georgia. At the time of filming, this collection served as the home of the Goat Farm Arts Center. While still sporting a dreary, industrial look, this rendition of District 12 holds little in common with that of the first film, let alone the version described within the novels. In the film, "Catching Fire," the square is now surrounded by nineteenth-century brick industrial buildings. Granted, the Goat Farm location provides an appropriately aging industrial scene for the purpose of framing the story. That said, some might still find this imagined urban pattern lacking a certain authenticity compared to what Collins had envisioned.

The Philadelphia Plan

Aside from the mishmash of District 12 townscapes offered through the films, the version provided by Collins could not be any more quintessentially American. To find the source of inspiration for this most common form of American town planning, one need only look to Philadelphia once again. According to geographer Peirce Lewis, the leaders of colonial Pennsylvania created the most radical departure from their European predecessors than what had yet been seen on the eastern seaboard.[2] Philadelphia emerged along the Delaware River as America's first significant planned city, serving as the urban hub of William Penn's "Holy Experiment" discussed earlier.

In his 1683 "Philadelphia Plan," Penn settled on a Renaissance-style, rectangular street layout. What could not have been predicted was the extent to which Philadelphia's grid of uniform city blocks would serve as the favored model for future town settlement across the continent. American settlers and town founders were absolutely enamored with the elegant simplicity and efficiency of the Philadelphia grid plan. For more than a century of town building and settlement efforts, Americans created literally thousands of miniature Philadelphias for small and large cities alike. It should therefore be of little surprise that Suzanne Collins simply followed suit, offering up a perfectly standard version of an American small-town grid plan punctuated by a central public square.

The geographical origins of the Philadelphia Plan provide for an intriguing story. As for where to locate the new colonial settlement, the original plan for Philadelphia was situated strategically between two navigable waterways. Penn's surveyor general, Thomas Holme, was the one responsible for drawing up the plan back in London, well in advance of Penn's arrival in America. Titled "Portraiture of the City of Philadelphia," Holme's visionary plan for the new city was of a monumental scale well ahead of its time. Its design was motivated largely to attract new settlers to the fledgling Quaker colony and to encourage shareholders to invest in the place.

Encompassing an impressive area of some 1,200 acres (480 hectares), the plan depicted a *rectilinear*—that is, a rectangular—Renaissance-inspired grid of broad, intersecting streets that stretched for two miles from east to west. The two principal avenues were designed with an impressive width of 100 feet (30 meters) and intersected at a prominent central square. The city's north-south streets were named for simple numbers, while the east-west streets were named for various trees. Like its rectilinear grid plan, Philadelphia's street-naming convention was widely adopted as it diffused into the plans for newer cities and towns across the nation.

Given the necessity to access navigable waterways, Philadelphia was wisely sandwiched between the expansive Delaware River on its eastern side, and the narrower Schuylkill River to its west. By extending the grid to connect the riverbanks, they created a city with two accessible riverfronts to maximize the potential for commerce and oceangoing trade directed back to Europe. The rivers would also provide reliable access to drinking water. Completing the urban plan was the inclusion of five public squares. The grandest square was reserved for anchoring the center of the city plan, while four additional, smaller squares provided a geographical focus for each of the city's four quadrants. As indicated within the original plan, rows of inviting shade trees would adorn their peripheries.

In reality, Penn's vision required quite some time to materialize. Much of the city's early development naturally clustered within the blocks nearest the Delaware River. This unbalanced emphasis on the city's eastern margin continued apace well into the nineteenth century. In turn, the land allocated for the public squares was prioritized instead for rubbish dumps and burial grounds, a far cry from the green spaces once envisioned. The people's devotion to the plan remained steadfast, however, and the city expanded slowly to the west and generally prospered throughout the nineteenth century. With some necessary patience the 1683 Philadelphia Plan eventually filled in. The smaller squares became the focal point of their neighborhoods and remain so to this day. These public spaces now constitute an indelible part of Philadelphia's very identity.

Aside from Renaissance town-planning ideals, Penn's original vision for the city was influenced by two recent crises that had devastated London. These involved the most recent scourge of the plague, or Black Death, and the great London fire of the 1660s. Similar disasters had occasionally befallen the Empire's colonial cities as well. Having wisely learned from such design pitfalls, Penn provided expansive city blocks and uniform streets from one river to the other, with each spacious block featuring an isolated family home at its center. In his memorandum of 1681, Penn provided instructions for his intended layout of the new town:

> Let every house be placed … in the middle of its plat, as to the breadth way of it, that so there may be ground on each side for gardens and orchards, or fields, that it may be a green country town, which will never be burnt, and always be wholesome.[3]

The plan for Philadelphia and countless cities like it were therefore contingent upon the knowledge of events and histories that preceded them. It stands to reason, then, that Penn had actually not envisioned a densely built city at all, but a "green country town." As Peirce Lewis explains, "Penn himself had expected that his big Philadelphia blocks would permit farmers to live in town and plant large gardens around capacious houses, each block a kind of mini-farm."[4] Of lower priority for Penn was setting aside land for public spaces or civic institutions, aside from the original squares. There is no articulated urban center. Certainly, the city's central square would catch the imaginations of town founders for generations to come.

From the perspective of Renaissance urban planning, however, this central feature of Philadelphia was rather unremarkable.

It is instructive to note that Penn himself was a Quaker, a faith that relied on neither a hierarchical ministry nor a fixed place of worship. Thus, as Peter Kostof explains, Penn's Philadelphia was "much like the planned estates of 17th-century London, not a city so much as a residential district."[5] This Renaissance grid plan, along with its absence of designated spaces for urban civic functions, was therefore in part a product of Penn's Quaker value system.

While Penn's original plan remains indelibly imprinted into today's urban landscape, his rather utopian-like garden approach did not come to pass. In the spirit of capitalist enterprise championed by colonial settlers, the "land in Philadelphia soon became too valuable to fritter away on mere gardens."[6] Instead, land speculators proceeded to divide the larger blocks into much smaller parcels to sell at a profit. In a classic case of migration diffusion, they promptly chopped down the trees to make way for Georgian-style, brick row-houses like the very ones they had inhabited back in London. Named to honor Britain's King George III, the modest, Renaissance formality of the Georgian style of architecture was adopted widely throughout America's colonial towns up and down the eastern seaboard, as well as deep into the American Midwest.

To be clear, Penn's rectilinear street grid was not the first on earth; rather, it represented the latest in a lengthy succession of urban grid plans implemented around the world. The Chinese invoked a grid plan for its administrative capitals beginning more than two thousand years ago. The Greeks likewise latched onto the conveniences of rectilinear planning, especially within their colonies as early as the seventh century BCE.[7] Perhaps more relevant for purposes here was the Roman Empire's standardized approach to colonial town settlement. The Rome of Julius Caesar's time made use of a central forum (public square) intersected at 90-degree angles by two principal arteries. With a renewed interest during the European Renaissance of Classical Greek and Roman art and architecture, the focus of town planning on a central forum or public square made quite the impressive comeback as well. Though settled some two thousand years apart, there is little to distinguish Philadelphia's central square and main avenues from those of the original Roman forum.

Although Collins may have intended some loose association with the Roman forum as a central public space, the story of District 12's townscape is more closely rooted to the Philadelphia grid plan which diffused into and well beyond the Appalachians. As the First Law of Geography teaches us, Philadelphia's relative proximity to the central Appalachians allowed Scots-Irish and other colonial settlers to simply transport their favored town planning traditions into their newer mountain settlements.

To be fair, such Renaissance-era grid planning was attempted elsewhere in the North American colonies as well. The first true rectilinear street grid on the eastern seaboard is actually credited to the 1638 plan for New Haven, Connecticut, with its nine square-shaped city blocks. But its plan was much more modest in its scope and did not catch the imagination of New England settlers moving west. More influential in the colonies of New Spain was the standardized town plaza heavily prescribed by the Spanish court and monarchy. Their own set of rules for settling the Spanish colonies became part of the *Laws of the Indies*, which were likewise a genuine product of Renaissance planning ideals.[8]

Generally, the towns of New Spain were referred to as *pueblos* or *villas* and were spatially organized within a square grid of streets. Most notably, two principal thoroughfares intersected in the middle at a large public square, or *plaza*. The blocks immediately surrounding the plaza were subdivided and sold to leading settlers. The plan diffused northward from Central America into the borderlands of New Spain, which Americans now recognize as the southern tier of states stretching from California to Texas, as well as Florida. Cities as prominent as San Antonio, Tucson, Santa Fe, and St. Augustine saw their beginnings in the town plans specified within the *Laws of the Indies*. Many of their original Spanish street grids and architectural legacies remain very much in place today, a visible legacy of Spanish colonial patterns.

Not to be outdone—at least not yet—was New France, which settled various grid-plan towns along the Mississippi River and, in the north, along the St. Lawrence Seaway. Perhaps the most famous of these places in the United States is the *Vieux Carre* or "French Quarter" of New Orleans. Returning to the East Coast, other English variations of the Renaissance grid appeared as well, though not before that of Penn's Philadelphia. The Oglethorpe Plan defines historic Savannah, Georgia, to this day, implemented by its own eastern colony during the 1730s. From its original inclusion of six equally spaced public squares created by the city's founder, James Oglethorpe, the city grid later expanded to include no less than 24 of them.

By 1730, however, Philadelphia's gridded city was already up and running. For their part, Appalachian settlers preferred this booming northern port city as their primary source of inspiration, which made good geographic sense given its relative proximity to the mountains.

Main Street and District 12

The public square—the very kind where Katniss visits the market or ogles the goodies in the bakery—became one of the more important ingredients of town design by the early American period. "Upon this square may be found public buildings, or, as is often the case, the square may remain unbuilt upon and will then be faced by the public buildings," explains Richard Francaviglia.[9] Importantly, the open square is spatially defined by the buildings and activities surrounding it. This is why communities which have demolished one or more sides of their commercial business blocks—usually to make room for more parking—have discovered that the square's original sense of place has been compromised as well. The square and what surrounds it consequently form a symbiotic relationship.

These modest business districts were replicated across the United States as new towns were settled throughout the nineteenth century. Americans came to refer to their centers of downtown retail trade as *Main Street.* As described by Francaviglia, a visual synergy is found on Main Streets, with the central thoroughfare usually defined by rows of commercial buildings lining both sides. Sometimes they are joined by occasional civic functions such as a city hall, courthouse, or church. Either way, the Main Street business district historically featured the highest density of structures in town and served as the "architectural climax of two- and three-story buildings set close together."[10] Should the original town plan additionally be blessed with a public square, the commercial landscape of Main Street simply wraps around it. Welcome to the town square of District 12, the heart of its Main Street business district.

One can find two variations of the public square in American towns or cities. The *closed square* is typically utilized for seats of local government, such as the political hub for a county seat. In this case a rather elaborate county courthouse is placed in the center of the town square, though still allowing for some open space around it. This layout is quintessentially American, with the rows of main-street commercial buildings placed around the courthouse—a downtown landscape often referred to as the *courthouse square.* For its part, the county building typically overshadows its more humble commercial blocks around it, providing a recognizable landmark and a potent symbol of democracy at the heart of town. By one count, out of 3,066 county seats across the lower 48 states (which include Louisiana's 64 parishes), approximately one-third include the familiar courthouse square layout.[11] Most are found in the South and Midwest, though curiously the plan diffused as far west as Prescott, Arizona, providing quite the "eastern feel" for the place.

In contrast, one can imagine the *open-square plan* by simply removing the government building placed at its center. The public space thereby remains empty of permanent structures, though it is still bordered by commercial buildings on three or four sides. This is the plan we find at the center of District 12. Any public buildings, such as a city hall or county courthouse, either face onto the square themselves or—in numerous cases—are relegated to unimportant city blocks nearby. In District 12 the equivalent to a local government facility would be the so-called Justice Building. In this case the Hunger Games films portray this hub of central authority quite accurately. The architecturally distinct symbol of Panem's governing apparatus appropriately occupies one of the square's four sides as we have seen.

For its part, the Justice Building fronts the square as more of a democratic equal with its commercial counterparts. This may not have served as the ideal visual symbol of authoritarian control the Capitol would have preferred. As for the "shops," as Katniss calls them, their own specialized businesses operated by the "merchant class" speak more of the largely free, capitalist enterprise that one would find along American main-street business districts. As Peirce Lewis explains, "the business of an American town was business—only incidentally the creation of social community."[12] Downtown business districts were therefore principally designed to promote commerce. As envisioned by Suzanne Collins, District 12 appropriately follows suit.

Even the shops which, as Katniss clarifies, "serve the wealthiest townspeople" must be fairly substantial structures of two floors or higher. We know this because Katniss tells us the "merchants live above their businesses" (*THG* 29). Likewise, typical main-street commercial buildings were fashionable, architectural affairs that accommodated multiple functions: commercial retail and services on the ground floor, and residential, office, or civic space on the floors above.[13] This mixed-use design for downtown buildings allowed property owners to either rent out their upper floors or to live upstairs themselves. Prior to the automobile age, commuting into downtown everyday was out of the question for most residents of modest means. Many merchants therefore simply lived above their shops, precisely as Katniss describes.

An Outdoor Living Room

American main streets and their occasional public squares have always played a role in forging a sense of community. While the primary intent of these places is to encourage business and trade, the space between the buildings provides an opportunity for people to engage and interact with fellow community members. These are some of the most democratic, or egalitarian spaces within our towns and cities. Public spaces are those where any law-abiding member of the community is welcome, regardless of socioeconomic background, race, or gender. Community planners often refer to public squares as "outdoor living rooms" because of their vital role in community building.

Municipalities, or local city governments, tend to favor these downtown public spaces for sponsoring a variety of community events throughout the year, such as parades or local festivals. Such activities can be mutually beneficial to local businesses and the community at large. They also tend to attract a wide array of people from both within and beyond the immediate locale. Should a public square be present, all the better. Whether oriented along a linear main street or perched around a public square, such public spaces play a generally positive role in fostering community interactions.

The public square of District 12 serves this community-building role especially well during the first novel. The role of its town square is most poignant, of course, when much of the local population is gathered for their mandatory viewing of the reaping. As perhaps the first silent protest in defiance of the Capitol, nearly everyone in the crowd displays the District's signature symbol of mutual support and respect, the three-finger salute. Katniss tells us that it is an old, rarely used gesture sometimes used at funerals to convey thanks or to say good-bye to a loved one (*THG* 24). In a way the crowd was indeed saying a final goodbye to Katniss, as they might do during a funeral. This was most powerfully accomplished, one might argue, within the public square where community members could express a unified voice. This touching sign of solidarity and mutual support affects Katniss to the point that she finds herself in danger of crying.

As Rickie Sanders explains, such smaller public places "are important staging areas for individuals and communities and may indeed be the only sites outside of the voting booth where they can give shape to their ideas and practice their notion of freedom."[14] It is a place for local residents to keep up on the latest news—mundane or otherwise—and for people to connect with one another and share ideas. As Sanders implied, this also represents a community's most democratic space where citizens might express their discontent in protest of some form. Public space therefore "belongs to everyone … and to no one."[15]

District 12's "outdoor room" further encourages community members to gather and to support one another during the actual Games. People are at least given a choice as to where they can watch the events, either from the privacy of their own homes, or on the square with the larger, clear screens (*THG* 280). Once again, the square is the designated place in town both to provide, and to seek out, community support for one another. At the same time, however, the Capitol's presence is undeniable, marked by its intrusive video equipment and related infrastructure and staff—all of which claim this space throughout the Games.

Still, certain aspects of democratic involvement remain possible at this point of the first novel. Should Katniss' family desire a kind word or to share some food with others, as Katniss explains, they can obtain "support in the square" (*THG* 280). Likewise, Katniss can even imagine the shouts from the crowd, urging her and Peeta onward. Specific friends and acquaintances from within her community come to mind, particularly Greasy Sae, Madge, and even the Peacekeepers who buy her fresh game. With these thoughts from Katniss we gain a brief window into her own community network which she has nurtured with her father's assistance since childhood. In this case her own sense of community is playing out within the town's most important public place.

Behind the Bakery

If the public facades of commercial buildings face onto Main Street or the town square, what is going on behind them? Early town planners typically—and wisely—included smaller lanes or alleys that bisected the larger city blocks. Most neighborhoods settled before World War II included these narrower lanes through the middle of their blocks to provide access to carriage houses (stables for privately owned horses and carriages) and first-generation automobile garages. Alleyways behind main-street commercial buildings further provided access for utilities, trash pickup, and deliveries. For these reasons, cultural geographers sometimes view the varied mish-mash of alleyway landscapes to be some of the more intriguing places to interpret. They often exhibit rather haphazard collections of hastily-built garage spaces, metal or wood-frame sheds, refuse piles of rusting furniture and construction implements and—as I've personally encountered more than once—discarded ceramic toilet bowls converted into flowerpots. If the alleys themselves are pre-planned features of a city layout, what we find along them is often less predictable.

More to the point of District 12, one of the most poignant and memorable scenes of the original series occurs along one of these very alleys. During the reaping for the 74th Games, Peeta Mellark has just been picked as the boy tribute when Katniss flashes back to the desperate times following the death of her father. In short, the family had been nearly starving to death in the midst of winter. Practically out of options, Katniss found herself "stumbling along a muddy lane behind the shops that serve the wealthiest townspeople" (*THG* 29). Following a disheartening attempt to pick through trash bins recently emptied, Peeta appears and plays out one of the story's most famous scenes. In the novel, he throws not one, but two loaves of perfectly good bread out to Katniss for her to collect. It is after this heartfelt event that she survives to find the first dandelions of spring, only then realizing how she will feed her family. Not only does this pivotal scene with

Peeta occur in a rather traditional alley behind the storefronts, but it reveals yet one more clue about the spatial layout of District 12's town center.

Possible Prototypes for District 12

To better gain a visual sense of District 12's public square, it may be helpful to consider a small subset of comparable places. Any number of downtown business districts with open-square plans could more or less serve as prototypes for District 12. One could consider the expansive, grassy square of Medina, Ohio, though its sheer scale would be too large for District 12's smaller population. A more modest-sized square is found in the comfortable public plaza of Santa Fe, New Mexico. This latter southwestern city was originally laid out through the Spanish *Laws of the Indies* in the 1600s. Back on the East Coast, many of the renowned Oglethorpe squares in Savannah, Georgia, could serve as District 12 models as well, though perhaps Wright Square is among the best. Its compact open space is largely surrounded and defined by two-story, nineteenth-century brick buildings.

Together with Santa Fe Plaza, Wright Square likely best represents the scale of District 12's own public space. With its towering Live Oaks, shady Spanish moss, and grassy pathways, Wright Square has the makings of a stunning outdoor room. And connoisseurs of urban design would agree. The place was included as one of America's "ten great public squares" by the Congress of the New Urbanism (CNU) in 2019. Adding even a portion of this natural beauty to the square in District 12 would undoubtedly make for quite the pleasant public place as well!

Beyond these examples, one could also consider the comfortably-sized open-square plan of Bentonville, Arkansas, on which we will now focus in some detail. The town also happens to be found in the Ozarks, an ancient mountainous area connected geologically (mostly underground) with the southern Appalachians. Like many of its counterparts, one of its central city blocks was reserved as an unbuilt public space. The various two-story commercial buildings facing the square further approximate those of District 12. And, as with the Justice Building, one side of the square is occupied by a civic government facility, in this case housing the Benton County Circuit Court. It would be difficult to imagine a more quintessential American downtown landscape as the one found here in northwestern Arkansas.

Among its historic commercial buildings facing the square is the Walton Five and Dime Museum. Such "five and dime" general stores were once the hallmark of downtown retail businesses, not unlike those found around the square of District 12. And perhaps something like the Mellark Bakery, this one has an intriguing story associated with it. On this site, an entrepreneurial young man named Sam Walton had purchased Luther Harrison's Variety Store facing the town square after moving to Bentonville with his family in 1950. Walton's new store was part of the Ben Franklin five and dime franchise at the time. Dime stores like this one—also known as five-and-ten-cent or variety stores—emerged onto America's Main Street retailing scene during the late nineteenth century. The business model was nothing short of revolutionary at the time, providing a new approach for selling discounted merchandise that caught on like wildfire by around 1900. Buying into this approach, Walton acquired the barber shop next door and expanded his operation to what became a fixture on the town square. He named it Walton's 5 & 10. Walton's represented one of countless retail variety stores that could be found in virtually every American downtown business district throughout the mid-twentieth century.

Some of the larger national operations included those of the F.W. Woolworth Company, Ben Franklin Stores, and W.T. Grant Company, not to mention numerous other regional chains. At its peak during the 1970s, Woolworth's operated more than 2,200 stores nationwide and had launched the Foot Locker shoe store chain. One of its national competitors, Ben Franklin was founded in 1927 by George and Edward Butler. At its peak their company boasted of approximately 2,500 stores nationwide, including the one in Bentonville operated by Sam Walton. By the 1980s, however, America's retail habits continued to shift in ways not kind to five and dimes. Ben Franklin Stores declared bankruptcy in 1996 with only about 860 stores remaining. The F.W. Woolworth Company experienced a similar fate upon the closing of its remaining 400 stores in 1997.[16]

What of Sam Walton and his own Five and Dime? After enjoying some impressive success with his expanded store downtown, he eventually launched another little operation focused on discount retailing. We know it as Walmart. With its earlier name of Wal-Mart Stores, Inc., the company's strategy was to locate its retail outlets in rural areas outside the major cities, thereby avoiding competition with the likes of Kmart, Sears, and Target. By 1990 Wal-Mart had become the largest discount retail chain in the United States. The corporation expanded into international markets during the 1990s and became the world's largest private employer by the turn of the millennium. With its global sales eventually surpassing Exxon Mobile, Wal-Mart ranked by 2001 as the world's largest corporation.[17] It is instructive to keep in mind that the vast majority of today's larger national and global corporations began as very small, local business affairs like that of Sam Walton. Interestingly, Walmart's global headquarters remain in Bentonville as of this writing.

Retail operations had also shifted geographically during the twentieth century. Once located at the heart of downtown business districts, the developers of larger retailers and department stores came to favor freeway interchanges and other automobile corridors for their sprawling supercenters. These days, one single "superstore"—providing various departments of merchandise and groceries—replaces the equivalent of an entire downtown business district like that of District 12. This is due to their ability to operate at *economies of scale*. That is, the larger the operation, the more efficient and cost effective it becomes. This allows such retail giants like Walmart to offer relatively lower prices for their consumers while undercutting their competition.

As for Walton's original five and dime store on the Bentonville square, it is now home to the Walton Five and Dime Museum (or Wal-Mart Museum), preserving some of the history that led to the founding of this global corporation. Those earlier, locally owned retail stores along America's Main Streets had thus transitioned into the incredibly larger-scale operations that characterize discount retailers (or "big-box" stores) today. Had District 12 been an actual place and continued to grow into the present day, it just might have found its own Walmart and related shopping centers on its periphery. This would have likely come at the expense of numerous locally-owned businesses struggling to compete, with Mellark Bakery likely being one of them.

With the rise of shopping centers, strip malls, and—most recently—big-box discount retailers since the 1960s, America's main streets and public squares have lost much of their former luster as central places within their communities. Only recently have local leaders turned to amenities, such as tourism and entertainment, to revitalize their once ailing downtowns. The so-called *adaptive re-use* of historic downtown buildings for more contemporary functions has likewise become fashionable, restoring them once again as stalwarts of local pride. Had District 12's business district survived this American era of small-town decline—as well as its unfortunate firebombing incident—it might find itself springing back to life once again as a re-imagined arts or entertainment district. Within this context, Mellark Bakery would certainly become a popular source of favored treats and baked goods, complete with outdoor café tables oozing onto the town square. And Katniss and her young family would surely become regular customers when not playing amidst the grasses of their favored Meadow.

6

Portraying the Seam

Much like the District 12 square, many of us probably conjure an image of the Seam as portrayed in the original film, "The Hunger Games." The Seam represents a distinct place within the broader District landscape as discussed earlier and is especially noteworthy as the location of Katniss' original home. It is here, amidst the Seam's derelict, uniform residential dwellings where Katniss forges the lion's share of her childhood memories. To represent the area's gritty, coal-centric sense of place, the producers of the first film chose the abandoned company town of Henry River Mill Village, located on a picturesque forested ridge about 70 miles east of Asheville, North Carolina. The Village's neglected housing from its textile mill days provided an arguably realistic perspective of how housing within the Seam might have actually appeared. First let's look at some historical and recent background of the Village itself as a filming location. This will set the stage for later discussions surrounding the role of company towns in authentic coal mining communities of the Appalachians.

Henry River Mill Village

The real history of Henry River Mill Village began around 1905 with the establishment of a textile mill by the Henry River Manufacturing Company. The nearest town was—and is—Hildebran, located only one mile north of the mill. As of 2019 the remaining structures on the 72-acre site included a two-story company store building and 20 nearly identical wood-frame homes of former textile workers. The original village had included 35 houses, and the mill itself had been closed in 1970 before being consumed by fire in 1977.[1] Since then the village's boarding house has also been destroyed.

Fans will recognize the village in various scenes within "The Hunger Games." Most notably we find the old company store, which served as the Mellark bakery, and one of the dilapidated houses featured as the Everdeen residence. What may be less familiar is the site's more recent developments that have played out since the filming had concluded. Following the Village's own "dark days" of abandonment since the 1990s, the place is now being transformed as a visitor attraction. Marla Milling of the *Asheville Citizen Times* relates the recent story of how the village is acquiring a new, and somewhat transformed life beyond its recent Hunger Games fame.[2] The entire village property was purchased in 2017 by Calvin Reyes, along with his mom and stepfather, only weeks before a tornado caused some damage to the remaining village property. "The roof on the company store got peeled back during the tornado, but none of the houses were damaged," Reyes recalled. Since the windows had already been removed, the tornado caused no further damage to those.

Reyes discussed how he and his parents had acquired the property. At one point he had been scouting potential sites large enough to accommodate members of his extended family, where they could all live in close proximity to one another. Upon surveying the Henry River landscape, he was instantly transfixed. He wasted no time in calling his mom to proclaim his love for the place and to garner her support for bringing it back to life. He and his family then purchased the entire village for $360,000 in 2013 from its former owner, Wade Shepherd, who would pass away two years later.[3] Even prior to filming for "The Hunger Games," Shepherd had complained about recalcitrant visitors and vandals on the site. Such acts of trespassing only became more frequent following the blockbuster film's release.

Regarding the condition of the property at the time of purchase, Reyes recalled, "[t]he grass was overgrown. It looked like a war zone." As for the country store that served as the Mellark bakery, the dilapidated structure was "stacked to the roof with junk. It was a hoarder's paradise."[4] For their part, the houses were in various states of decay, including the one used by the movie company for Katniss Everdeen's home. The entire village had essentially suffered from what historic preservationists refer to as *benign neglect*. In such cases buildings and other historic structures are simply abandoned and left to the elements of nature without intention to either destroy or renovate them. This dereliction through abandonment has been replicated thousands of times over throughout the United States, leading in part to the burgeoning historic preservation movement by the late twentieth century.

In the spirit of transforming historic structures to more contemporary purposes—defined earlier as *adaptive re-use*—Reyes sought to accomplish something similar by restoring the buildings and converting the property into a visitor destination. As of this writing, that initial vision has in part come to fruition, complete with the property's own promotional web site. Due in part to its fame as a popular filming location, the outdoor site is also monitored more thoroughly with video surveillance. Likewise, activities for visitors are more organized and prescribed in the form of scheduled tours.

The village was also recently listed on the National Register of Historic Places, a federal level of recognition for the property's historic significance. Reyes had sought the designation because his family "wanted to be the ones who got this property the recognition it deserves," he explained. His family has also established the Henry River Preservation Fund as a nonprofit organization to help preserve remaining historic artifacts still scattered around the property. Future plans for the site include a new museum, gift shop, and perhaps even renovated houses to accommodate guests. One structure has already been fully restored for that purpose. Reyes has proposed additional ideas, including a restaurant in the former country store, a banquet hall upstairs, and even accommodations for wedding ceremonies.[5]

The village is further officially recognized as a "historic district" given its inclusion on the National Register. While the web site acknowledges the property's role in "The Hunger Games" film, the listing on the Register is justified more on its historical association with the nation's textile industry. In brief, the village provides an excellent example of a typical textile mill and its associated company town within the Carolinas. Not unlike the impoverished conditions of District 12, the village had never enjoyed a sewer system or running water. This is why it may surprise some to learn that the last native resident to move out of the village did so rather recently, around the year 2000.

Was the choice of Henry River to represent the Seam appropriate for a coal-mining community? On one level, sure. The derelict, unkempt structures resemble an underprivileged, rural community within its intended Appalachian setting. It further represents a realistic—if rather small-scale—company town, where its mill workers and their families were substantially dependent upon the company for their livelihoods. Perhaps most true to the intent of the novel was Katniss' home residence, essentially a run-down, company-built, wood-framed structure. Likewise, the rows of derelict cabins in Henry River Mill Village could certainly reflect the curving roads and sprawling nature of the Seam.

One passage within the prequel provides a description of the Seam's geographic layout. This follows the same scene discussed in Chapter 5 when Coriolanus and Sejanus were searching for the home of Lucy Gray and the Covey. After Sejanus trades some of his best chewing gum for a loaf of bread at the bakery, the "beet-faced" woman points them in the direction of the Seam. The narrator then takes us along their route, allowing us to see what our two young Peacekeepers are witnessing along the way. We are told that the Seam sprawls for miles beyond the center of town, defined by an irregular pattern of winding lanes that emerge and disappear in an unplanned manner. Some of these lanes feature rundown, makeshift structures serving as the homes of Seam residents.

Not surprisingly, this description corresponds well enough with that described in the original series, and also with that of Henry River Mill Village. Granted, this filming location is overall cleaner and more charming than a coal-dependent mining landscape would likely appear, with nary a hint of coal dust or village residents to be found. But no matter. The setting provides a realistic perspective on the realities of working-class families dependent upon their corporate overseers.

One could even interpret Henry River as an educational opportunity. As indicated by the historical research for its National Register listing, the place exemplifies how corporate owners predetermined the spatial layouts of their communities, and how they monopolized the bulk of local employment opportunities. While Collins admittedly invented a more extreme case of community desperation under the guise of crippling authoritarian control, the Henry River site exhibits various geographic and social qualities that would have generally mirrored such conditions. The film producers could have done far worse than Henry River in choosing a filming location for the Seam—not the least being a false movie set in the rear of a California studio lot.

To enhance the gloomy and depressed appearance of the Seam and District 12, the film producers creatively varied the color palette. The film's director, Gary Ross, explained that "the palette of District 12 is much bleaker than the palette of the Capitol," which can be controlled through the production process and costume design.[6] Perhaps one notable example occurs during the reaping in front of the Justice Building, when Effie Trinket's eye-popping Capitol costume contrasts starkly against the grungy blue and gray hues of District 12. This was a strategic approach to accentuate the vast socio-economic disparity between the Capitol's privileged population and those merely surviving within the districts.

The Social Geography of Coal Mining

One finds a curious juxtaposition between the human landscape of the Seam and the center of District 12. On the one hand, Collins presents readers with a fairly realistic coal-mining scene, thereby shedding light on the history of mining companies and their control over employment and livelihoods. At the center of District 12, however, is a rather typical small-town landscape built atop a Philadelphia-style grid—the primary intent of which was to champion free-market commerce. Would these two very different types of places co-exist within an Appalachian coal-mining community? And, to what extent were free-market business activities allowed to carry on in District 12 under the auspices of Capitol control? Certainly, the vibrant local trade in Katniss' home town may be another unintended consequence of negligent Capitol authority, not unlike its derelict fence. But how likely would we find such a collection of main-street businesses within a true mining town? These questions provide an opportunity to further compare the juxtaposed landscapes of District 12 with their authentic coal-mining counterparts of central Appalachia.

First, there is certainly precedence within the Appalachian coal fields to find District 12-type places. While relatively rare, not all coal towns of central Appalachia were owned or operated by the companies themselves. The other extreme was admittedly more common, that of an entire town being designed, built, and operated by a corporate entity headquartered outside the region. The Seam would represent such a place. Unincorporated company towns, as they are termed, were for all intents and purposes considered private property. There was one landowner—the corporation—which allowed for no civic representation through a democratically elected town council or equivalent municipal body. The company purchased and owned the land, and thus it was fully responsible for constructing and maintaining the town's physical infrastructure of streets, utilities, and housing. Corporate personnel doubled as landlords for miners and their families. They likewise provided some semblance of police and fire protection and could even provide churches and general stores. The company store often became the focal point of a mining community. Residents of more isolated places within the coalfields often had few alternatives for obtaining household goods and services.

Of course, not every place or company was the same. This diversity of operations generated a wide array of possible living conditions and degrees of corporate control. Company towns could range from crudely constructed coal camps thrown up overnight to model communities that resembled fully functioning towns. Many came with all the latest modern conveniences and relatively benevolent if paternalistic owner-operators. What they all held in common, however, was their extraordinary level of local influence, both for the residents who lived and worked there, and within the greater regional political system.

It is worth emphasizing that these operators all consisted of large-scale, privately owned entities. This meant that standard democratic and free-market processes did not apply to them, nor to whomever lived on their properties. According to Robert Lewis, it was this type of unincorporated operation that became one of the defining geographic features of the central Appalachian region. More than three quarters—and in certain areas upwards of 90 percent—of all miners lived in these corporate-controlled places.[7] Though missing the characteristic company store or related community services, the Seam of District 12 generally represents the oppressive social and working conditions experienced in such places during the late nineteenth and early twentieth centuries. Suzanne Collins did not invent this scenario, nor did she need to greatly exaggerate the living conditions of such places for a fantastical dystopian story. She merely had to pull from existing places and situations to find her inspiration. This is sad news, indeed.

At the other extreme of corporate control were the more conventional towns overseen by a democratically elected governing body. These are the incorporated towns, most of which—outside New England—operate through the mayor-council form of municipal city government. With few exceptions, most of these communities had been platted and surveyed in advance, adhering to some version of the Philadelphia plan described earlier. Such places were largely characterized by their focus on local enterprise, expressed through a downtown business district focused on a main street or a public square, complete with privately owned residential and business properties. Likewise, these places were often platted conveniently at the junctions of rail lines, crossroads, or near waterways that offered various geographic advantages for future development and population growth. This scenario more accurately describes what we find with the public square and its associated town plan of District 12. There is even a town mayor, though to what extent that position is democratically elected is anyone's guess.

One characteristic of mining towns, regardless of the extent to which the coal companies held sway, was their segregation largely along racial or socio-economic lines. This strikes a familiar chord with how Collins separated her mixed-race, working-class community of the Seam from its more Caucasian, middle-class town center. While often considered somewhat idealistically as "melting pots," the geographical situation on the ground often played out quite differently. Mining companies sometimes encouraged local segregation along racial or socio-economic lines—or both— thereby creating areas of town designated with names such as "Colored Town," "Hunky Hollow," or "Little Italy," to name a few.[8] This segregated social geography typically carried over to employment opportunities as well. Discrimination was blatant and systematic in the kinds of jobs available, based principally on one's racial or ethnic background. In this way the segregated neighborhoods of District 12 follow suit, most visibly between the merchant class of the town center and the people of color relegated to the Seam.

Despite systematic and corporate efforts to reinforce patterns of segregation, a true ethnic "melting pot" could still evolve elsewhere within the community. The most rigid geographies of segregation often became blurred within the mines and during various community social events featuring entertainment, music, and dance. Much of the second half of this book provides highlights of such racial blurring, especially as experienced through the joys of Appalachian music making, performance, and related folk traditions. Down in the mines themselves, workers often shared in one another's economic challenges. No matter their ethnic background, miners were eventually able to organize themselves in support of their mutual, common interests. They focused their ongoing fight for better working conditions and wages, for instance, through the United Mine Workers of America, which afforded miners with the ability to exert some measure of influence.[9]

This pattern of solidarity seen down in the mines may reflect a similar pattern within the Seam. Both fathers of Katniss and Gale—and later Gale himself—were apparently able to conspire more adequately during their time below ground. A similar case is presented within the prequel, involving the allegedly rebellious activities of Arlo Chance. As the Capitol presents the case, Arlo was summarily arrested and hanged for killing a Peacekeeper and two District 12 bosses down in the mines. Discussing the background of the incident, Sejanus tells Coriolanus he overheard that Arlo had accidentally killed the three while trying to sabotage coal production (*BSS* 346). Also working against his cause, Arlo had been known as a rebel leader during the war. Of course, this very incident is what inspired the prequel's Lucy Gray to pen the "The Hanging Tree," a murder ballad that would resurface in the time of Katniss Everdeen. Thanks in large part to Katniss' father, the song would exact quite a powerful influence on fomenting the rebellion and its eventual success.

Within real-life mining towns as in the Seam, hazardous working conditions were all too common. One situation involved a regional disparity. Wages in Appalachian mines were fixed 15–30 percent lower than in those located north of the Ohio River. Moreover, hazardous conditions permeated all aspects of mining work. Tens of thousands of miners lost their lives within Appalachian coal mines, including some 21,000 deaths in West Virginia alone between 1883 and 2004. One of the most common causes of death was the collapse of mine roofs, though it was more often than not the "explosions that attracted the press and captured the nation's imagination."[10]

Despite deplorable conditions and risks, mining companies were overtly hostile to the formation of unions. Corporate owners fought their creation at every turn. Miners who eventually joined the United Mine Workers of America (UMWA), for instance, were often blacklisted and then evicted from their properties. Companies further sought the wholesale dismantling of these organizations through combinations of court injunctions and company guards deployed on the ground. Such scenarios devolved into the so-called "mine wars" during the first three decades of the twentieth century, characterized by protracted conflicts and violence.

The tide in favor of workers' rights did not improve substantially until the Great Depression, when President Franklin Roosevelt initiated the New Deal. Numerous reforms were included within the new legislation to improve conditions faced by coal miners and their families. Of particular note was the Wagner Act of 1935, which granted the right of workers to organize into labor unions. "Almost overnight," explains Ronald Lewis, "the Appalachian coal fields became organized, though union organizers continued to face fierce resistance in some sectors."[11]

Within the Seam of District 12, of course, there was no recourse like the Wagner Act through which coalminers could organize. Any attempt to express dissent was summarily squashed by Capitol authority. In this way, the miners of District 12 were operating under the oppressive conditions that largely characterized the early twentieth century. Collins basically replaced the authority of the mining company with that of Panem's own authoritarian regime.

Life in the Company Towns

In the mining towns under complete corporate control, community social life often depended upon services and entertainment provided by the company itself. One of the most visible influences on daily social life was the company store, sometimes augmented by additional specialized services such as pharmacies. For their part, these corporate-owned facilities played multiple roles in the local community, as demonstrated by the recollections of Shirley Glass about her own hometown of Dante, Virginia:

> When I got out of high school, one of my first jobs was working in the company drugstore. And they had like a restaurant in there, and they would serve food every day to the people that worked in the office building.... My sister-in-law used to work in the company store, and my cousin. I would catch a ride down with my cousin to work, or sometimes I'd even have to walk home. But it was real exciting working over there, especially when the officials from up north come, so we could get some extra money. About $90 a month was all you made; that wasn't very much. We got a little discount, but it really helped.
>
> When I was a little girl, we used to come to Dante to buy our groceries, furniture—anything that you wanted was at the company store. And at Christmas time they had a special place, and they'd open it up with toys, and you looked forward to that. And now we don't have nothing, it's just really sad. Like grocery shopping, you have to go to St. Paul.[12]

In towns where the land, housing, and local trade were all overseen by the corporation, reminders of who controlled their lives were pervasive and constant. As Glass indicates above, the company store not only provided goods and services but also local employment and holiday festivities to boot. Glass and her family depended upon the company for securing low-wage employment, social activities, company discounts, and spending money. Everyday household goods were provided by the same corporation, from furniture to toys.

In some ways this situation represented a greater degree of centralized control than the one Katniss experiences within District 12. Though largely reserved for the privileged merchant class, the shops of District 12 operated within more of a free-market, capitalist scenario as we have seen. Even the Hob—though officially illegal—provided more of an organic, unregulated, laissez-faire approach with its individual stalls, food, and vendors like that of Greasy Sae. Perhaps ironically, the Hob would not have easily persisted within a corporate-controlled town.

Of course, when the coal ran out or was no longer easily obtained, the corporation fenced in its facilities (or simply left unprotected holes in the ground), locked its doors, and left the town to fend for itself. This was the typical *boom-bust cycle* that characterized communities dependent upon extractive industries. Eventually the valuable resource would be exhausted, and the corporation would move on with little concern for those left behind. The extent to which a company town could weather its own economic collapse was correlated with its former dependence on the corporation. Incorporated towns not owned by the mining companies were generally more effective with transitioning to alternative economic activities. Peter Crow emphasizes how such communities left to their own devices could use education to their advantage:

> So, education became important, and not just education tied to economic interest of the coal companies. With education came greater likelihood of using courts to settle problems, town council debates to steer a community's future, and understanding of how state and national decisions are made and how to work the system. Over time, women took leadership roles, often with less confrontational leadership styles than men. And environmentalism began shaping "get along" in an ecological image to which many mountain people seem particularly receptive.[13]

In contrast, many corporate-owned towns have not been so fortunate in their recoveries once the mines were shut down. Few local options have emerged to prevent wholesale economic collapse and the ensuing outmigration. In perhaps a desperate attempt at optimism, Crow adds, "[b]ut persistence and resourcefulness have enabled at least some former company towns to 'die' at least partially on their own terms, perhaps not even to end up 'dead.'"[14]

In a way, this last phrase might describe the eventual rebirth and reinvention of District 12—during its own postindustrial, post-mining era. While wholesale firebombings may not have occurred in real life, the ultimate effect was comparable for towns which had lost their sole economic rationale for existence. Likewise, the District 12 to which Katniss returns after the revolution is but a shell of its former self. As discussed in Chapter 3, she and Peeta begin a family there, and coal mining gives way to the manufacture of medicines. Like countless former mining communities—reliant on coal or otherwise—some people find ways to remain there because, well, it's home.

Aside from Peeta, Haymitch, and Greasy Sae, some 200 others have joined Katniss to rebuild their community and carry on. In whatever ways she might decide, and all in good time, she will most likely participate once again within the place she was born and raised. Welcome to the postindustrial era, Katniss!

7

Designing a Capital City

What is the city center of the Capitol supposed to look like? As with District 12, the films and novels portray widely disparate versions of the Capitol's urban center. With respect to the City Circle itself, the films of the original series remain true to its description within the novel, made most apparent during the tribute parades and the chariots moving around it. Beyond the paved circle, however, the films diverge markedly from what Katniss relates from her various experiences. In this chapter, we will explore the urban design of the Capitol's city center as specifically envisioned by Suzanne Collins, allowing for a more nuanced comparison with that of the films. And now with the more recent prequel, readers are provided with even more clues as to the Capitol's urban layout, essentially allowing us to piece together more of the city's intended design. For purposes here we will focus especially on the geographical characteristics and inspirations for the City Circle and the Corso, followed by a more architectural interpretation of the president's house, Victor's Village, the Justice Buildings, the cornucopia(s), and the Capitol's urban cityscape overall. As with the Philadelphia-style grid plan of District 12, the design of the Capitol is no accident; rather, Collins once again relies strategically upon a combination of European and American precedents of city planning in which to ground her dystopian story.

Channeling the Grand Manner

If the uniformly rectangular grid plan of Philadelphia provides a tangible symbol of American democracy, Collins chose a very different type of urban layout to represent her authoritarian Capitol. The spatial pattern described within her novels represents the antithesis of egalitarian city blocks and public squares. Rather, we find that Panem's own capital city comes right out of the playbook of European Renaissance–era dictators and monarchies. Just as the iron fist of Coriolanus Snow oversees Panem's unforgiving regime, the Capitol's own urban landscape only reinforces the role of centralized political power and authority.

It turns out that the Capitol described within the novels is fundamentally based on a European pattern dubbed the *Grand Manner*. This general approach to urban design was based largely on Renaissance-era planning principles favored by Europe's most powerful monarchs and—in Rome— the Popes, roughly from the 1500s through the 1700s. This was an innovative time during the Enlightenment, when art, architecture, and urban design were variously influenced by a newfound fascination in all things *Classical*—particularly related to the artistic, mathematical, and formal design modes of the ancient Greeks and Romans. As we saw earlier, such Renaissance-era planning approaches also inspired America's rectilinear street grids and public squares, of which Philadelphia became the primary source of inspiration on this side of the Atlantic Ocean.

As for Panem's own Capitol, its street layout relies heavily upon a later Renaissance trend known as the *Baroque* aesthetic (pronounced "Bar-OKE"). In brief, the primary indicator of a Baroque urban plan is its "hub-and-spoke" pattern of broad avenues radiating away from strategically placed central nodes, or circles. It is a distinctly hierarchical pattern designed to accentuate the symbolic importance of central government and its autocrats. The visual impact on the ground is striking. All major roads lead to the city's power centers which, in turn, provide daily visual reminders of who is in charge. All one need do is to scan up or down the street to catch a glimpse of colossal statues, monuments, or palaces of the state. As Peter Kostof asserts, the European Baroque is "a phenomenon of capital cities. It served the tastes and representational needs of absolutism."[1] The Grand Manner can thus be interpreted as a fusion of the straight, broad avenues of the Renaissance with this later radial pattern of the Baroque.

A distinct social hierarchy was built into the system as well. The expansive, central boulevards were intentionally lined with the grand palaces or spacious townhomes of the urban elite. In contrast, working-class neighborhoods and industrial districts were relegated to more distant— and less visible—spaces placed well away from the central thoroughfares, conveniently unseen by the upper classes.

Hints of the Baroque ideal could be traced to the rise of *signorie*— essentially the lords of ruling families in fourteenth-century Italy. They were followed in turn by the rise of royal authorities in France, Spain, and England throughout the next two centuries. The "progress of autocratic rule," as Kostof refers to the process, encouraged the growth and development of capital cities designed to concentrate the lion's share of national power and influence in one central place.[2] Madrid was the first to demonstrate this pattern of growth, followed by similar cases in Paris, London, Amsterdam, and Copenhagen.

Joining its larger capital counterparts was Rome, with its own Renaissance revival being led by a rather ambitious succession of popes. This is where the Baroque aesthetic was first embedded prominently within a capital city's urban street plan and design. During the sixteenth century, the Grand Manner culminated there with the imposing city master plan of Pope Sixtus V (1585–1590) at the hands of his architect, Domenico Fontana. What largely came to fruition was an expansive network of straight, radial streets, a focus on central vistas placed strategically at the end of broad thoroughfares (known now as *terminated vistas*), and an "overarching principle of geometric order."[3] Following Rome's lead, France appropriated Baroque-style urban planning during the 1600s and continued to develop its radial system right up through World War II.

From Paris the Grand Manner diffused across Europe, as far eastward as Russia's St. Petersburg. In the opposite direction, its ideals spread across the Atlantic to the "backwoods Baroque" as some referred to its appearance in Detroit, and to various other North American cities, as we will see below. And perhaps even more to the point of Suzanne Collins' Capitol, the Grand Manner's appeal for totalitarian regimes became most apparent through the likes of Mussolini, Hitler, and Stalin. What better urban design for Panem's authoritarian hub of control than that favored by the West's most notorious autocrats?

The City Circle

Though portrayed rather vaguely within the films, the Capitol's street layout described by Katniss takes the shape of a quintessential Baroque-style urban plan. Like that of District 12, the Capitol's urban *morphology*—or spatial layout—can easily go unnoticed by readers more intently following the story line. Still, Collins once again provides plenty of descriptive clues to help piece together the Capitol's appearance and functioning. And we find that the bulk of these descriptive breadcrumbs focus on one particular place of some importance—the City Circle.

Our first true experience within the Capitol of the original series occurs during the Roman-inspired tribute parade. Katniss brings us along for the chariot ride, during which she details the 20-minute gallop into the City Circle. It is further noteworthy that Collins capitalizes this central place as a proper noun. From Katniss' vantage point in the chariot, the City Circle is expansive enough to accommodate all twelve tribute pairs, lined up in single file. This aspect is portrayed quite accurately within the films as well. From here, however, Katniss' description diverges from that of the films. She notices that buildings surround the circle, upon which every window is packed with prestigious Capitol citizens to enjoy the festivities below. Their horses and chariots pull "right up" to the president's mansion (*THG* 71). The social hierarchy is evident here, exhibiting a quintessential Baroque urban plan. The Circle is lined with buildings of multiple floors, clearly representing some version of elegant townhouses or mansions owned by the city's wealthiest families. The president's house is fittingly placed prominently among them.

More of the city's Baroque elements become evident later in the first novel. As Katniss prepares for her interview with Caesar Flickerman, she explains that the event occurs on a stage directly in front of the Training Center. This, too, is located somewhere at the City Circle. We know this because Katniss mentions that, upon arrival at the Circle, the tributes are provided first with an official welcome, followed with a rousing version of Panem's national anthem. Afterwards, they are escorted right into the Training Center. It must therefore be located on site to allow for such a speedy transition between these activities.

As for the president's mansion, it is likely placed along the periphery of the Circle with its taller counterparts, though still signifying a central location within the city's hierarchy of authority. This is counter to the president's house seen in the films, in which the palatial structure is set back far from the street surrounded by its own spacious estate. Katniss tells us at the conclusion of the tribute parade that the president provides his official welcome from "a balcony above us," even as they still remain in their respective chariots (*THG* 71).

Notwithstanding the necessary sound system to project his voice, he and his mansion must be very close indeed. One additional clue corroborates this conclusion, found much later in *Mockingjay*. In this scene, Katniss approaches the City Circle dressed as a Capitol refugee. Upon arriving, she recognizes the City Circle and declares that it consists of a wide expanse lined with grand buildings including the president's mansion (*MJ* 345). This implies that the center of the Circle remains open and unbuilt. In actual Baroque-era cities, some form of monument or related symbolic feature would typically be located here, though Katniss never describes one.

In another diversion from the films, we learn that the tribute interviews with Caesar Flickerman actually take place outdoors. This is very different from the impression one receives from the films, where everyone appears to be seated within an expansive indoor theater. After arriving on stage with the fear that she will trip, Katniss describes the crowd and the surrounding scene. Evening has fallen, she notes, though the City Circle is brightly lit up, not unlike a summer's day (*THG* 124). Elevated bleachers of some kind have been assembled to seat the more prestigious guests—reminiscent of any major American parade route. The stylists are in the front row to honor their presence. A large balcony on a nearby building is reserved for the Gamemakers, providing them with a commanding view and signifying their elevated importance within the spectacle of the Games. Other balconies are filled mostly with television crews. We therefore have an interview scene that occurs completely outdoors, while the surrounding buildings all face onto the Circle.

Then the final clue clicks into place during the same tribute interviews. Katniss observes, "the City Circle and the avenues that feed into it are completely packed with people. Standing room only" (*THG* 124). Well, then. Here is our Baroque, radial street plan with its characteristic hub-and-spoke pattern of broad thoroughfares radiating outward from the city's central hub. People are crowded into the Circle and sprawl into some or all of the radial streets. If there is any geographical indication how important the Hunger Games were viewed as part of the political apparatus of control, this is it. All roads lead to the president's house—and to pivotal events and infrastructure that constitute the Games. Baroque urban planning, indeed.

America's Capital City and the Capitol

One need not look toward Europe to find an appropriate model for Panem's capital city. It turns out that one of the world's most inspirational and widely replicated Baroque urban plans is found much closer to home. Given prior comparisons between Panem's thirteen districts and America's thirteen original British colonies—not to mention the ensuing American Revolution, it would not require a large leap to consider that Collins based her fictitious Capitol on the urban layout of Washington, D.C. It is this particular city which exhibits by far the most elaborate example of the Grand Manner to be found in North America. The extent to which the Capitol of Collins' Panem resembles the radial pattern of America's own capital city is uncanny. As geographer Wilbur Zelinsky has noted, it was a "supreme irony" that an urban design intended specifically "to magnify the glories of despotic kings and emperors"—was actually adopted as a national symbol of American democratic ideals.[4] Let's take a look at the fascinating story of our own capital's origins to better understand how it might have inspired that of Panem.

The site chosen for the City of Washington, as it was originally dubbed, was itself a compromise. As George Washington, Alexander Hamilton, Thomas Jefferson, and other luminaries of the time sought to build a new democratic nation from the ground up, they faced a rather delicate decision of where to place the new federal hub. In 1790 an act of Congress authorized the creation of a federal district that would offer a relatively easy inland route to access the western frontier. After considering a number of options, President Washington himself chose a 100 square-mile area of land nestled between the Potomac River and the Eastern Branch (now the Anacostia River), which would provide future access to the lucrative water route of the Ohio River Valley. Just as important, this location was roughly equidistant between the antagonistic northern and southern states, so that neither region would be disadvantaged with their distance from the new federal capital.

The western boundary of the city's plan was placed flush up against the original settlement of Georgetown, which for its part had been founded in 1751 along the Falls of the Potomac. This was the furthest inland that merchant ships could navigate upstream before running into the ancient metamorphic rock of the Appalachian Piedmont. This geographic situation, and its ability to capture inland trade along a naturally protected river, would come to benefit the new capital city as well.

The purpose of the urban plan for the City of Washington was to showcase the world's first-ever completely synthetic capital designed entirely from scratch.[5] Its spatial layout and monumental structures were intended to both impress and intimidate foreign powers that may not have yet gained confidence in the permanency of this new American government. The original plan for the new city is likely what attracted Suzanne Collins to adapt it for her own capital of Panem. Of course, hers is curiously spelled "Capitol," which more typically refers to a "Capitol Building," such as the U.S. Capitol. After all, what is now Washington, District of Columbia (D.C.) has inspired the designs of numerous other capital city projects around the world, not the least being Ottawa, Canberra, Brasilia, Islamabad, New Delhi, Ankara, and some other more recent efforts. So, why not the capital city of Panem?

The original plan for the City of Washington is largely the product of Major Pierre Charles L'Enfant (1754–1825), who came to the American colonies from France in 1777 to assist with the Revolutionary War. Once a military engineer with Major General Lafayette, L'Enfant served on George Washington's staff at Valley Forge. He eventually became the trusted city planner for Washington himself, who personally asked L'Enfant to do nothing less than design a plan for the capital city of their shiny, new democracy. In that role, L'Enfant would then survey the area and recommend locations for the capital's prominent buildings and streets. He essentially enjoyed a clean slate on which to design the city of his dreams. And this is precisely what he did.

The grand challenge, however, was that the chosen site was—to use a modern phrase—in the middle of nowhere. For his part, Thomas Jefferson had already sketched out his own version of a reasonably sized, if rather unremarkable, federal town in 1791. He favored a more compact plan for the new capital city and provided two draft versions. One was situated near the confluence of the Potomac River and the Anacostia, where Carrollsburg was already situated. His second was a similar grid plan near Georgetown to the west. His gridded city would also allocate three adjacent blocks for the future president's house and gardens, and three blocks for the Capitol building nearby. Both of these architectural symbols of the new democratic republic would be connected appropriately by public walks.[6] If nothing else, the plan was pragmatic, keeping in mind the need for shorter distances to facilitate communication prior to automobiles and telephones.

Well, Jefferson's ideas were apparently not grand enough for showcasing the world's new aspiring pillar of democracy. L'Enfant scoffed at these uninspired proposals. First, he wrote to President Washington that the design should be created at a scale grandiose enough for the "aggrandizement & embellishment" of the future city, allowing for a much larger urban population and an elevated sense of global importance.[7] Second, Jefferson's plan had envisioned a street grid laid out on flat ground—which this site decidedly was not. L'Enfant further considered such rectilinear planning to be "tiresome and insipid." What was called for in this case was a design "proportioned to the greatness which … the Capital of a powerful Empire ought to manifest."[8] To that end, he turned to the familiar Baroque-era precedents of Europe.

One particular such plan known well to L'Enfant was that of Versailles. The entire French royal palace and grounds represented the epitome of Renaissance and Baroque-era planning with their formal, symmetrical designs for both architecture and landscaping. L'Enfant had even spent his childhood there, his father having been employed under commission as a painter. He also knew of other exemplars that would collectively inform his own plan for America's new capital of "Empire." These included an existing multi-centered, Baroque plan to reinvent Paris, the new capital city of St. Petersburg begun in 1703, and a "German Versailles," with its 32 radial streets all focused on the royal palace. This latter example was even included within a collection of city maps Jefferson had brought to L'Enfant at L'Enfant's request, hoping they would serve as inspiration for his own plan.

With this former knowledge at his disposal, L'Enfant carefully surveyed the topography of the site, as accomplished Renaissance-era designers would do. He thus identified the two highest points of elevation—hills, if they could be called that—on which to place the nation's grandest government buildings. He was especially "riveted by the commanding position" of Jenkins Hill, which "stands as a pedestal waiting for a superstructure." Of course, this would become the location of the nation's new "Congress House," as it was originally dubbed. The new Capitol building would be devoted to conducting the business of the legislative branches of government—complete with a Senate and a House of Representatives. Its location would be destined to become one of the most recognizable government landmarks in the world. We know it in common parlance as "Capitol Hill." A second natural rise would serve nicely, he determined, for the proposed "President's House." The eventual British, Georgian-style mansion would come to be called the White House only after its rebuilding in brilliant white stonework in 1815.

As the most prominent democratic seat of government, L'Enfant's plan presumed that the Capitol building would become the physical and symbolic center of the city. In contrast, the President's House would be located a stunning one mile away and would be connected to it by the future Pennsylvania Avenue. In true Baroque fashion, an extensive radial street plan was then oriented around these two buildings, with numerous avenues converging on Capitol Hill. Named for the existing states of the Union, these wide boulevards allowed for ease of transportation and offered strategic views of these and other important nodes from a great distance. These would become the stately terminated vistas as Baroque planning tradition would have it. Space for public squares and parks was created at the remaining hubs where boulevards converged.[9]

What of the so-called democratic ideal? To complete his grand scheme, L'Enfant overlaid his Baroque-style city plan with an expansive rectilinear street grid, thus allowing for the future in-filling of residential and commercial land uses. Today as always, the visual effect of this plan as it plays out on the ground is arguably stunning. the American-style rectangular streets and blocks intersect almost haphazardly with the hub-and-spoke plan of the radial boulevards. While stressful for visitors to navigate with a car, this innovative street plan makes for a wonderfully walkable city.

The National Mall, for its part, was originally designated by L'Enfant as a garden-lined "Grand Avenue." This east-west axial corridor would provide a linear focus to the plan and extend for about one mile to another public space in front of the President's House. Following its expansion and enhancement through the MacMillan Plan of 1901, this linear public space had also been intended as a major nod to the new democracy and its egalitarian principles. In true European fashion, however, this broad thoroughfare was originally intended to be lined with the city's more fashionable mansions and townhouses of prominent citizens and politicians. With time, however, it was Pennsylvania Avenue—serving as the more direct link between the White House and the Capitol—which would evolve into the city's true, grand boulevard.

It comes as no surprise, therefore, that the plan L'Enfant submitted to President Washington was many times more ambitious than anything Jefferson had in mind. L'Enfant envisioned nothing less than a world-class metropolis rising out of an otherwise swampy, rural, mosquito-infested backwater. While others considered the idea just plain crazy, he ultimately won over his most important ally—the President himself.[10]

In some ways L'Enfant was ahead of his time, and his work was greatly under-appreciated in his day. For its first half-century of existence, much of L'Enfant's massive scheme remained unbuilt, and the capital city remained more of a national embarrassment that sat festering unfinished within the mucky swamps of the Potomac.[11] Its few major buildings—most notably the isolated President's House and Capitol—remained separated by a full mile, a rather inconvenient commute prior to the advent of rail transit or automobiles.

Throughout much of the nineteenth century, cows regularly grazed on the National Mall, which at that time comprised a twisting, tree-covered park with winding paths.[12] Adding insult to injury during the railroad era, steam trains regularly crossed the Mall on the Capitol Building's back (west) side, causing enough of a racket to interrupt Congressional debate. For his part, L'Enfant's term as chief architect of the nation's new capital city ended disappointingly. Following a contentious period of debates over his plans, Washington let him go and he was never compensated for his work.

Much of the planned city only began to develop in the 1870s following the Civil War. And, as we saw earlier with Philadelphia, urban plans have a funny way of deviating from their original intentions. In this case, L'Enfant had originally expected the capital city's business district to develop eastward from Capitol Hill toward the Anacostia River. Thus, the Capitol building was constructed with its "formal face" aimed in that direction. In reality, things turned out just the opposite. The Anacosta River became a noisome industrial area while the more elegant, ceremonial capital city expanded toward the Potomac and Georgetown to the west. It is thus a curious case that for two centuries our presidential inauguration ceremonies actually take place on the wrong side of the Capitol building—that is, on its back elevation, facing westward.[13] *Oops.*

What L'Enfant never lived to see, however, was the culmination of his plan as it matured into a fully developed, bustling metropolis during the twentieth century. His grand system of radial streets, squares, and monumental government buildings remain prominent features in the city's urban landscape. Moreover, the democratically-inspired street grid now allows for the vibrant and well-connected walking city it is known for today. L'Enfant's dream has thus become, according to Wilbur Zelinsky: "the world's capital city par excellence, a metropolis of dazzling symbolic expressiveness, a nearly ideal pronouncement of the nation-state creed in material terms. L'Enfant's plan has been fleshed out—triumphantly."[14]

If Suzanne Collins was indeed looking for a suitable model on which to inspire Panem's own capital city, there is likely no better choice than Washington, D.C. We know that she adopted Baroque-style planning for the City Circle and its radiating boulevards. As for potential American models, nothing comes close to the scale and grandeur of L'Enfant's capital city. Yes, there is the smaller-scale radial street plan of Annapolis, Maryland. This colonial capital city was named in honor of Princess Anne, heir to the British throne at the time. Its street plan was also based on Baroque principles, complete with radiating streets and circles as central nodes. They all remain a distinctive pattern within the city's landscape to this day. The scope and extent of its street plan are much more modest, however, as compared with the enormity of L'Enfant's grand design.

Then there is the curious, Midwestern example of Indianapolis, located at the geographic center of Indiana. Its original mile-square street plan features a Baroque-style central circle with four broad avenues radiating outward along all four diagonals. The whole ensemble is overlapped with a more typically American grid plan, quite similar to that of Washington, D.C. Further, the broad, diagonal avenues are named for—you guessed it—select U.S. states. Briefly placed at the center of the circle was the governor's mansion, in true Baroque splendor. It would later be replaced with the more democratically inspired Soldiers' and Sailors' Monument (1888) which remains the prominent downtown landmark to this day. City blocks were also reserved along the east-west corridor of Washington Street (notice the name) for a statehouse and county courthouse. This approach was more akin to the plan of Philadelphia, where few allowances at the plan's center were made for civic buildings.

If one digs deeply enough, we learn that the city's design was platted in 1821 by a surveyor named Alexander Ralston. Perhaps not surprisingly, Ralston had worked directly under the tutelage of one Pierre Charles L'Enfant while planning the nation's capital. Still largely exhibiting its original street plan to this day, Indianapolis is fittingly dubbed the "Circle City"—a coincidental reversal of Panem's "City Circle" of the Capitol. And the plan had been directly inspired by the nation's capital itself.

Indianapolis therefore serves as an impressive case of imitation diffusion, the product of personal connections between urban designers who had worked together at the time. On a more speculative side, it is difficult not to consider the time Suzanne Collins spent at Indiana University in Bloomington, where she had ample opportunity to interact with the Circle

City itself. Regardless of whether she considered Indianapolis a model or not, the size, scale, and placement of the original circle, governor's house, and prominent buildings around it provide an uncanny resemblance to the City Circle of Panem's Capitol. From the perspective of geographic scale and layout, there is perhaps no better likeness to be found anywhere in the United States.

The Corso: From Rome to Panem

Aside from her adoption of a Baroque urban plan, Collins alludes to another famous exemplar of urban geography. Her naming of the Capitol's primary thoroughfare as the *Corso* is easy to overlook, though its symbolism within her prequel is highly significant. Immediately in the novel's first chapter, the narrator informs us that young Coriolanus—along with his cousin, Tigris and his Grandma'am—live in the penthouse of a prominent if crumbling "apartment" building located along one of the Capitol's main boulevards. This avenue is so wide, the narrator states, that eight chariots could ride side by side. This was most typically accomplished back when the Capitol had staged military parades (*BSS* 12). Coriolanus' family had thus identified with the Capitol's upper echelon of elite residents who could afford to reside along the city's grandest boulevard. The Corso, as it is called, thereby serves as the Capitol's principal, Baroque-style thoroughfare.

One need only look to Rome to find the Corso's main source of inspiration. With this designation for the Capitol's principal thoroughfare, Collins is most certainly referring to Rome's own *Via del Corso* in Rome, which was considered that city's veritable main street of the nineteenth century.[15] Given her proclivity to borrow from ancient Roman precedents, the Corso provides yet another direct historical link between Panem and the Classical period of Julius Caesar and friends. The eight-chariot width of the Corso is in itself a direct reference to the ancient Roman, horse-drawn vehicles. This association is played out in full during the tribute parades of the original series. It was only logical, therefore, that Collins chose this geographical reference to continue her theming around the original Roman Empire.

As for the original Corso, Rome's principal main street can likewise be traced back to the city's Classical era. During that time, however, it was referred to as Via Lata, which essentially translates as "Broad Way." The thoroughfare was thus already recognized as a principal urban corridor. The historical record points to its construction during the second century BCE as part of a new overland route to connect the center of Rome with the Adriatic Sea. As the city grew in population and expanded northward during the early imperial era, the road became the favored corridor for

monumental public structures. Somewhat ironically these structures ultimately punctuated the road's width and restricted the ease of movement.
This created bottlenecks, where the right-of-way was narrowed to accommodate the city's triumphal arches. Nonetheless, these monuments were
viewed as necessary icons of imperial power and authority. It is somehow
captivating to think that this very road had already served as a gateway to
the city during Julius Caesar's time.

Even then, the corridor followed a path that remains to this day. Its
route began on the edge of the original Roman forum, near present-day
Piazza Venezia. At its opposite end the road met the imperial city's new-
est northern gate (Porta Flaminia), at the location of present-day Piazza
del Popolo. From here the road parted from the city proper and led into the
northern countryside on its way to the Adriatic Sea. It was none other than
Julius Caesar who, along with various successors, expanded Rome's government center beyond the earlier confines of the Roman Forum. This expansion had the effect of pushing the Empire's urban center right up to the
southern terminus of Via Lata. According to James McGregor, these developments consisted of "vast and impressive structures that were associated
historically with Roman autocracy rather than republicanism."[16] The Via
Lata thus became a central focus for imperial political power. For this reason alone, this predecessor to Rome's future Via del Corso provides a fitting
model for Collins' own authoritarian capital city.

Fast forward to the Rome of the Renaissance and its later Baroque
period. The now-renamed Via del Corso developed into a fashionable corridor of renovated churches and grand palaces of the city's noble families.
Its newfound urban fame came at the behest of a lengthy line of Popes who
gradually transformed Rome from a densely packed medieval city to one
of Renaissance splendor. It was during this period when the Palazzo Venezia was constructed at the southern terminus of Via del Corso. The Palazzo
became one of the first grand palaces of the Renaissance era in Rome. As
for the palace's architectural design, it represented the diffusion of earlier
Renaissance palaces in Florence and the ideas of Leon Battista Alberti, one
of the Renaissance era's leading architectural figures.

Various successions of Popes, who essentially controlled Rome during
these centuries, found ways to impose more order and regularity to the
Corso. They were all too aware how the corridor had devolved somewhat
into an ad-hoc collection of irregular-shaped palaces, unfinished churches,
and unsightly building projections. Their collective efforts sought to reinvent Rome's densely-packed medieval urban landscape into an exemplar of Renaissance urban planning. Along the Corso, various properties
were demolished or refashioned so as to present a more regular, linear
appearance.

Due to the relocation of the Papal Palace to Quirinal Hill, Via del Corso gained new prominence as a central corridor into the city. The street became a major urban priority for Pope Alexander VII, who desired to impress whatever foreign dignitaries might pay him official visits. The Piazza del Popolo was cleared and reworked, creating the landscape seen there today.

Likewise, the road's main gateway to the north, the Porta del Popolo, was likewise redesigned as a grand, Baroque-style entrance into the city. Once redesigned, the expansive Piazza del Popolo became "Baroque Rome's opening statement."[17] Bernini had redesigned the gate and worked with Rainaldi to plan the now-iconic twin churches that flank the entrance to the Corso. Three radial avenues were then fashioned as the principal corridors into the heart of the city. From their point of convergence at Piazza del Popolo, they fan out into the city's historic core and channel traffic into the three major zones of the Baroque city. At the center of it all, the Via del Corso cuts between the twin churches and their iconic Renaissance domes as it leads to the center of town. As in the past, the corridor terminates at Piazza Venezia and the Capitoline Hill.

In this way, Via del Corso became the effective main street of Baroque-era Rome. For much of this period the fashionable corridor became the favored location for a variety of social and cultural activities, not the least being an annual round of parades, horse races, religious processionals, candlelight marches, and even the Roman Mardi Gras up through the nineteenth century. One of the earliest events featured the racing of riderless horses, an activity that temporarily converted the avenue into a veritable racetrack. This was a cherished, annual event held as part of the Roman Carnival. The running of the horses was referred to as the "corsa dei barberi," which became the inspiration for the renamed Via del Corso.

Given the demand from locals and visitors alike to view such events, buildings and balconies along the route were constantly remodeled to provide evermore seats. One insightful visitor experienced this very scene while traveling with his family through France and Italy in 1844. His name was Charles Dickens. The writer was supposed to be taking time off from his novels. Instead, his experiences as a tourist led to his own travelogue titled *Pictures from Italy*, published in 1846, in which he provided a colorful description of the scene along Via del Corso:

> There are verandahs and balconies of all shapes and sizes to almost every house—not on one story alone, but often to one room or another on every story—put there in general with so little order or regularity that if, year after year, season after season, it had rained balconies, hailed balconies, snowed balconies, blown balconies, they could scarcely have come into existence in a more disorderly manner.[18]

It comes as no surprise, therefore, that the Via del Corso of Renaissance-era Rome gained the attention of Suzanne Collins. Still, she did more than simply replicate the corridor for her own purposes. Rather, she scaled it up as a reimagined grand boulevard that was many times wider than its predecessor in Rome. Though always one of its city's most prominent thoroughfares, the actual Via del Corso is by comparison considerably narrow. Today as in the past, the corridor remains a mere ten meters wide, barely enough room for two lanes of traffic and flanking sidewalks. Consequently, there is no way to accommodate eight chariots side by side as Collins' version in the Capitol can do.

Similarly, the Via del Corso's Renaissance-era buildings rise to only six floors in height. Of course, they may appear considerably taller due to their relatively high ceilings. Such spacious floor plans were nearly universal prior to the age of steel-frame construction and elevators, necessitating some serious stair climbing. Quite simply, humans the world over have demonstrated a curious proclivity to avoid climbing higher than six floors. For this reason, rents for upper-floor apartments were typically the least expensive, reflecting a cost of housing that was inversely proportional to the number of stairs one was forced to climb. Apartments closer to the ground floor are understandably more desirable—and expensive. It is thus safe to conclude that the twelve-story buildings envisioned for Panem's capital city came complete with structural steel, central air, and—when they were functioning—elevators.

The Corso of Panem further demonstrates a common feature of public transportation still popular during the early twentieth century. This grand avenue is served by some version of "colorful trolleys," on which Coriolanus depends for commuting to and from home (*BSS* 45). A "trolley," one might recall, is the colloquial term for America's traditional form of electric streetcars, harkening to a time when urban residents were still accustomed to daily commuting on public transit. Every mid-sized and large American city once depended upon vast networks of streetcar railway lines connecting entire metropolitan areas. Of course, America's streetcar companies and related infrastructure were summarily ripped out by the 1950s and replaced with buses and a newfound reliance on automobile traffic. Only in recent decades has the trolley's modern-day equivalent, light-rail transit, been making a comeback in more progressive cities. For whatever reason, Panem's capital city still relies upon a 1920s-era cityscape, complete with trolleys plying the Capitol's main thoroughfares during the time of the tenth Games.

One additional curiosity along Panem's Corso involves the scale of the Snow family's apartment building. First, we know that it is situated amongst its neighboring "grand palaces," which the narrator admits will soon be placed on the market for sale. This is due to the economic depression that has since followed in the aftermath of war (*BSS* 19). Of course, Coriolanus' apartment is one of them, which incites much angst within the family and plays not a minor role within the prequel's overall story line. Perhaps most notable, however, is the aforementioned fact that their apartment building is precisely 12 stories high. At times when the elevator is not working—through the early part of the prequel—Coriolanus is forced to speed down twelve flights of stairs before spilling out onto the Corso (*BSS* 12). The Snows live in the penthouse suite of the twelfth floor, complete with a roof garden where Grandma'am grows her infamous roses.

One might note a curious similarity between Coriolanus' penthouse and the spatial layout of the Tribute Center from the original series. Is it mere coincidence that the Center includes precisely twelve floors, a penthouse, and rooftop area that can be accessed only by the District 12 tributes? Given Suzanne Collins' penchant for placing breadcrumbs into her narrative, this is a potentially striking one. Why are the District 12 tributes assigned to the penthouse of the Training Center when they are disadvantaged in so many other ways? It is further reasonable to presume that—as Panem's leading autocrat—President Snow likely either designed the Training Center or in the least approved its final floorplan. Could this particular facility of the original series reflect some lingering sentimentality for his own childhood home, or for certain individuals who once lived in District 12?

Renaissance Architecture in the Novels and Films

In addition to the Baroque-style urban plan of the City Circle and the Corso, the art and design of Renaissance Europe shows up elsewhere in Panem. It may come as a surprise that an array of settings—namely, the Justice Building of District 11, the president's house, and the Victor's Village—are all derivative of Renaissance-era design traditions. Some design elements are emphasized within the films more than others. Curiously, the inspiration for the District 11 Justice Building is generally rooted within one of America's grandest architectural masterpieces, the U.S. Capitol building. While this connection might at first glance appear to be a stretch of the imagination, let's see how this plays out. Those familiar with the iconic U.S. Capitol will instantly recognize its stately, neoclassical-style dome. This is in fact the Capitol building's third and grandest edition, enlarged to its current size even while the American Civil War raged on. Architectural historians sometimes interpret the structure as the last great architectural dome of the Renaissance.

On the flip side, the first dome to usher in the European Renaissance was designed by the innovative fifteenth-century mind of Filippo Brunelleschi, himself considered a pioneer of Italian Renaissance architecture. He happened to be the first architect since the Roman Empire to successfully engineer a scheme to construct large, masonry domes to be placed atop the Church's elaborate cathedrals. When the Romans all but disappeared after the fifth century CE, their engineering knowledge disappeared with them. Brunelleschi's primary accomplishment thus consisted of solving the ages-long puzzle of how to design a massive dome for the Cathedral of Santa Maria del Fiore in Florence, Italy.[19] His ingenuity kicked off a three-century span of Renaissance-style dome construction in Europe and North America. The magnificent U.S. Capitol dome of the mid-nineteenth century served as a fitting bookend to that architectural era.

This latest dome placed atop Capitol Hill soon became an inspirational model for architects tasked with designing statehouses, county courthouses, and even city halls scattered around the country. Numerous other federal buildings likewise adopted *neoclassical* forms—with their Greek temple fronts and round, marble columns representing early Classical-era, republican forms of democratic government. There was probably no better way at the time to symbolize America's revival of these long-lost democratic ideals. However, it was the U.S. Capitol building—our nation's "symbolic anchor," as Zelinsky described it—that became the favored prototype for the design of local and state government buildings across the country. Many of our state capitol buildings and county courthouses thus include their own iconic neoclassical-style domes, thereby imbuing the nation's democratic ideals into their own local architecture. In some cases, notably the statehouses of Providence, Rhode Island, and Austin, Texas, we find virtual replicas of the U.S. Capitol.[20] At the level of county seat, it is not uncommon to find courthouses adorned with similar neoclassical facades and domes, serving as iconic landmarks at the center of America's public squares.

This is the connection necessary for understanding why Collins placed a dome atop the District 11 Justice Building. We earn an unexpected tour of this apparently historic facility when Katniss, Peeta, and Haymitch regroup following their ill-fated Victory Tour speeches. Through the eyes of Katniss, we find that the building's interior is replete with Renaissance-style design elements. These include a "magnificent curved marble staircase," which takes the three of them to an aging yet elegant room upstairs. The walls and perhaps ceiling are adorned with imagery of fruit, flowers, and "fat children with wings" (those would be cherubs) looking down from all angles (*CF* 64). The ceilings are a neck-breaking twenty feet high, as one would find within a palace of Renaissance-era nobility.

Beyond its characteristic artwork (possibly frescoes), Haymitch finds his way even higher into the structure where no one can hear their ensuing conversation. After climbing a ladder to a trapdoor, they somehow find themselves "in the dome of the Justice Building" (*CF* 64). While we do not have—to my knowledge—a description of the District 12 rendition, it is a safe bet that it includes a standardized, replicated architecture foisted upon the outlying districts by Capitol planners. In this way the uniformly symbolic architecture of centralized authority diffused into the human landscapes of the districts, inspired loosely by the European Renaissance. The description of the District 11 building's interior only confirms this supposition. Had this been an American county seat, this modest-sized dome with its four small windows would most certainly have been inspired by its larger prototype in Washington, D.C.

Consequently, the notion of placing domes atop local government buildings is owed directly to their association with America's democratic ideal. The dome as a distinct element of American institutional architecture ultimately diffused down the urban hierarchy from Washington, D.C., and similar large cities to smaller towns like that of District 11—and likely to District 12 and others as well.

Back at the center of the Capitol, the president's house located on the City Circle provides another instance of Renaissance influence. In this rare case, however, such Renaissance imagery is exhibited primarily within the feature films. For their part, the novels provide little descriptive detail regarding the mansion's exterior appearance. Within "Catching Fire," the mansion comes into prominent view during the Victory Tour's final party scene, hosted by President Snow. These scenes include a smattering of interior and exterior shots of the Renaissance-inspired building. The filming location for these scenes was the estate known as Swan House, located in the countryside north of Atlanta, Georgia. Snow's office was filmed inside the Morning Room of this same residence.

Constructed in the late 1920s, the mansion and its formal landscaping are derived straight out of the Grand Manner. What one sees in "Catching Fire" is actually the back side, or rear elevation, of the house and its Baroque-inspired gardens which face west. Its more formal entrance on the eastern side includes a tall-columned portico as described by the property's National Register nomination form. Its Italian Renaissance-Revival architecture is adorned with various Baroque elements on its façade. Such architectural flourishes include the segmented pediment and scroll brackets above the central entryway, reminiscent of Renaissance-era churches in Italy. One also finds Baroque niches for statuary on both sides of the entrance. The floor plan is completely symmetrical, with one half of the building precisely mirroring the other. Such "bilateral symmetry" was a quintessential trait of formal Renaissance architecture.

franchise. Although known more for her superb acting skills than for her singing, Lawrence's version of "The Hanging Tree" had already reached number two on the iTunes song charts and was streamed by fans more than 4.8 million times as of 2014.[15]

While Lawrence earned much of the credit as the star singer, the rather eerie, haunting version for the film was the product of a collaborative effort. Author Suzanne Collins had written the original lyrics in the form of an Appalachian ballad for her third novel, *Mockingjay*. The lyrics were then handed off to the *Lumineers*, a folk-pop group, to invent a melody which has been described as "a caricature of an Appalachian ballad."[16] A dramatic symphonic score was then embedded into the tune by composer James Newton Howard, who was responsible for the music throughout the four films. In this way the original lyrics from the novel turned into a sensation and centerpiece of the film itself.

Long before the film industry added its own interpretation, this particular murder ballad was believed to represent a coded slave song from the American South. Prior to the Civil War, slaves had used such songs as attempts to communicate with one another, largely under the radar of their overseers.[17] For some observers, the lyrics of "The Hanging Tree" closely resembled the theme of "Strange Fruit," a dark Billie Holliday anthem which protested lynchings of African Americans in the United States. Self-proclaimed "Hogwarts Professor" John Granger wrote that you "can't talk about a 'hanging tree' song if you're in my generation and not think immediately of *Strange Fruit*."[18]

The parallels between the two songs are even closer, given that "Strange Fruit" was inspired by an image of two lynched Black men. A similar image is conjured in the lyrics of "The Hanging Tree," which invites the lover to "wear a necklace of rope, side by side with me."[19] Just as "The Hanging Tree" serves as a call to revolution in Panem, "Strange Fruit" aligns with America's Civil Rights Movement as one of numerous protest songs of the time. It is therefore difficult to not think of Civil Rights protests when encountering this music through much of the third novel.[20]

In a broader context, "The Hanging Tree" further serves as an invitation to revolt, to "risk death in the hope of a greater life," as Granger elaborates. Of course, such a revolution becomes the principal story line for the original series, and much of the song's backstory is now found within the prequel. In his original blog post dedicated to "The Hanging Tree," Granger suggests that the idea of rebellion may have even predated the birth of Katniss, specifically through various clandestine efforts of her father. We know that he taught the song to Katniss before he was summarily killed in a mine explosion with many of his peers. We do not yet know what caused the explosion. Granger hypothesizes that Katniss' father was singing the song

Swan House thus represents the cultural diffusion of the style from Renaissance Italy into America around the turn of the twentieth century when the United States was enjoying its own self-proclaimed Renaissance prior to the Great Depression. In one sense, the property reflects the last gasp of that booming American industrial era, as the house's design and construction in 1928 preceded the infamous stock market crash by only one year. After serving as the home of the Inman family for four decades, the house and estate was transferred to the Atlanta Historical Society and was converted into a museum for public tours—and for apparent use as the occasional movie set.

Likewise, the well-manicured gardens we see on the home's west side directly reflect Renaissance-era precedents of landscaping. Within "Catching Fire," these gardens serve as the setting for our Victory Tour guests of honor as they ascend to the mansion's rear entrance. The classical, orderly layout of the gardens is reminiscent of Baroque-era landscaping found at Versailles and around countless smaller European villas and estates. Like the façade of Swan House, its grounds are bilaterally symmetrical. The plantings are geometrically arranged on both sides of the formal, axial walkway leading to the house. Other Renaissance elements of the lawn include numerous stone retaining walls, two stone obelisks, and two stone fountains. Thus, although the Swan House is certainly Americanized in various ways, the entire estate reflects the symmetrical formality of its Renaissance predecessors.

An additional influence of the Grand Manner is found in the Victor's Village of District 12. It is further safe to presume that its particular design and layout are standardized and replicated elsewhere across Panem. As discussed earlier, government-sponsored projects typically exhibit uniform, mass-produced floorplans and designs, reflecting a national presence. Once again, much of what we see of the Victor's Village is found within the films, particularly those of "Catching Fire" and "Mockingjay, Part 1." In contrast, Collins provides relatively little description within her narrative. Katniss does offer some tidbits of information, including a history lesson about the "dozen fine houses" built by the Capitol back when the Games had begun (*THG* 304). Strangely, there is nothing mentioned about these villages within the prequel.

Katniss later expands on her initial comments, near the beginning of *Catching Fire*. At that point, much of the story's early action and drama occur within the Victor's Village itself. After confiding with Greasy Sae about dreading the upcoming Victory Tour, Katniss tells us more about the Village and its spatial layout. She describes it as a separate community designed around a beautiful open green with flowering bushes. It is likely on the edge of the town's original street grid, as she describes it as a half-mile walk from the square (*CF* 12). Describing the twelve houses located there, she estimates that each one is ten times the size of her original house in the Seam. This sense of scale not only sheds some light on the sheer massiveness of these places, but also likely implies a social disconnect and striking injustice as well. While so many Seam residents remain clustered inside unhealthy, substandard shacks, much of the space in the Victor's Village remains vacant and will continue to remain so.

Within the film version, the producers of "Catching Fire" appropriately bring the Renaissance architecture of the Capitol back to District 12. The Village seen in the film presents a Renaissance-styled urban neighborhood straight out of eighteenth-century Europe. Rather than an American town grid and public square, the Village—based on the film's rendition— provides the look of a very different type of place. It is decidedly more grandiose as Katniss describes it, and is probably more suited to an upscale, wealthier urban scene. In the film we see orderly rows of stylish, symmetrical, and standardized brownstone houses all facing onto a straight, formal pathway—the development's central axis or main thoroughfare. This is straight out of Renaissance and Baroque urban planning traditions, once again harkening back to the Grand Manner. The Village is bilaterally symmetrical, with the buildings equally spaced within their own individual lots on either side of the central axis.

In short, a miniature version of the Grand Manner has thus been imposed within the District 12 landscape, signifying an architectural extension of the Capitol's elegance into this otherwise rural and underprivileged place. From a geographical perspective, the Capitol's architecture and urban design principles have diffused down the urban hierarchy, from the nation's capital city and cultural hub to the outlying districts. This is typically the process through which cultural trends become adopted elsewhere, following their innovation with a larger urban center, or culture hearth. In one respect, then, what we find in the Victor's Village is District 12's first planned suburb. Only a half-mile walk from the town center as Katniss describes it, this particular suburban neighborhood may find itself largely uninhabited, but also separated socially and culturally from the rest of the community. Its imposed—and imposing—urban landscape represents a stark disconnect between Capitol-esque culture and the quintessentially Appalachian small town into which it has landed.

Modern Architecture in the Hunger Games Films

Aside from their various Renaissance-inspired filming locations, the producers of the franchise films turned to modern-era designs of the mid-twentieth century to represent the Capitol's urban landscape. As discussed above, the European Renaissance had relied upon the revival of Greek and Roman precedents. In stark contrast to this fascination with all things Classical, the premise of *modernism* flipped that around to focus principally on the promise of an industrial, technological future. What became known as the Modern Movement involved numerous European and American architects who sought out new and innovative approaches to design and construction that purposely did not point back to historical precedents. Their modernist thinking began to galvanize around the time of World War I and largely came to fruition after the war's conclusion in 1918.

While not a coordinated effort on their part, these early pioneers of modernism included the likes of Walter Gropius, Ludwig Mies van der Rohe, and Le Corbusier. They did not really work together in a collaborative fashion, but they all had one thing in common: a collective vision that pointed to the future rather than to the past. As Ian Sutton explains, these architects who were dabbling in modernist ideas believed that "the 20th century was a new era in world history, whose citizens had needs different from men and women hitherto; and that a new architecture would evolve to answer those needs which would be universal, democratic, functional, economical, and beautiful."[21]

Following the global disruptions of the Great Depression and World War II, modernist architecture and related urban design became the dominant mode for building nearly everything on both sides of the Atlantic Ocean. This trend would continue apace right through the 1980s and linger for years thereafter. In this way, four decades of our human landscapes reveal an unhindered fascination with the materials of reinforced concrete, structural steel, and expansive plate-glass windows for our office towers (skyscrapers), schools, churches, government buildings, train stations, airports, and virtually every other building designed for civic purposes. By the 1960s this international modernism had swept across both Europe and America and had become the favored mode of architecture for democratic, capitalist nations.[22]

It was this era of modernist architectural design that would become the favored approach for portraying the Capitol within the Hunger Games films. In an interview with the director of "The Hunger Games," Gary Ross recalled how they honed in on one particular variation of modern architecture: "I will say that Phil Messina, my production designer, has such wonderful tastes that he and I wisely began with a lot of reference and we looked at a lot and we wandered into this area of architecture … called 'Brutalism,' which uses, like, massive concrete form. It's very imposing. It's very stark. It's very authoritarian."[23]

If reinforced concrete had become a fashionable feature of modernism, this variation known as Brutalism ultimately elevated this heavy medium to a new level of prominence. In fact, this modernist style relies fundamentally on rough-textured concrete for its own distinctive look. Though tempting to associate the style's name with an appearance of "brutality," its namesake is actually derived from the French term, "beton brut," meaning "rough concrete."[24] Still, the style's massive, austere appearance certainly gives it an impression of brutality—for proponents and critics alike. The early founder and principal champion of Brutalist design was none other than the storied modern architect himself, Le Corbusier. He purposely experimented on various applications of concrete and was responsible for devising the enormous block housing projects of that time. That Gary Ross and his designers landed on brutalist architecture to portray aspects of the Capitol should thus not come as a surprise.

The paradox here is that the European dictatorships that replaced democracy during the early twentieth century held little interest in modern architecture to forward their agendas. Rather, the likes of Stalin's Soviet Union, Mussolini's Italy, and Nazi Germany all chose to adopt simplified—though exaggerated and imposing—variations of revived classicism. They consequently preferred to once again adopt the time-honored symbolism of Greek and Roman classical architecture to connote their own imperialistic intentions. Still, the colossal concrete forms of these overpowering structures still remind one of early modernist practices with their shared focus on geometric simplicity. In Russia, an obsession with "megalomaniac classicism" took hold, which was ironically intended to demonstrate and symbolize the power of the people on a massive scale.[25] Likewise, Mussolini looked to Rome for his inspiration to convey his own thirst for a renewed empire. However, his own version of Roman architecture was greatly reduced to mere abstract forms, utilizing bare cylinders for columns and unadorned triangular pediments. Not far away, the Nazis adopted a similar form of pared-down classicism similar to that of Italy, also with a heavy concrete presence and exaggerated scale symbolizing autocratic power and authority.

Despite the political connotations symbolized by the architecture of these regimes, both modern and neoclassical styles diffused back and forth across the Atlantic Ocean. Italy still welcomed various modern architectural designs during the 1930s, for instance, and numerous excellent examples appeared there in the face of Mussolini's fascism. The railway station in Florence provides an excellent example, designed by Giovanni Michelucci in 1933. Even during the height of the Cold War, Stalinist architects looked to the United States for inspirational models. Some of the ornately designed classical skyscrapers that encircle Moscow, for instance, were clearly inspired by American counterparts found in Chicago and New York City. Going in the other direction across the Atlantic, the heavy, abstract classicism of 1930s Europe found its way to the United States as an alternative to full-blown modernism. This mode especially found a home in Washington, D.C., and remained popular for the design of massive government buildings up through the 1950s. The National Gallery comes to mind, designed by John Russell Pope in 1941.[26]

In reality, then, the association of modernist styles with the despotic regimes of the early twentieth century is tenuous at best. Architects hailing from a variety of capitalist, communist, and fascist societies were sharing their work with each other and around the world. That said, there is little doubt that Brutalism provides an imposing form and aesthetic approach that are certainly appropriate to connote the heavy-handed might of centralized power, authority, and control one finds in Suzanne Collins' Capitol.

The architecture of Brutalism was carried over in some ways to the franchise's second film, "Catching Fire," in the form of Atlanta, Georgia's Marriott Marquis Hotel constructed in 1985. Along with Singapore's Marina Mandarin, the Marriott Marquis is credited with having popularized Brutalist architecture even beyond Le Corbusier's earlier championing of the style. The film's producers chose the hotel's imposing, modernist interior to represent the luxurious victors' quarters leading up to the 75th Games.[27] Viewers enjoy an impressive panoramic shot of the interior's central open atrium as Katniss and her entourage—joined humorously by Joanna Mason—ascend to their respective quarters. The keen viewer will further notice something else that is curious. The chosen panorama displaying the hotel's curving, U-shaped interior further resembles—whether intentionally or not—the winged bird featured on the Seal of the Capitol. This image is presumed to derive logically from the Bald Eagle, given that Collins devised Panem as a post-apocalyptic revision of America.[28]

Beyond the showcasing of Brutalist architecture within the films, this chapter would not be complete without considering those chilling, futuristic cornucopias that adorn the centers of both arenas. As for the first one in "The Hunger Games," its design represents another offshoot of modernist architecture, though from somewhat later in the twentieth century. As discussed previously, these cinematic, outrageous contraptions connote the "horns of plenty" traditionally found on Thanksgiving dinner tables throughout America. Of course, Suzanne Collins has turned this tradition on its head. In her world the cornucopia serves as the symbolic centerpiece of their respective arenas and serves as a storehouse of weapons within her Games.

Speaking of the cornucopia's design in the first film, Jimmy Stamp of the Smithsonian Magazine believed that the production designers "just nailed it."[29] In his eyes, they created "something dramatic and memorable that subverts the familiar woven symbol of nourishment by transforming it into an unfamiliar, menacing cavern."[30] Indeed. Phil Ross, a production designer for the first film, had voiced his own determination for getting the cornucopia's appearance just right. Though initially concerned about how it would ultimately appear on the ground, it turned into one of Ross' favorite creations of the film. Their version of the cornucopia was, as he put it, "a huge, nasty sculptural horn in the middle of a field."[31] He then revealed its inspiration: "We looked at Frank Gehry designs and a lot of modern architecture with folded planes and fractured surfaces and kind of riffed on all of that. It looks like it fell from the sky onto this field."[32]

This raises the question, just who is Frank Gehry? For his part, Gehry's architectural brand is often described as belonging to another subset of modernism, known as *Deconstructivist*, or Deconstructivism. This more radical style essentially devolves, or explodes, a building into a collection of related fragments that overtly challenges traditional building design and construction.[33] Buildings in this mode appear like something altogether different from conventional, boxy, modernist structures, taking on any variety of abstract shapes and sizes. They rarely include right angles and usually require remarkable feats of engineering. So too does the contemporary, unique architecture of Frank Gehry, who "strives to translate emotion into his structures, to evoke passions through them, and to bring them to life with reflected light dancing on undulating surfaces."[34] Beginning first as a local architect from southern California, Gehry rose to fame almost instantly with his design for the Guggenheim Museum in Bilbao, Spain (1991–97). Not a single, flat surface is to be found on the structure, but is more abstract and sculptural. Its underlying steel frame is covered in glossy, reflective titanium sheathing.

While the design was quickly declared a masterpiece, his work has invited detractors as well. They claim that his architecture is designed for its shock value rather than for more functional or aesthetic concerns that might be more pragmatic. A number of his projects can be found throughout the United States as well, for those who wish to see their resemblance to the cornucopias of the films. The Walt Disney Concert Hall in downtown Los Angeles (opened 2003) comes to mind, as does the Weisman Art Museum in Minneapolis, Minnesota (completed 1993). Other projects in Cleveland Ohio (the Peter B. Lewis Building) and in Seattle, Washington (at the base of the Space Needle) exhibit his characteristic reflective titanium paneling and curvilinear surfaces.

Perhaps one of Gehry's more well-known, public projects is found in the Jay Pritzker Pavilion in Chicago's Millennium Park. As the centerpiece of this reclaimed railroad yard, Gehry's performance venue is framed in brushed stainless-steel ribbons that have the appearance of reaching out into the Great Lawn in the form of steel piping.[35] Collectively, all of Gehry's projects have helped establish him as one of the most universally acclaimed architects since Frank Lloyd Wright.[36] It is perhaps fitting, and appropriate, that his characteristic approach to Deconstructivist architecture ultimately landed in the two successive arenas of the Hunger Games films.

8

Panem as World System

As discussed in Chapter 1, the First Law of Geography helps explain the lack of Capitol oversight within District 12. But what factors contribute to Panem's severe extremes of wealth and poverty? The original Hunger Games series is widely viewed as an allegory, in that Collins aims in part to focus attention on socioeconomic disparity facing America and the world as a whole. The ongoing concentration of wealth into the hands of a few is arguably one of those global challenges which Collins emphasizes. Had we been contemplating her dystopian tale during the mid-twentieth century, social scientists may have compared Panem's binary system of "Capitol" and "Districts" with the so-called First and Third Worlds, respectively. Even today the rather outdated concept of a "Third World" is regularly invoked within various media outlets to connote the poorest, most disadvantaged nations.

In the decades following World War II, the concept of a Third World was widely adopted to describe the poorer nations of Africa, Asia, Latin America, and the Caribbean.[1] This naming lexicon was somewhat rooted in the experience and context of the Cold War between the United States and the now-former Soviet Union until its breakup in the 1990s. As defined during that time, the Third World generally comprised the planet's poorest, agrarian, and less "developed" nations. Also included were those nations belonging to the Non-Aligned Movement (NAM)—that is, those which supported neither the capitalist United States nor the communist Soviet Union.

If there is indeed a Third World, then, what of the First and Second Worlds? Again, these definitions are rooted in the history of the Cold War. The First World came to primarily represent the more capitalist and industrialized nations of Western Europe, the United States, Canada, Australia, and Japan. In contrast, the Second World consisted primarily of the communist bloc of the Soviet Union and Eastern Europe—essentially the portion of Europe located eastward of the so-called Iron Curtain and the Berlin Wall.

Fast forward to the twenty-first century, and we find this three-tier distinction rather irrelevant and out of date. The Cold War has more or less concluded with the disintegration of the Soviet Union, and its Second World status along with it. Further, the largely futile effort to divide our incredibly diverse planet into three distinct categories was recognized as overly simplistic at best. Socioeconomic differences within nations were virtually ignored and overgeneralized with labels indicating whether a place was rich or poor. The terminology further connoted a competitive hierarchy, whereby industrialized nations somehow came in "first place" while poorer, less advantaged populations came in "third," or last place. For these and related reasons, reliance on this constructed hierarchy has been downplayed in the realms of academics, government agencies, and non-governmental organizations (NGOs).

One alternative, geographic perspective can shed some light on the economic connections and disparity between the Capitol and districts of Panem. Recognizing as he did the expanding role of capitalism around the world, sociologist Immanuel Wallerstein devised a perspective known as *World Systems Theory* in the 1970s.[2] Building upon the tenets of *Dependency Theory*, which posits that more powerful, industrialized nations will tend to exploit disadvantaged populations elsewhere, the world-system perspective recognizes that *trans-national corporations* (or multi-national corporations) have actually gained more power and authority than many of the world's national governments. Global trade, digital communications, and more efficient transportation have overall reduced the political and geographic influence of national borders. Even the smallest of companies is now able to operate internationally with little constraint. Further, companies are now freer than ever to relocate at nearly a moment's notice, should local conditions become unfavorable. This ability for global business to move about the planet on a whim is sometimes referred to as the *mobility of capital.*

Within this world system, it follows that the activities of global corporations easily transcend the political borders between nations, and national governments are relatively powerless to control them. Further, proponents of dependency theory had argued that peripheral nations were doomed to be forever exploited and marginalized for their cheap labor and raw materials. Though such global relationships were certainly occurring, Wallerstein noticed that a number of peripheral countries were demonstrating their own economic development and were gradually rising out of abject poverty.[3] These "newly-industrializing countries" (NICs) included the so-called "Asian Tigers" of South Korea, Hong Kong, Singapore, and Taiwan, along with countries elsewhere including Brazil.

This was perhaps a bit of good news, in that countries—or, perhaps more accurately, metropolitan areas within them—could influence their own economic status and standards of living. As Katie Willis explains, countries in our globalizing world "do not follow a linear pathway of progress, rather at different times as the global economy changes, certain countries may be able to make economic advances, while others lose out."[4] This more dynamic and uneven distribution of global capitalism and wealth is what defines Wallerstein's world system. Let's see how this perspective might help us understand the relationship between the Capitol and the districts of Panem.

World Systems Theory views the planet as structured around three general types of capitalist zones: a core, semi-periphery, and periphery. The world is thus organized into a spatial division of labor, not unlike the economic specializations of the Districts of Panem. In peripheral regions we tend to find low-skilled, labor-intensive production and extraction of raw materials. In stark contrast, the world's core areas consist of the wealthiest nations or cities. This is where we find a disproportionate number of the world's most influential global corporations and their headquarters. These core regions tend to control wages and monopolize the production of manufactured products elsewhere on the planet. Their operations within the core tend to provide higher-skill professions while relying upon some of the best access to educational institutions and their recent graduates. They further enjoy a political clout which allows them to pay lower prices for raw materials and to exploit cheaper labor—through low wages—in peripheral regions or nations.

Where are these core regions located? Geographers have identified three primary economic power centers: those of North America (centered on New York City), Western Europe (centered on London), and Japan (centered on Tokyo). Of course, other global cities have emerged in recent decades to exert more influence on global financial trade, such as Singapore, Seoul, Hong Kong, and Shanghai. Somewhere between the extremes of core and peripheral regions, Wallerstein and his proponents have recognized a fuzzier category dubbed the *semi-periphery*. Places with semi-peripheral characteristics maintain influential urban centers and exert their own economic dominance on surrounding regions. They still remain influenced by the core, however, and they typically include enclaves of rural poverty that resemble places in the periphery. They are somewhere in the great in-between, the middle-ground of the world system. Nations such as Mexico, Brazil, India, South Africa, and even China tend to represent the semi-periphery.

Then there are the peripheral nations or regions which represent the world's most exploited populations. Workers tend to endure low-wage jobs or labor-intensive agricultural occupations and benefit little from their role in the global supply chain of consumer goods. These places, now mainly in Africa and parts of Asia, Central and South America, the Caribbean realm, and much of the Middle East, focus on growing cash crops like sugar and tobacco, and sending raw materials back to the core and semi-periphery for processing. Those in the periphery therefore are typically burdened by the greatest degree of physical labor and the least capacity to benefit from their production.

Like all attempts to explain complex human patterns, World Systems Theory does have its shortcomings. It is said that this perspective places too much emphasis on the role of economics and capitalism in explaining uneven development around the world. Though admittedly a significant influence, the decisions of global corporations are also supplemented by an intricate blend of cultural factors, political oppression and authoritarian regimes that hoard resources for an elite few. Further, what defines whether a nation or region is part of the core, semi-periphery or periphery is difficult to define and determine.[5]

With these aspects in mind, Collins' dystopian nation of Panem provides an arguably excellent—albeit fictitious—exemplar of how the theory can play out on the ground. Panem's geographic division between the Capitol, "career" districts, and peripheral districts is analogous to Wallerstein's core, semi-periphery, and peripheral regions respectively. The Capitol clearly serves as the dominant core—both politically and economically. It is this metropolitan hub which controls investment, industry, and in turn, employment—to the extent it can be called that—within the outlying rural periphery of Panem. Within this conceptualization, Districts 1, 2, and perhaps 4 apparently play the role of semi-periphery within Panem's own political-economic system. On the one hand, these districts do not enjoy the political or social clout—nor the level of economic wealth—of that found in the Capitol. Likewise, their populations are still highly regarded as an unworthy "Other" by their superior Capitol counterparts, and they are forced like all other districts to participate in the Games. Capitol citizens therefore still regularly perceive the populations of these more well-off districts as foreign outsiders.

That said, Districts 1 through 4 are still portrayed as more economically diverse with a higher standard of living than those on Panem's periphery. They are also more closely tied into the economic investments and industrial developments of the Capitol. District 2, for instance, plays a fundamental role in munitions, weapons development and manufacturing. As world systems theory would have it, these semi-peripheral districts are also physically closer to the Capitol, thereby creating stronger economic linkages between them—a benefit afforded by the First Law of Geography. And, although they still participate in the Hunger Games, there is a hierarchy of privilege among the districts themselves. Most notable are the "Careers," who enjoy an unfair advantage given their relative level of social and economic status, and overall higher quality of life. And although considered illegal, these tributes find ways to train at home before the Games. Katniss teaches us about this relative inequity in the first novel through her description of the volunteer tributes from the wealthier districts. These "Careers" are typically from Districts 1, 2, or 4 and usually win the Games due to their distinct advantages (*THG* 94).

Of course, in true Katniss fashion, she finds a silver lining to this structural injustice and thereby flips this situation to her advantage. In particular, the Careers have never learned how to be hungry like impoverished residents of Districts 11 and 12 (*THG* 208). Still, this is of little consolation to the vast majority of district populations forced to endure abject living conditions and poverty throughout their lives.

In contrast, the higher-numbered districts (with the exception of District 13) find themselves in Panem's rural, relatively impoverished periphery. As now famously known, each district generally emphasizes the production of a single commodity for its economic well-being. As with many of our own world's peripheral nations, they represent the most unfavorable end of the spatial division of labor, with low-wage jobs focused on growing cash crops for export (District 11), or the extraction of minerals or related natural resources (Districts 7 and 12). Also mirroring reality, we learn through dialogue between Katniss and Rue that district residents benefit little from their own labor. Cash crops are sent back to the nation's wealthy core, just as sugar, cotton, tobacco, and related commodities were shipped from British colonies back to Europe within its own colonial economic system.

This inability for local populations to benefit from their own labor comes to light once again while Katniss is befriending Rue. Katniss expresses surprise that Rue's district does not have more to eat, given their focus on agricultural production. As Rue's eyes widen, she exclaims that they are not allowed to eat the food they produce. The punishment for doing so is no less than a whipping that everyone else is forced to watch. In return, Rue asks if Katniss is allowed to keep all the coal she wants, to which Katniss replies similarly, adding that they can only use what they purchase or manage to track in on their boots (*THG* 203). Like most countries that rely on similar extractive industries for their economic well-being, what they produce is designated for export back to the core region and not for local consumption.

Districts 11 and 12 therefore find themselves on the extreme end of the world-system continuum, as they represent the most impoverished, oppressed, and extractive regions of Panem. The First Law of Geography kicks in here as well; those districts more distant from the Capitol tend to find themselves most disadvantaged. They are separated economically and physically from the wealth and economic opportunities available within the core or semi-periphery. In this respect, Panem portrays a world system in miniature.

Ronald Lewis invokes world-systems theory to explain the historical situation of Appalachian coal mining. He describes the central Appalachian coalfields as a peripheral region, where "raw materials are extracted to support more developed spheres within the system."[6] He further contends that many of Appalachia's future land speculators and entrepreneurs were first introduced to the region's potential for natural resource extraction during the Civil War. Leaders of both the Confederate and Union Armies, including various majors and generals, were known to have heavily promoted the future development of central Appalachia's coal deposits. Industrial capitalists therefore found their way into the mountains much sooner than many people realize.

In the final decades of the nineteenth century, for instance, the mountains were already undergoing a "wrenching industrial transition." Industrial society advanced into the Appalachians "behind armies of resident and imported laborers who laid the tracks for three major railroad systems."[7] Essentially, the Chesapeake & Ohio and the Norfolk & Western railroads extended their lines into central Appalachia from the east, while the Louisville & Nashville Railroad extended its own track into the Kentucky coalfields from the west. Not long afterward, the entire central Appalachian region was linked into the national rail network beyond the mountains. An elaborate system of main lines, branch lines, and feeder lines was built specifically to transport natural resources out of the mountains to America's manufacturing core in the Northeast and Midwest. For these reasons, the powerful myth that Appalachia remained a place "where time stood still" could not have been further from the truth.[8]

A Capitalist Panem?

Appalachia's connections with the American industrial core were analogous to the relationship of District 12 to the far-away Capitol. Collins provides an even richer pool of information about Panem's economic geography within her prequel. For those clued into such things, the indicators she provides are revealing. Despite its sluggish recovery and reconstruction following a crippling war, the Capitol and its industrial leaders were still apparently participating in a rather typically capitalist system of enterprise. The complete shutdown of the nation's free-market economic system had not yet transitioned to the state-controlled *command economy* witnessed within the original series. Corporations and the industrialists who owned them could still benefit from the mobility of capital.

By the time of Katniss Everdeen, it appears that any hint of remaining capitalist trade between the districts and the Capitol had been all but eliminated. The central regime controlled the flow of all commodities. At some point Panem's political-economic system transitioned from one focused on free-enterprise to one resembling a command economy characteristic of the former Soviet Union. Most likely, President Snow plays a signature role in that transition, though we will need to await future novels to confirm whether this is the case.

What is evident from the prequel, however, is that the Snow family fortune had been dependent upon capitalist investment in munitions. And where was the bulk of their operations located? Unfortunately for them, in District 13 of all places. "Their sprawling complex, blocks and blocks of factories and research facilities, had been bombed to dust," the narrator bluntly tells us, taking the family's fortunes with them. With the ensuing elimination of District 13 by nuclear weapons—or so we are told—the Capitol's military manufacturing had shifted to District 2, a situation that persisted throughout the more successful revolution of Katniss' time.

In no small touch of irony, we learn that the Snow family's nemeses, the Plinths, end up profiting handily from their own investments in District 2 munitions. One cannot help but wonder how Coriolanus feels when he discovers later that District 13 has not been destroyed at all. Throughout the prequel novel, he is led to believe that his family's fortune had been eliminated. Yet District 13 survives through a secret agreement with the Capitol, allowing it to remain as one of Panem's foreboding nuclear powers. *Oops.* In this case, Snow didn't land on top.

Within the prequel we learn of similar capitalist—or corporate—activities between Panem's core and periphery. Livia Cardew, for instance, who was prone to gloating we are told, had been awarded the District 1 boy for her mentoring assignment. The narrator suspiciously hints that her favored status was more the result of her mother's role in running the largest bank in the Capitol and less on her own merits. Collins is likely pointing toward the typical privileges and perks enjoyed by corporate owners and their families. Then there is Festus, who had existed within Coriolanus' inner circle of friends since birth (*BSS* 6). Representing old money, his family fortune had been built upon their investment in District 7 timber, which had taken a hit during the war but was rebounding. Likewise, District 10 practically serves as Arachne's second home, she tells us, bragging outwardly of her own various forays into that district. She had also traveled extensively elsewhere in Panem, which indicates that Capitol-district movement and leisure travel were still encouraged prior to and following the first war. Her family had even developed luxury hotels in vacation destinations, the primary source of their own fortune.

Just as a booming railroad network played a fundamental role in America's industrial growth, so too did Panem's own rail system. During the prequel we learn of Panem's national rail network that connected districts with the Capitol and with one another. Descriptions of this network within the prequel—and to a lesser extent within the original series—were probably intended to mirror the heyday of American railroads during the early twentieth century. Coriolanus and his Peacekeeper counterparts all travel long-distance by train, and they apparently receive their mail by train as well. There is no mention of overland, interstate highways or of widespread air travel except for what is authorized by the military.

Thus, just as America was a nation of railroads and related public transit prior to the 1950s, so too was Panem reliant upon its own railroad network. This is further indicated by Panem's postal system. As indicated by regular deliveries and care packages for Coriolanus and his Peacekeeper peers, their mail seems to have arrived by train. This, too, reflects America's own railway system and its role in distributing the nation's mail. Long-distance delivery once depended almost entirely on passenger trains outfitted with special mail cars operated by the United States Postal Service. They were, quite literally, America's rolling post offices.

In these ways, Collins was once again pulling from the history books of early twentieth-century American life. And, despite the rather bizarre magnetic-levitation trains portrayed in the films, the aesthetics of the train interiors and exteriors also pull from this same historical period. Railroads by the 1930s were designing their sleek locomotives and fashionable passenger cars with *Art Moderne* and *Art Deco* design motifs, often represented by an emphasis on smooth, metallic finishes and horizontal elements to signify speed and technological advancement. This was the age of the streamliners, sporting a standard, sleek appearance for America's passenger trains between the 1930s and 1950s. It was a celebration of the machine, of industry, of speed. This was a bold, if ultimately ill-fated strategy to encourage continued travel by rail in the face of the burgeoning automobile era.

Perhaps most curious for purposes here, there is some point between the prequel and the original series when this capitalist-based economic system all but collapses under the heavy hand of authoritarianism. It remains unclear as to why, or when this occurs. While the extreme economic and social contrasts between the Panem's urban core and the peripheral districts remain largely unchanged—and unimproved—much of the corporate, capitalist-driven world system becomes but a shadow of its former self. But no matter. A second, more successful revolution will soon be underway.

9

The Ballads of Appalachia

The World of Lucy Gray Baird

Katniss Everdeen may have introduced us to various cultural traditions of central Appalachia, though it is the prequel's Lucy Gray Baird who effectively brings them to life. Through Lucy Gray's own colorful character traits, Collins introduces us to the *ballad* style of folk song, which has played a prominent role in Appalachian culture and music history. Readers are suitably educated when Lucy Gray is introduced to the Capitol audience for the first time prior to the tenth Games. During her interview with Lucretious "Lucky" Flickerman, she introduces herself as Lucy Gray Baird of the Covey Bairds. She then prepares to sing a song she had started to write back in District 12. With its lyrics "set to an old tune," she further explains that this style of song is called a ballad "Where I'm from" (*BSS* 170).

The passage above can be interpreted as a heavily coded introduction to Lucy Gray's family, home, and cultural heritage. Given that "covey" refers appropriately to a flock of birds, Collins likely chose the obscure term to symbolically link the theme of songbirds—and more specifically, mockingjays—to the characters and plot of the prequel. Likewise, the connections between Lucy Gray and Appalachian culture are pervasive throughout the story line. Not only has she written a ballad as a metaphor for her own life story, but it is also set to an "old tune," which is likely an Appalachian folk song handed down orally through the generations. This appears to indicate that the Covey Bairds do originate—in the world of Panem—elsewhere in Appalachia.

It is perhaps more revealing that Lucy Gray had become familiar with ballads where she's "from," though she makes it clear later that District 12 is not her true home. During her first interview with the Capitol's Lepidus Malmsey, Lucy Gray clarifies that she and the Covey are not really from any district in particular, but rather they move around from place to place on a whim (*BSS* 52–53). This revealing dialogue clarifies that neither Lucy Gray nor the Covey are sentimentally attached to District 12, as this is not their original home. Their music, however, is decidedly Appalachian in its varied styles and character, as we will consider in future chapters.

While ballads could be found anywhere the British settled on America's eastern seaboard, Collins purposely sets her story in the central Appalachians and intentionally ties the ballad to Appalachian culture. As we will see, this reflects an accurate historical precedent. Researchers have documented that British colonial ballads had actually survived centuries later within the central mountains, whereas they had largely disappeared elsewhere. Through the principle of association, then, it is reasonable to presume that Lucy Gray's original home is likewise somewhere else in Appalachia. It is, as she says, "where I'm from."

A Broadway Musical?

Compared to the original Hunger Games series, the prequel focuses even more centrally on Appalachian music traditions. No less than eleven full-length songs and their lyrics are woven throughout the novel.[1] For those songs handed down from the original series, they are now provided with additional backstories. Among the most prominent examples are "The Hanging Tree" and the so-called "valley song," which is based on an early country tune called "Down in the Valley." Numerous additional song fragments and instrumental tunes are also performed by the Covey, including key verses of the well-known "Clementine."

The Covey's performance style is distinct in its own right, something that is safe to interpret as traditional bluegrass music. Chapter 12 is devoted to this very topic. Once referred to as "folk music with overdrive" by folklorist Alan Lomax, the up-tempo style played with purely acoustic instruments was derived from a multicultural blend of folk and early country music.[2] Additionally—and quite appropriately for Collins' mountain setting—the origins of bluegrass are primarily found in the central and southern Appalachians, as we will explore in later chapters.

To discover that country and bluegrass music play prominent roles within a Hunger Games novel is perplexing enough. Even more amusing is that some observers have compared the prequel to the likes of a Broadway musical. This distinct form of theater can be generally defined as a stage or film production featuring popular songs, either to tell a story or to showcase the talents of writers or performers.[3] All chuckling aside (my students were unanimously opposed to the idea), the notion of configuring The Ballad of Songbirds and Snakes into a theatrical production is not a preposterous one. Like in the musical form of theater, various songs in the prequel are repeated—or reprised—later, sometimes with a twist, or to re-emphasize an earlier mood. As one prominent case in point, the representative Appalachian murder ballad "The Hanging Tree" is repeated numerous times in various contexts. In perhaps one of its more darkly romantic performances, Lucy Gray reprises the song as a coded invitation for Coriolanus to meet her at the very tree for which the song is named.

The early country song "Keep on the Sunny Side" provides another case. Author Valerie Estelle Frankel notes that this number is first sung as a sing-along by Maude Ivory, and is reprised later as an "ironic juxtaposition."[4] That is, while the Covey band entertains the crowd with this happy song, dramatic acts of teenage violence and murder are transpiring in the garage nearby. Then as a musical finale, "The Hanging Tree" is reprised once again as the novel's closing song. Lucy Gray sings it as a diversion— somehow gathering her wits enough to perform it flawlessly in the woods— with Coriolanus in full chase. No, *Hunger Games: The Musical* is not that far off base.

Appalachian Ballad Origins

The tradition of ballad singing demonstrated by Lucy Gray and Katniss is rooted in the folk music of the British Isles. The ballad thus naturally came to the mountains along with the musically-inclined Scots-Irish and English settlers discussed in Chapter 4. It is important to note that Appalachian music includes a wide array of styles—not the least being ancient folk songs, lullabies, play songs, chants, and hymns. But the core of the region's musical heritage is found in its folk ballads and instrumental dance tunes.[5] By choosing the ballad as a centerpiece for her novels, Collins successfully integrates a key Appalachian cultural form into her own dystopian world.

Appalachian songs were often sung by women and were usually unaccompanied by other singers or musical instruments. In one sense the women who sang them were "fulfilling roles as keepers of the families' cultural heritages and rising above dreary monotonous work through fantasies of escape and revenge."[6] Perhaps "Deep in the Meadow" best represents the daily ritual of singing by Appalachian women and their families. Both Katniss and Lucy Gray sing the peaceful lullaby several decades apart to sooth the younger Prim, Rue, and Maude Ivory. Katniss further describes the song as a "mountain air," a term she had learned from her music teacher rather than from her father.

As European settlers populated the backcountry, the subjects of ballad lyrics began to reflect their new American settings, occupations, and natural environments. Still, many of the earlier stories and ballads from Europe survived to be retold as well. Many were also sung as personal narratives, or life stories rooted within their earlier British traditions.[7]

While it is not incorrect to describe the origins of Appalachian folk songs as "British," it is probably more accurate to define their origin as broadly "Anglo-Celtic." The "Anglo" part of Anglo-Celtic refers to those with English ancestry, while "Celtic" refers to those originating from one of the territories of the Celtic Isles.

Well, then, just where are the Celtic Isles? The six territories they comprise include Scotland and Ireland, as well as Cornwall, Wales, Brittany, and the Isle of Man. These places are sometimes referred to collectively as the Celtic nations, given their common languages and cultural identities which have more or less survived to this day. Their ballads often featured folk tales of love and family but were also related to their own true-life stories, hard times, and loss of loved ones.[8]

A large proportion of immigrants from England and the Celtic Isles came from highly artistic backgrounds. Enough settlers therefore could "hit the ground running" to perform and teach music upon their arrival in America. Once entrenched within their colonial American homes, these northern Europeans were influenced throughout successive generations by a blend of Native American and African folk ways. In the central and southern Appalachians, traditional songs of the Cherokee, black slaves, and later free blacks influenced the Anglo-Celtic music of these early American settlers.[9] This cultural mixing of music forms will be discussed in more detail below, particularly with respect to the development of Appalachian string bands, early country music, and a later energetic derivative called bluegrass.

Three Forms of Ballads

To recall from earlier, any ballad can be defined generally as a song that tells a story with various characters involved. Beyond that, ballads can be classified into one of three specific types—namely, folk (or popular), broadside, and literary. Since all three varieties make an appearance within the prequel, it might be helpful to distinguish between them. Folk ballads are typically the oldest of the three types, the original sources for which are often lost to the passage of time. Their themes most often revolve around rather serious topics of love or death, though humorous ones can also be found. One classic example would be "Barbry Allen," for which the Covey character Barb Azure is named. It is common to find numerous variations of folk ballads, to the point where sometimes their total quantity is impossible to determine. For instance, researchers have documented no less than 158 variations of "Barbry Allen."[10] Talk about an identity crisis for Barb Azure, whose first name is derived from that very ballad!

As a second distinct type, broadside ballads rely to some degree on true stories that have been enhanced and converted into catchy songs. They are so named because of their traditional means of distribution well prior to our digital age. Up through the nineteenth century, the lyrics of such ballads were printed on a single "broadside," or piece of paper, and distributed on the streets to local populations. Many of them rely on stories of homicide, which is why they are sometimes referred to as *murder ballads*. More often than not, the victim in such ballads is a young woman, and a large share of them feature "unwary young women murdered by their lovers, often to conceal an illicit relationship or unwanted pregnancy."[11] Whether a man owed a debt or murdered his wife's lover, as Amelia Mason describes, the summative act of hanging "was a likely punishment in the ballad universe."[12] It should come as little surprise that "The Hanging Tree" serves as the most prominent and recurring murder ballad within the Hunger Games saga, and is discussed in more detail below.

The third type is the literary ballad, perhaps derived from a poem or other artistic creation.[13] The Wordsworth Poem of "Lucy Gray"—on which the character of Lucy Gray Baird is based—generally reflects this tradition, as does the more comical ballad of "Clementine." While such literary ballads can resemble their broadside or folk counterparts, they are authored by specific individuals and crafted largely from imagination. All of the songs written by Suzanne Collins herself can be described as literary ballads.

Lucy Gray's primary antagonist, Coriolanus Snow, takes us on a veritable tour of methods for killing people that are common to traditional ballads. Coriolanus is ultimately responsible for killing three individuals in the prequel's story line—if we don't count the Epilogue, where there is a fourth. All of Snow's homicidal methods are "quintessential ballad fodder," explains Elizabeth Hardy.[14] They essentially include the "variety pack" of bludgeoning, shooting, and unjust hanging. Speaking of which…

"The Hanging Tree"

Probably no other ballad or song within the Hunger Games saga has earned more attention than "The Hanging Tree." Oscar-winning actress Jennifer Lawrence generated Hollywood news of her own with her performance of the song in "Mockingjay, Part 1," the third film of the Hunger Games

to express his revolutionary sentiments and was actively recruiting others to join him in revolt. It was thus "probably safe to assume," says Granger, that he and Gale's father died at the hands of a paranoid Capitol, which had gotten wind that the coal miners were conspiring to begin an uprising.[21] This is not an unreasonable assumption, one which has led to much speculation surrounding the incident.

Beyond "Strange Fruit," there is actually a real country-western song titled "The Hanging Tree." This one served as the title song for a popular Gary Cooper cowboy film in 1959. The song is basically about a man who enjoys a reunion with his own true love after nearly being hanged at the gallows himself. Granger suggested that if one were to "graft" this country-western song into the spirit and lyrics of "Strange Fruit," we would come very close to the Collins song—along with its varied meanings that are peppered throughout *Mockingjay*.[22]

Without discarding these initial interpretations, it turns out that Collins was really preparing a surprise for all of us. In the prequel we learn that the character of Lucy Gray actually wrote the song, thus adding another layer to its prior meanings. Lucy's song specifically references an actual event within the story line, namely the hanging of Arlo Chance who apparently "murdered three." Just before his body drops from the gallows, Arlo notices "a young woman with olive skin and long black hair" shrieking to Arlo through the crowd. Arlo eventually yells back, "Run! Run, Lil!" To Coriolanus' absolute horror, the slew of mockingjays within earshot begin to repeat his cry. We further learn that such events occur regularly at the Hanging Tree of District 12, given Lucy Gray's quip, "The show's not over until the mockingjay sings" (*BSS* 352).

According to Valerie Estelle Frankel, the entire story line of the prequel reflects the "Hanging Tree" song itself. Lucy Gray is in the fight of her life—first within the tenth Games, and later in District 12 at the hands of various troubled characters. She then ultimately chooses between a likely death and fleeing into the mountains, rather than enduring a perpetual life of slavery. The prequel further establishes that "The Hanging Tree" lyrics will live on, specifically through the young Maude Ivory, a child who "never forgets anything with a tune" (*BSS* 173).

We had learned in the original series that Katniss learns the song from her father, and we might presume that her father learned it from older members or descendants of the Covey—quite possibly from Maude Ivory herself (see Chapter 15 for further discussion). Beyond this, keen readers will note that the Covey was banned from performing at the Hob—but not at other potential functions within District 12. It follows that the enduring music of the Covey and "The Hanging Tree" in particular will likely live to see daylight in future novels, should they ultimately appear.

Child Ballads and the Covey

One inspiration for early Appalachian folk songs was the so-called Child Ballads. This is an impressive collection of 305 ballads primarily from England and Scotland, though some American variations are included as well. Most of the ballads date to the seventeenth and eighteenth centuries, though at least a few of them come from much earlier times. Contrary to what one might presume, this is no collection of children's tales. Rather, this was the work of Francis James Child who collected and published an eight-volume series entitled *English and Scottish Ballads* in 1860.

Child had collected many of the ballads from broadsides, like those mentioned earlier. Broadsides were a particularly popular form of published material in Great Britain as well as within the American colonies. In addition to ballad lyrics themselves, broadsides could include news stories, rhymes, and similar short narratives. A later version of Child's collection was published in the United States as *The English and Scottish Popular Ballads* in five total volumes beginning in 1882. Over time the Child Ballads found their way into the folk customs of Appalachian communities. Although the content of many ballads was changing to reflect a distinctly Appalachian sense of place, "many nineteenth century versions of the Child Ballads still refer to Lords and Ladies, castles, and ghosts, and retain as their central theme love affairs and interpersonal relations."[23]

That said, Americans were not merely content to stick with the British and Victorian predecessors. More contemporary ballad topics expanded to stories of male-dominated occupations such as logging, ranching, and mining, along with tales of environmental desecration, tragedies, and murders. Adding to this diversity of topics was an ongoing African American influence that highlighted the emotional moods of grief or celebration. For them, real historical characters and events were highlighted in their stories.[24]

It appears that Collins is enamored with the Child Ballads as well, given her subtle nod to the collection within the prequel. Perhaps most prominent is her naming system for the youthful members of the Covey. As explained by the character of Maude Ivory, their respective first names are generally derived from a ballad while their second names are based on colors. Barb Azure owes her name to the ballad, "Barbara Allen," for instance, while her own name comes from "Maude Clair" and the color ivory found on piano keys. Lucy Gray is special, of course, since her whole name is owed to the ballad of the same title (*BSS* 436).

The names of the Covey characters are thus directly intertwined with the Anglo-Celtic ballad tradition. As author Valerie Estelle Frankel explains, two of their names directly reference specific Child Ballads. Tam

Amber, the Covey's esteemed mandolin player, can be associated with Tam Lin, the focus of Child Ballad number 39. This is a "very famous" ballad and a "very feminist tale" as described by Frankel, in which the queen of the fairies abducts a young man. A woman and property owner, Janet, is pregnant with his child, and she ultimately wrestles him away from the queen.[25]

It is suggested that Tam Amber's name reflects his own experience with being "stolen by the fairies"—that is, by the Covey family when they find him abandoned as a baby on the side of a road. As Coriolanus walks with the Covey to the lake in the woods, Maude Ivory describes Tam Amber as "a lost soul." Asked to elaborate, Maude explains that Tam was found in a cardboard box on the side of a road when he was a baby. The joke is on whoever left him there, says Maude, given that "he's the finest picker alive" (*BSS* 380). Aside from her commentary on Tam Amber's mandolin skills, this may very well be the link between his given name and the Child Ballads.

Frankel further posits that fiddler Clerk Carmine's name was similarly inspired. His first name likely references "Clerk Colvill" which is Child Ballad number 42. Upon conducting my own search for alternative naming origins, it appears that Frankel's suggestion makes the most logical sense. In Ballad number 42, Clerk Colvill ignores his own lady's advice and allows himself to be seduced by a mermaid. In a strange bit of irony, the mermaid then curses him for his infidelity before Colvill meets his own death.[26] How exactly the tale of Ballad number 42 reflects the life of Clerk Carmine remains unclear, unless more of his story has yet to be revealed in future books.

Appalachian Ballad Collectors

Not unlike Child's earlier mission to preserve ballads from the British Isles, similar efforts gained steam to "collect" authentic Appalachian folk songs before they, too, disappeared. These determined individuals tended to be academics or folklorists enamored with an image of what they believed to be "authentic folk" culture.[27] Around the time of World War I, for instance, the English folk song collector Cecil Sharp and his assistant, Maud Karpeles, managed to document more than 100 ballads from Old-World Britain that were still being sung in Appalachia.[28] Prior to his work in America, Cecil Sharp had taught music in England and had gained experience with collecting British dances and songs passed down through aural tradition, along with researching their background and histories. In 1914 and 1915 he visited the United States to consult and lecture on topics of dance. He eventually met another avid song collector from North Carolina, Olive Dame Campbell. She had already founded the John C. Campbell Folk School in Brasstown, North Carolina, and she willingly shared her own song collection with Sharp.[29] He then returned to the United States with his assistant and dance troupe member, Maud Karpeles and secured support from the Campbells to launch a multi-year expedition into the Appalachian backcountry to collect folk songs.

Their circuitous route took them through the mountainous back-country of Virginia, Kentucky, Tennessee, and North Carolina—essentially within and around our District 12 core area. For a total of 46 weeks between 1916 and 1918 the pair visited families and collected more than 500 such songs and their melodic variations, or tunes. Having devised their own division of labor, Sharp transcribed the songs' musical melodies while Karpeles recorded their lyrics. Their hard-fought efforts culminated in their seminal 1917 publication, *English Folk Songs from the Southern Appalachians*. Inside one finds no less than 274 songs and ballads and 968 tunes (melodies) to which they were sung. Thirty-nine of the tunes had been contributed by Olive Dame Campbell.

Well before Cecil Sharp had first visited America, another diligent researcher had tried tirelessly to publish her own collection of Appalachian folk songs. Katherine Jackson's story has been little known until very recently, and more than a century had passed before her original manuscript was finally recognized and published in 2020. This book was authored and compiled by Berea College professor of music education, Elizabeth DiSavino.[30] Already by 1909, Jackson had accumulated more than 60 ballads from her travels in the hills of eastern Kentucky. Her efforts were singly impressive, given that she ended up with five more ballads than would be found later in Campbell and Sharp's own 1917 publication. Berea College offered to help publish her collection in 1910 but never followed through. A large number of her ballads were therefore lost over the years, and fewer than half her original collection remains today. This consists of 28 ballads (25 of British origin and three native to Appalachia) with 43 total variations. These are supplemented with one additional thirteenth-century song and one Appalachian tune.

As DiSavino laments, the inability to publish and receive credit for her work through Berea represented a significant failure within a lifetime of otherwise impressive professional accomplishments.[31] Prior to venturing into the backwoods of Kentucky, Jackson had studied medieval literary balladry at Columbia University and went on to become the first woman in Kentucky to earn a Ph.D. She had been told about Appalachian ballads by some of her classmates, and her previous interest in historical ballads naturally led to her curiosity about what might be found in the Appalachians.

It turns out that the ballads her classmates had told her about were the descendants of those collected by Francis Child back in Britain. Jackson and some of her contemporaries thus sought to flush out these "escapee" ballads that had settled along with their immigrants deep within the mountains. Had Jackson's effort to publish her manuscript been successful, "hers would have been the first large and scholarly collection of southern Appalachian balladry ever published."[32] Instead, that honor ended up going to Campbell and Sharp in 1917.

The admittedly significant contribution these collectors made to advance our knowledge of music history was in some ways a mixed bag. It is important to note that all of them were a product of their time, in that they all maintained personal motives for pursuing these old Appalachian songs. Looking back on their efforts now in the rear-view mirror, DiSavino cautions that these collectors from a century earlier were biased in various ways and "sometimes demonstrated a wishful racial identification."[33] Specifically, the songs they found residing within the Appalachian Mountains were more often than not purposely credited as purely *Anglo-Saxon* in their origin. This largely ignored the fact that the ballads discovered in America were derived from both English and Scottish precedents. As we have seen earlier, most of those immigrants who had migrated into the central and southern Appalachians had been Scots or Scots-Irish, not English. Many of them had first fled from the Scottish Lowlands to Northern Ireland (the Ulster Scots). These people were neither Anglo nor Saxon; rather, their origin was more correctly placed in the Celtic Isles.

Somewhat amazingly, this intentional favoritism toward pure English, or Anglo-Saxon origins remained unchallenged for nearly a century. Folk song collectors were further known for downplaying or purposely ignoring the reality that was Appalachia's 300-year mixed-race heritage. Sharp, for instance, was an avowed nationalist who intentionally avoided the collection of folk material from non–Anglo, or non-white people.[34] This meant that songs of decidedly African, Indigenous, or mixed-race origins were often misrepresented. Of course, this type of cultural appropriation or favoritism was not exclusive to Appalachian ballad collectors; the contributions of black, Indigenous, and mixed-race people have been undervalued generally. It is thus good news indeed that the early twenty-first century has produced a much more inclusive pool of scholarship and creative writing to help rectify this oversight. Many of the authors cited herein provide a collective case in point. As for Suzanne Collins and her otherwise dystopian series, she is providing yet another opportunity for us to celebrate and learn from the multi-cultural, melting-pot character of her favored heroine, Katniss Everdeen.

Oh My Darling Clementine

The ever-popular ballad of "Clementine" is one of the prequel's more recognizable songs, and it is one that Maude Ivory clearly adores. Like many folk ballads, its origin is murky, with competing historical accounts. Still, its fundamental story revolves around the character for whom the song is named. Clementine is the daughter of a California gold miner who is also the singer's sweetheart. Following this? She ultimately drowns in some kind of rough water after the singer—who cannot swim—decides to not save her. The singer then essentially wipes his hands of Clementine with nary a tear shed, then—in one common version—pursues Clementine's sister instead.[35] *Ouch!*

One connection between the song and District 12 consists of their mutual focus on mining occupations. Suzanne Collins even chose to provide two verses of the song within her narrative, including the phrase "Excavating for a mine, dwelt a miner, forty-niner" (*BSS* 431). Curiously, the song refers to the mining of gold, not coal, which may raise some eyebrows. The "forty-niner" reference gives it away, of course; those who joined the initial rush in 1849 were known generally as "forty-niners."

There may be an additional, more historically obscure rationale for including this song within the prequel. As we have seen, the ballad tradition heavily influenced the central Appalachians during the 1700s and 1800s with the arrival of Anglo-Celtic immigrants. But the lyrics of this ballad are attributed to Percy Montrose around 1884, based on the earlier song "Down by the River Liv'd a Maiden." While the origin of the song's melody remains unclear, author Gerald Brenan claims that it originated as an old Spanish ballad he had originally heard in the rural village of Yegen after moving there in 1919.[36] Following the song's diffusion to Spanish-speaking Central America, Mexican miners made it popular during the California Gold Rush. Regardless of how its lyrics and melody came together, the song is rather lengthy. The version indicated above contains no less than eight successive verses—not including the repeated chorus, which Maude Ivory enjoys belting out within the prequel.[37]

The ballad's popularity has persisted to the present day, largely due to its rather continuous appearance in recent recordings, TV shows, and films. Its various cameo TV appearances over the years have ranged from episodes of *M*A*S*H* and *Columbo* to a *Star Trek: Voyager* episode in 1999, and later still within season five of the *Outlander* series. In this latter case, the time travelers Breanna and Roger sing the song to their son while living in the mountains of western North Carolina in the 1770s, in the heart of a Scottish immigrant community.

How might we rationalize the connection between coal mining in

District 12 and gold mining in California? Perhaps their common focus on mining and the ballad tradition was enough for Collins. However, there are some intriguing historical connections we might consider. Before there was coal mining in the Appalachians, for instance, there was gold! America's first gold rush occurred not in California but within the southern Appalachians not far from the District 12 core—particularly in western North Carolina and northern Georgia. Launched in 1829, this earlier Appalachian rush came to a crashing end two decades later when California became the next great hope for striking it rich. For this reason, we can seriously claim a legitimate gold-rush connection with the fictional realm of District 12.

Unfortunately for the Cherokee, their very livelihood and future became entangled within the politics surrounding this first Appalachian gold rush. The story began during the summer of 1828, when a black slave happened upon a nugget of gold in a branch of the Chestatee River. The news spread quickly, though no one knew in which of the river's tributaries the gold had been found. The first crowds that gathered within one week expanded to a small village of shanties with a particularly potent mix of aggressive miners, thieves, and gamblers.[38] As Brian Hicks explains, the village attracted "the worst kind of settlers. The prospectors were ruthless and violent. Fights broke out over small claims, swindlers found ways to make money off the suckers, and local Indians were robbed weekly."[39] The unruly camp in turn grew into a makeshift town named Dahlonga, a corrupted Cherokee word which loosely translated to "yellow money." The problem? Dahlonga was sitting atop traditional Cherokee land, and there was absolutely nothing the Cherokee could do about it.

Cherokee leaders had no experience with negotiating mineral rights, but they could see the writing on the wall. If gold fever continued to grow, Georgia politicians would be more inclined to confiscate their ancestral lands. Unfortunately their worst fears proved to be accurate. The state's militia occupied Dahlonga under the false pretense of policing the rowdy prospectors. Their main goal, however, was to prevent the Cherokee from absconding with any gold from their own land. The principal chief of the Cherokees, John Ross, asked Hugh Montgomery, the Indian agent, to send federal troops to protect their land and gold. After waiting several months, however, Montgomery apologized for not being able to obtain authorization. Without Ross knowing about it, Montgomery was actually quietly encouraging Cherokees to move westward. Even worse, President Andrew Jackson had ordered Montgomery to entice as many families as possible to leave their Cherokee homes. By the end of the year some five hundred families had been persuaded to move out.

Pressure was also coming from the Georgia legislature, which passed its own laws declaring authority over the Cherokee. They had been attempting to find ways to secure their land for years. The state was experiencing growing pains, they felt; Georgia's population expanded steadily to more than a half-million people by around 1830. Beyond that, Georgia had a profit motive to consider. As one of the original thirteen colonies, any land declared as public domain within its borders was owned by the state, which meant the Cherokee were standing in the way of potential land sales from which Georgia politicians could make a handsome profit. For his part, President Jackson believed the best solution was for Native American peoples to relocate west of the Mississippi River. Long story short, Congress soon began deliberating the details of a comprehensive bill that would legally remove Native Americans from their land, once and for all.

Meanwhile, the Gold Rush had expanded to include parts of Alabama, Tennessee, and Virginia—thereby overlapping with our District 12 core territory. The "fever" was so intense that state and federal governments were finally persuaded to remove the Cherokee once and for all from their ancestral lands to the newly formed "Indian Territory" comprising much of modern-day Oklahoma.[40] All of these factors had conspired terribly against the Cherokees' cause. It was within this context that politicians pressed hard for the removal of all Native Americans from the eastern seaboard, which ultimately led to the passage of the Indian Removal Act of 1830. For the Cherokee in particular, it was the Appalachian Gold Rush that provided the final excuse to have them removed permanently from their ancestral Appalachian homes.

What eventually followed was one of the most tragic events in American history. By 1838 some 16,000 Cherokee were still inhabiting previously ceded lands in North Carolina. That spring, the U.S. Army moved into the mountains and led them on a forced march on foot to Oklahoma, which has since become known as the Trail of Tears. Somewhere between 4,000 and 8,000 Cherokees died before reaching their destination, and many died in staging (concentration) camps before their journey had even begun.[41] Amazingly, a portion of the Cherokee people had escaped the Army's grasp and hid in the mountains. By 1900 some 1,400 of their ancestors had successfully formed the Eastern Band of Cherokees, now with their new capital at Cherokee, North Carolina. Many worked as poor subsistence farmers while some earned wages in the lumber industry.

While they were finally declared U.S. citizens in 1924, they did not receive the right to vote until after World War II. The latter half of the twentieth century saw some measured improvements for their struggling community, capped by a sizable tourism economy and a venture into casino development. In 1997 the $85 million Harrah's Cherokee Smoky Mountain Casino was opened, with every Cherokee member receiving a portion of its profits. They were also provided with preferential hiring for jobs involving the casino. As summarized by C. Clifford Boyd, Jr., after some 300 years of dependency, acculturation, and warfare, "they are now in a position to choose the direction of future change and their own destiny."[42] For all of these reasons, the Cherokee legacy remains indelibly etched into Appalachian culture.

A second way the Clementine ballad relates to gold mining and Appalachia involves another gold rush, this time in California. After gold was discovered at Sutter's Mill in Coloma, California, in 1848, some 300,000 people from the eastern United States and elsewhere around the world were attracted with the hope of striking it rich. One sizable migration stream came directly from the central and southern Appalachians, though mainly from North Carolina, Georgia, and surrounding states. In more cases than not, they were also accompanied by their slaves. Thus, many of the California forty-niners were, in fact, Appalachian transplants—whether by choice or not.

It would be negligent to not highlight one particular, more recent ballad titled "Fire on the Mountain." This one speaks to the connections between the Appalachian Mountains, the California Gold Rush, and the ballad tradition. The song tells the story of an ambitious if naïve man who drags his family away from their Carolina homestead and endures six months on a cross-country trail with the hope of striking it rich in California.

The story ends in a sad touch of irony. The man's widow weeps by his grave after he is shot down for a worthless claim. The song is a rather recent addition to the ballad tradition, one which still makes the association between Appalachia and the Gold Rush of 1849. It was written by a guitarist for the Marshall Tucker Band, George McCorkle, released in 1975. The ballad rose to become the band's second biggest hit, after their famed "Heard It in a Love Song."[43] Still, the 1970s birth of this particular ballad was probably too recent for the tastes of Suzanne Collins, who relies more on historical associations from the early twentieth century.

One might ponder whether Collins intended a deeper connection between Katniss' gold-colored mockingjay pin, the gold bangles in *Catching Fire*, the gold-plated cornucopia within the first novel, and of course Effie's gold-tinged hair. One could make a case for an underlying "gold" theme within the original series. And now this same theme reappears within the prequel, this time in the form of "Clementine." Granted, Collins' infusion of gold into her story line may have more to do with symbolizing the wealth and luxuries enjoyed within the Capitol, in contrast to the impoverished districts. Still, it is difficult to ignore the historical connections between the original gold rush of the Appalachians with that of California, and the litany of ongoing references to the precious metal within the story. Might Collins be subtly nudging us to uncover this little-known facet of Appalachian history?

Lucy Gray and Her Ballad

A considerable amount of conjecture has occurred regarding the possible fates of Lucy Gray Baird near the end of *The Ballad of Songbirds and Snakes*. True to form, Suzanne Collins leaves her readers puzzled about the whereabouts of Lucy Gray, along with a number of other loose ends. Given a rash of fan-site posts following the prequel's release, an untold proportion of readers seem to believe Lucy Gray to be deceased, and for thoughtful reasons—not the least being that Coriolanus may have shot her. Beyond the mystery of whether she was hit by bullets or not, one might also consider the ballad for which she is named. The original "Lucy Gray" was a poem written by William Wordsworth in 1799, which happens to be one of his most well-known works. It was later published in Wordsworth's *Lyrical Ballads*, which earned the poem even more attention.

The poem's story is based on a true event about a little girl in Yorkshire, England who became lost in a snowstorm. Her parents traced her footsteps to the middle of a canal lock, where they mysteriously disappeared. Sadly, the girl's body was eventually found in the canal. Wordsworth had learned of this story from his sister, thereby providing the inspiration for his future poem. In his own version, however, the lost girl simply vanishes into nowhere, likely as a spirit which, some say, can still be seen "upon the lonesome wild."

Collins' Lucy Gray Baird is clearly meant to parallel Wordsworth's own character. However, some liberties were taken to alter a few things. As Maude Ivory explains within the prequel, "We mixed it up a little" by altering the words of the original poem to better represent Lucy Gray's life within the Covey (*BSS* 424). Those who believe Lucy Gray Baird actually perishes can rationally point to both the original and altered poems, which insinuate that she becomes a ghost at the story's conclusion. A supporting argument relates to the confusing exchange when Coriolanus wildly chases Lucy Gray through the woods and attempts to shoot her through the trees. He cannot see her, however, and there is no clear indication as to whether his bullets hit home (fatally or not). He does hear "a faint cry," which some interpret as Lucy being hit (*BSS* 503). The intended meaning of her cry, however, is left intentionally ambiguous.

Adding to the confusion, a flock of birds takes flight at the same time Coriolanus hears her cry out (*BSS* 503). And she is nowhere to be seen when he reaches her former location. If the level of ambiguity was not enough at this point, Lucy Gray somehow manages to keep her composure enough to capably sing "The Hanging Tree" as a final symbolic gesture to Coriolanus. Of course, the mockingjays quite fittingly pick up the song with not a little irony. It is further important to note that Lucy Gray knows the forested area like the back of her hand, which Coriolanus does not. She knows where to run and how to get around. A possible clue that foretells her familiarity with the woods occurs earlier in the prequel when an unsure Coriolanus asks Lucy Gray how Tam Amber knows his way to the lake. She replies matter-of-factly that they all know the way because it's their "second home" (*BSS* 430). This breadcrumb may have been included as a clue for later, indicating that Lucy Gray can easily find her way around the lake and through the forest. With all of these considerations, there is consequently very little if any decent evidence that Coriolanus actually kills her.

That said, Lucy Gray does indeed disappear at the end of the prequel, in parallel fashion to her counterpart in both versions of the poem. One possibility is that she summoned the courage to return home and deal with the mayor while rejoining the Covey. She does admit to Coriolanus earlier that she is not too keen on living in the wild. Aside from her numerous positive attributes, Lucy Gray is no Katniss Everdeen when it comes to wilderness survival. About the prospect of living in the woods, she says, "It's not just how hard it will be. It's too lonely. I might've made it for a few days, but then I'd have come home to the Covey" (*BSS* 491). Of course, she also admits that the Covey can "get by," and that Maude Ivory will be old enough to lead the group in a few years. But this reflection on her part came when she was still planning to escape with Coriolanus. Now suddenly without him by her side, it is very possible that she simply goes back home. Her one true concern in life was to protect her Covey family, so it is reasonable that her determination in this regard is what finally motivates her to face the music, so to speak, and deal head-on with her remaining problems.

Aside from the mystery of Lucy Gray's whereabouts, the extent to which the final verse of the Wordsworth poem parallels her own situation is uncanny. Wordsworth's verse reads as follows:

> O'er rough and smooth she trips along,
> And never looks behind;
> And sings a solitary song
> That whistles in the wind.

It appears that Suzanne Collins purposely crafted Lucy Gray's disappearance to closely mirror Wordsworth's final verse. While being pursued by an enraged Coriolanus, Lucy Gray certainly "trips along" through the woods and, for some time at least, "never looks behind." Then she sings her "solitary song"—a reprise of "The Hanging Tree"—for Coriolanus' benefit, essentially giving her the last word on the matter. The song then effectively "whistles in the wind" as the mockingjays pick up the tune. Regardless of where she might have gone, this is arguably an impressive and fitting conclusion for Lucy Gray Baird and her own ballad of life!

10

Mountain String Bands

The Covey, the instruments they play, and the songs they sing are all descended from generations of Appalachian music history. Along with the Anglo-Celtic ballad tradition, various musical instruments accompanied the first generations of European migrants into the mountains. Most prominent among them were the fiddle, mandolin, and guitar, which arrived in waves with their European immigrant caretakers. Before long these were augmented with a diverse array of musical styles and instruments representing various Indigenous and African peoples. In this chapter we explore the history and multi-cultural origins of these musical styles that came to be associated with the central and southern Appalachians. This will serve as the next step in understanding just why Suzanne Collins decided to land a traditional Appalachian bluegrass band at the Hob of District 12. Prior to describing the characteristics of the bluegrass sound and the Covey's immersion within it, however, we need to step back and consider the origins of the Covey's musical instruments and the generations of settlers who introduced them to the mountains.

Colonial and early American mountain music often involved the combination of two contrasting string instruments that would normally be unlikely candidates for pairing—those of the European fiddle and the African banjo.[1] This unique combination enabled and encouraged generations of cross-cultural musical exchanges between Appalachia's black and white populations. One could even find common interactions between blacks and whites on slave-owning plantations when it came to music and dance. Black performers were regularly called upon to entertain or accompany social dances and related colonial functions within their own homes or towns. Eventually the dual, contrasting sounds of the fiddle and banjo became a fundamental trait of "old-time" Appalachian music, which has been described by Stephanie Ledgin as a "rough-edged, raw sound reflective of simple country life."[2] Black spiritual music was likewise integrated within the fiddle-banjo combination. Let's look first at how the fiddle came to the mountains and why it provided for a natural fit within District 12.

The Fiddle and Clerk Carmine

We should probably start with the basics. Exactly what is a fiddle, and why does it show up in the Hunger Games saga? The smallish string instrument appears in two distinct places within the novels. In *Mockingjay* the fiddle provides backup for the dancing at Annie and Finnick's wedding. As Katniss describes unemotionally, a choir of children provide the music, accompanied by the one fiddler who managed to escape District 12 with his instrument (*MJ*, 226). Then within the prequel, Collins elevates the fiddle to a more prominent role, as one of the four principal instruments of the Covey band. At the start of the Covey's first performance at the Hob, the spirited Maude Ivory introduces her fellow group members, as the story's narrator describes: "Next, the boy who'd set up the microphone appeared with a violin. 'That's Clerk Carmine on fiddle!'" (*BSS* 361).

In this single passage, Collins deftly reveals that the violin and fiddle are essentially the same, interchangeable instruments. Their difference comes primarily with the types of music they play. The term *violin* is principally used by players of classical and sometimes jazz music, while the fiddle has come to represent the music derived from Scots-Irish, Celtic, and French folk music and their various American descendants including Appalachian folk, country, bluegrass, and Cajun.[3] These latter styles are generally regarded as less complex than that of the classical violin. On the other hand, fiddlers have traditionally taken on the added responsibility of encouraging people to dance. This requires unique and intricate skills to produce the upbeat rhythms and melodies necessary to elicit human movement on the dance floor. The difference between the two instruments therefore largely boils down to a matter of semantics and the types of music they play.

The fiddle appears throughout the Hunger Games saga as another distinct cultural element of District 12 (and later, District 13). In the real Appalachians, generations of families and communities depended upon local fiddle players to back up their traditional dances. It was not uncommon for fiddles to accompany their Anglo-Celtic owners as they arrived in Pennsylvania during the 1700s. As successive generations settled into the central and southern Appalachians, they generated a repository of songs and reels—that is, Irish or Scottish dance tunes. These in turn were rooted in the older jigs, hornpipes, and yes—Anglo-Celtic ballads of the British Isles.[4] Thus, the fiddle and its music had accompanied the European colonists since their first arrival.

In the American colonies, the fiddle was typically played when accompanying community dances. It was also highly popular among amateur musicians who learned to play from family members or other local sources. Even Thomas Jefferson played the fiddle as an *amateur*—that is, someone playing for fun but not as a paid, professional musician. Slaves and indentured servants likewise adopted the fiddle for their own music, once again demonstrating the ongoing cultural exchange between black, white, and Native American populations. There are clear records of slaves having played the fiddle as early as the 1690s, and they even played the popular European music of the day.[5]

The fiddle was also commonly played at rural house parties and at community social and political events. It made additional appearances at local fairs, medicine shows, circus performances and, well, fiddle contests. The smallish instrument thus became well integrated into local cultural and social norms. As the cultural exchange process would have it, European fiddlers likewise adopted African stylistic approaches. In particular, black banjo music influenced fiddle playing and led to the emergence of a unique, syncopated type of Appalachian fiddle dance. The earliest musical exchanges between people of European and African descent often occurred through fiddle playing, which "provided one of the earliest, most long lasting, and most deeply influential musical and cultural meeting points between African and European people."[6]

Within the prequel, Lucy Gray informs us that the Covey band likewise entertains people at local events. When Coriolanus asks how the impoverished people of District 12 can afford to pay for entertainment, Lucy Gray explains that sometimes they pool their money and hold several weddings simultaneously. The Covey is thus hired to provide the entertainment (*BSS* 87). This signals a direct connection between the Covey and the weddings for which they perform, perhaps including a similar event featuring Finnick and Annie. Some Hunger Games fans have suggested that Clerk Carmine may end up being the lone fiddler who plays at Finnick's wedding in *Mockingjay*. Of course, Clerk Carmine's age in the prequel is unknown, aside from one description of him as a "boy." If we presume his age to be between 12 and 14, he would end up playing his fiddle at Finnick's wedding approximately 66 years later, nearing a venerable 80 years old. To reach this age in decent mental and physical shape would be a challenge, given his presumably hardscrabble life in an impoverished community— though it is certainly possible. Whether this scenario ultimately plays out will depend upon the release of future novels and whether Suzanne Collins decides to write about his later life.

The Banjo in Appalachian Music

Quite unlike the European fiddle, the banjo comes to us from a whole other continent. This was the first instance of a distinctly West-African musical instrument to develop in North America.[7] Through the process of migration diffusion, slaves brought earlier forms of the banjo with them from their original African homes. These earlier instruments went by a variety of names, such as the *banjar*, *bandore*, or *banza*, and various others. They all had in common a pole attached to a gourd that was strung with four strings. Historical records exist of the banjar showing up in Maryland and Virginia by the 1740s. Black banjar players were noted by the early 1800s in the emerging Appalachian settlements of Knoxville, Tennessee, and Wheeling, West Virginia.[8]

Thomas Jefferson took notice of the *banjar* as well, providing an impressive description of its construction in 1781.[9] Slaves were further known to construct their own instruments. As the banjar evolved through the next generations of both white and black musicians, later versions were improved upon with a flat fingerboard and tuning pegs. African slaves also brought the traditional down-stroke playing style to North America. By the 1830s people of Scots-Irish descent had learned to play these gourd instruments by adopting this down-stroke technique as part of the ongoing cultural exchange.[10]

By the middle 1800s the banjo had become a prominent feature of minstrel shows outside Appalachia. Also referred to as *minstrelsy*, the minstrel form of entertainment remained popular in America through the early twentieth century before becoming widely dismissed for its blatant racism. The typical minstrel show would feature a variety of acts, performances, music, and dancing that directly lampooned people of African descent as lazy, buffoonish, ignorant, and happy-go-lucky.[11] One characteristic of minstrel shows was the practice of non-black performers wearing blackface, which persisted as a performance tradition in American theater for approximately 100 years. Blackface performances became popular in both the United States and Britain and were most often utilized in minstrel shows. To darken their skin, white performers would apply burnt cork, greasepaint or shoe polish. It should come as no surprise in contemporary times that such flagrant caricatures of Black people only served to enhance existing stereotypes. By the middle twentieth century—amazingly not that long ago—changing attitudes toward race and racism finally led to the end of minstrel-type performances.

While the history and legacies of minstrelsy are too involved to treat effectively here, one of its significant influences involved the development of the banjo. As Charles Perryman notes within his own research, it was Thomas Dartmouth Rice who first introduced the imitation of slaves dancing on stage, usually with fiddle accompaniment. In turn, Joel Walker Sweeney became one of the first well-known white banjo players, though he had learned his playing style directly from black slaves.[12] Likewise, the renowned minstrel Dan Emmett learned his own banjo techniques from a fellow white man named Ferguson, though Ferguson had originally developed his own skills from black banjo players in the Appalachians. In this way, black musicians passed along their skills and techniques (through imitation diffusion) to white minstrel performers. As a result, the banjo continued to evolve, eventually leading to the more familiar instrument with five strings, wooden rims, and circular, open-backed bodies.[13]

Despite its continued development, the banjo became much less popular among black people and musicians by the late nineteenth century. For them the instrument had been culturally appropriated by white minstrel shows and thus became a symbol of racist stereotyping. As a result, their rich tradition and heritage of playing the banjo and its predecessors nearly died away. Eventually the minstrel performance tradition all but disappeared for its own part by the mid-twentieth century, and so too did the once-common imagery of the black banjo player. In no small amount of irony, the banjo would go on to become a symbol of white, hillbilly stereotyping across America during the latter half of the twentieth century.[14]

Adding the Guitar

The fiddle-banjo combination began to replace the lone fiddle in popularity during the late nineteenth century. In turn, the tradition of the lone fiddler accompanying traditional dances began to fall by the wayside. The musical emphasis shifted toward more complicated rhythms and less on the actual melodies—rhythms which the fiddle-banjo duo could more adequately provide.[15] These musical shifts set the stage, so to speak, for the emergence and flourishing of the *mountain string band*, which became commonly identified with Appalachian music. The string band's sound was based in part on the blending of black and white banjo playing styles. It also relied upon the addition of yet another instrument to the previous fiddle-banjo combination—that of the guitar. Of course, this is the very instrument that plays a fundamental role in the hands of Lucy Gray.

Historically, the guitar emerged in Europe along with a variety of other string instruments. Early versions had already become standardized by 1800 with its characteristic six strings and tuning mechanism. This more modern instrument later became a prominent feature within the parlors of elite European families. Its popularity as a so-called "parlor instrument" continued apace through the early American period.[16] As the precursor to today's middle-class "living rooms," the parlor was largely devoted to receiving and entertaining guests. As with the fiddle, guitars were brought over by various European teachers, performers, and working-class immigrants during the early nineteenth century. One early guitar maker was C.F. Martin who arrived from Germany in the 1830s. Martin's well-known company continues to thrive in Pennsylvania as of this writing.

Prior to industrialization, companies like that of Martin had not yet developed a standardized manufacturing approach. Rather, early guitar makers were capable of hand crafting only a few dozen guitars each year. Of course, the required time, labor and workmanship meant higher costs and expensive prices for customers. As factory approaches of production improved, the guitar became more accessible to a wider population. By the 1840s, for instance, Englishman James Ashborn had established his own factory in Connecticut and adopted some budding approaches for mass production. His company churned out as many as one thousand guitars per year, which were mostly marketed through New York City music stores.

Though resembling the guitars of today, those of Martin and Ashborn were smaller instruments and were not as loud.[17] Most were also destined for well-to-do parlors along with accompanying music manuscripts and teaching manuals. Photographs from the nineteenth century often feature middle- or upper-class women and their guitars in parlor settings, often while socializing or within party scenes.

With more prolific and inexpensive manufacturing techniques, the guitar expanded from its status as a parlor instrument. In one respect the instrument diffused down the urban and social hierarchies into smaller towns and rural areas. Because of the difficulty of travel into and out of the Appalachians, the guitar did not arrive in large numbers until much later, approximately between 1890 and 1920.[18] When it did arrive in the hands of eager Appalachian performers, however, the guitar's typical musical setting had shifted drastically. The earlier genteel, classical style of guitar playing was summarily replaced with the finger-picking techniques of black musicians. The earliest mentions of the guitar in the South, for instance, featured the instrument being played by black workers. They not only brought the guitar into the mountains, but they further developed a uniquely black style of music which was gaining popularity—a style that would become known as the *blues*.

Both the blues style and the instruments that played it came to the mountains in large part with black laborers. They came to find work in the coal mines, for railroad companies, and for other related working-class jobs of the time. Historical accounts from as early as 1904 reveal black musicians in Appalachia playing the blues on their guitars.[19] By that time, the guitar had continued to spread, or diffuse, through mountain towns and rural communities by way of their newer railroad connections with larger cities. People also acquired guitars and other merchandise through mail-order catalogs such as those distributed by Sears, Roebuck & Company. It was consequently not long after 1900 when the guitar found itself joining its fiddle and banjo counterparts. With the addition of this third acoustic, string instrument, the first mountain string bands were born.[20]

As one might imagine, the addition of the guitar encouraged some altered roles for all three instruments. (It is tempting to reference the "three's a crowd" cliché.) In the era of fiddle and banjo duos, both instrumentalists had played the melody together, thus sharing equal roles within the performance. Now with the guitar added as the proverbial third string—pun intended—musicians were freer to experiment with different roles for their respective instruments. In what would become the typical string band approach, for instance, the fiddle would play the melodic lead while the guitar would play bass lines and harmonies. The banjo was relied upon to maintain the rhythm and beat.[21]

As the instrumentation expanded, so too did the musical repertoire. These more contemporary groups performed not only Appalachian folk songs and instrumental tunes, but they now added a variety of popular music and jazz. The string band's overall sound likewise became more contrasting, rather than blended, which was an important contribution of West African musical tradition. This contrasting style, known as the "heterogeneous sound ideal," could be recognized most distinctly by the widely contrasting sounds produced by each specific instrument.

For instance, in the case of a string quartet, all the instruments blend into a single, homogeneous sound because the instrumental ranges all overlap. It is difficult to discern the contributing musical role of each specific instrument. In African and later African American music, however, the musical style is more contrasting, or heterogeneous. Olly Wilson provides the rather peculiar example of an ensemble composed of a drum, metal bell, and a flute. Each instrument provides a distinct, unique sound, each of which is likely discernable to the average listener.[22] It was this African American "heterogeneous sound ideal" that strongly influenced the development of Appalachian string-band and bluegrass music. This style came to be played largely by white Appalachian musicians, though the music they played could be described more accurately as "mulatto."[23]

Until the turn of the twenty-first century, there had been a persistent—and erroneous—collective thinking that Appalachian music was singly the product of earlier British folk music traditions. This simplistic conception of the region's rich musical heritage had conveniently omitted the contributing roles of African American music styles.[24] In truth, the influence of African and later African American sources has been pervasive and continuous since early colonial times. More specifically, the development of Appalachian music has been enhanced by the unique stylistic contributions of the blues, black gospel, rhythm and blues, and jazz.

Readers might wonder whether Suzanne Collins intended the Covey to represent the Appalachian string band tradition. Not quite. For one thing, the Covey's instrumentation does not match well. String bands only occasionally included a mandolin or string base, like those performed by Tam Amber and Barb Azure, respectively. Second, there is no banjo in the Covey's ensemble. Third, the earlier fiddle-banjo combination and the later string bands were still typically employed for backing up local folk dancing activities. For its part, the Covey does not perform primarily to accompany dancing. Rather, they are in the business of playing music, and their audiences come to listen and—at the Hob—occasionally holler, sing along, and otherwise root for the young performers.

However, there is a distinct, high-energy performance style into which the traditional mountain string band would evolve—something that would come to be known as *bluegrass*. The Covey most accurately represents a traditional bluegrass band, a topic to which several chapters are devoted below. For now, we turn our historical tour to the birth of the country music industry. Suzanne Collins carefully selected a handful of this genre's early songs for inclusion within her original series and her more recent prequel. These songs are brought to the fore by their now-famous Appalachian performers, none other than Katniss Everdeen and Lucy Gray Baird.

District 12 Goes Country

The next phase of Appalachian music adopted for the Hunger Games is directly tied to new media technologies of the early twentieth century. The proliferation of what became known as "country music" required a tie-in to the latest communication technologies of the radio, phonograph, and vinyl records. In addition to Maude Ivory's rendition of "Clementine," members of the Covey introduce us to songs that find their roots in actual American history. Two of these—"Down in the Valley" (the source for the "Valley Song") and "Keep on the Sunny Side"—actually point readers to the first generation of commercial country music. While some Hunger Games songs were originally written by Collins herself (in the form of literary ballads discussed earlier), it appears that she strategically chose these tunes to highlight the early generations of the country music genre.

On the surface, "Down in the Valley" and "Keep on the Sunny Side" appear to have little in common. They appear within two very different contexts of the saga and elicit widely differing emotional responses. What they do share is their parallel emergence within the burgeoning country music industry. Both songs had been performed and promoted by America's first country music stars, making them logical choices for Suzanne Collins. But just how did country music first emerge, and where? Let's take a look at the genre's beginnings to better understand how the likes of Katniss and Lucy Gray managed to learn these timeless tunes.

Discovering Appalachian Folk Music

Americans from outside Appalachia have been fascinated with the region's music since the time of the Civil War. As urban growth and industrialization swarmed around the mountains, the perceived difference between urban and rural lifestyles became more noticeable. As discussed above in Part I, it is true that industry, urban growth, and manufacturing found their way into the Appalachians as well—to the benefit of some people more than others. Still, the scope of industrial growth within the mountains was much less pronounced than that which occurred within the core manufacturing regions of the Northeast and Midwest. The lingering rural lifestyles of the mountains therefore gained increasing amounts of attention from urban outsiders.

The extension of railroads through and around the Appalachians coincided with the telegraph and, later, with the more modern telephone. Recall that even a remote place like District 12 had freight and passenger train service—even if under the auspices of Capitol control. Along with these urban innovations came the proliferation of local radio stations, downtown department stores, and mail-order catalogs. For these reasons, Appalachian people were not as isolated from their surroundings to the extent one might presume. While local communities became linked into the world outside the mountains, outsiders became more enamored with Appalachian culture and wanted to experience it for themselves. This included a burgeoning interest in Appalachian folk songs and mountain string bands.

Printed media of the early 1900s extolled the virtues of mountain culture as an escape from industrial life—juxtaposed with rampant derogatory stereotypes toward mountain people. Much of the literature that idolized Appalachian rural life was aimed primarily at urban populations elsewhere. On the heels of printed materials came one industrial invention after another, including the light bulb and electricity, telegraph, telephone, phonograph, record player, radio, and even motion pictures by the early twentieth century.

This flourishing of American ingenuity occurred mostly between the 1870s and 1920s—a period often referred to as the American Renaissance. Portions of Appalachia's population may have indeed remained rural and agrarian—if not bogged down near coal mines in company towns. But the trappings of urban America were infiltrating the mountains with speedy steam trains, radio waves, telephone cables, mass marketing, books, and related printed materials. This reduction of rural isolation at the hands of urban industrialism set the stage for a new "discovery" of Appalachian folk culture. Said another way, the best-kept secrets of Appalachian folk ways were now being revealed to the outside world.

Commercializing Appalachia

It was probably inevitable at some point that entrepreneurs would discover the economic potential of traditional mountain music. After all, there was money to be made on the wholesale extraction of mountain culture. In one sense, Appalachian music traditions were just as susceptible to extraction as the coal being dug out of the ground. Around the time of Cecil Sharp's expeditions, scouts for the nascent recording industry were conducting similar field trips into the mountains. They, too, sought out new potential markets for their records. Strangely, two expanding sectors of the music industry were already in serious competition by the 1920s: those of the commercial recording industry and the expanding network of radio broadcast stations.

Not unlike the widespread appearance of cell towers and mobile phones a century later, it was the radio and its required infrastructure that transformed life of the early 1900s. Curiously, the newfangled radio was already beginning to threaten the early growth of the music recording industry. As more people acquired radios and enjoyed their wireless entertainment, the sales of music records plummeted. Commercial record companies were thus compelled to get creative and intensify their search for new consumer markets. Already by 1918 such companies were marketing what was referred to as "race" records, consisting of recordings of Black music produced at makeshift studios in Atlanta and New Orleans.[1]

On the heels of these early efforts came the industry's "discovery" of rural southern music and Appalachian string bands. These latter groups had favored small-scale entertainment venues such as local house parties and church gatherings. The relentless push to commercialize—that is, to monetize and profit from—local cultural traditions has been traced to a series of studio recordings in New York City in 1922. Quite out of place, it was within this northern metropolis where Texas fiddlers Eck Robertson and Henry Gilliland performed recordings for the Victor label. Such early recording efforts set the stage for the genesis of the commercial country music era.

One year following those initial efforts in New York, Ralph Peer made the first "field recordings" in Atlanta, Georgia—focused on none other than old-time Appalachian music.[2] These early records were sold only in regional markets at first, though they were surprisingly quite successful. Such initial encounters between northern record companies and Appalachian musicians encouraged further forays into the mountains with the aim of generating greater profits. Even at this early stage of commercialization, these northern-based companies were already picking and choosing the qualities they felt would best represent their version of "Southern" or "Appalachian" music.

In this way, whatever authenticity had existed within traditional Appalachian folk music was being compromised from the outset by non-local commercial promoters. Looking back, this process could be interpreted as the commodification of local culture ways. A complex set of mountain cultural traits was being transformed into a packaged commodity to be bought and sold.

It was within this context that perhaps the most famous recording "field trip" occurred. In late July 1927 producer Ralph Peer brought his own recording crew to Bristol, Tennessee—a city which literally straddles the border separating Tennessee from Virginia. One of his goals was to capture the songs of mountain musician Ernest Stoneman, who had already demonstrated his ability to earn money from performing "The Sinking of the Titanic" and related traditional songs.[3] And quite wisely, Peer also advertised his visit in local newspapers, hoping to attract other promising acts into his makeshift recording studio. In terms of volume itself, the results were impressive. The music of nineteen different mountain groups or performers was thereby "preserved" through a total of 76 recordings. It so happened that at least two of those acts would ultimately make music history.

The Carter Family and "Keep on the Sunny Side"

One of Peer's advertisements managed to reach the Carter Family, consisting at that time of the husband-and-wife team of Alvin Pleasant Carter (known as A.P.), Sara Carter, and his sister-in-law, Maybelle Carter. Theirs was an authentic Appalachian family, hailing from Maces Spring in southwestern Virginia—District 12 territory. They were further dedicated to collecting and performing traditional ballads and other folk songs. The *Encyclopædia Britannica* lauds the singing group as "a leading force in the spread and popularization" of Appalachian mountain songs. With Maybelle's distinguished guitar playing, the group had gained a local reputation performing at house parties and church events, not unlike the Covey and countless other real-world groups of the day. The Carters would eventually include some 300 songs within their extensive catalog, one of the most far-reaching and significant repertoires of mountain music then in existence.[4]

Similar to Cecil Sharp, A.P. Carter was an avid collector of aural traditions. He would spend days on end traveling and collecting songs handed down through generations of mountain families. He drew on a wide range of existing musical traditions already embedded within rural mountain culture, including fragments of original British ballads, Victorian "parlor songs," African American material, gospel music, and nineteenth-century pop tunes.[5]

The Carters further demonstrated a fondness for the blues, a style of music with clear African American origins. Their regular performance of songs like "Worried Man Blues" and "Bear Creek Blues" showcased the significant contribution of Black music to their sizable repertoire. It is no surprise that A.P. Carter was sometimes accompanied on his "song-hunting expeditions" by a Black musician named Lesley Riddles, thereby forging yet another multi-racial connection. Ultimately the Carter Family's collection of mountain songs emerged from a substantial "reservoir" of music that was already well known to rural southerners.[6]

While the Carters had already been performing at small-scale venues on local circuits, their recordings with Ralph Peer quickly propelled them into the national spotlight. After 1927 the varied songs of the Carter Family collection became household melodies both within and beyond the mountains. Their earlier popular standards included the likes of "Wildwood Flower" and "Keep on the Sunny Side" in 1928, joined in 1932 with "Wabash Cannonball" and "Will the Circle Be Unbroken." These became four of their most famous numbers.

The rather catchy and uplifting "Keep on the Sunny Side" is of course featured within Collins' prequel, and sung enthusiastically by the Covey's own Maude Ivory. The song serves as one of her crowd-pleasing, sing-along tunes that is juxtaposed with the drama of murder and deceit taking place in the garage nearby. For its part, "Keep on the Sunny Side" was adopted nearly word-for-word for Collins' prequel. The song was written in 1899 by Ada Blenkhorn as a gospel hymn, apparently inspired by her disabled nephew who always wanted his wheelchair pushed down "the sunny side" of the street. The song became a national hit after the Carter Family's first recording in 1928.

The Carters and country music star Johnny Cash featured the song in various albums and performances for decades thereafter, and the upbeat tune became a sort-of family theme song. Of course, Johnny Cash entered the picture while developing a relationship with June Carter—the daughter of Maybelle and Ezra Carter. The entire Carter Family had already been performing with Johnny Cash for some time prior to their eventual marriage in 1968.

Suzanne Collins may have chosen "Keep on the Sunny Side" due to its prominent role in the early history of the country music genre. As summarized by music historian Bill Malone, "Drawing on nineteenth-century pop tunes, gospel resources, African American items, and some British folk fragments, the Carter Family recorded a body of music that breathed with the essence of the rural South."[7] The Carters ultimately recorded some 300 "sides" or numbers throughout their lengthy careers, and their style and music survive today through the more contemporary sounds of country and bluegrass musicians. What better way to honor another Appalachian music tradition within the Hunger Games than to pull from the Carters' own legacy?

The musical style offered by the Carters was likewise shaped by the

American cultural exchange discussed earlier. Their music reflected a variety of Anglo-American and Black sources of inspiration, similar to that of earlier mountain string bands. Of particular note was Maybelle Carter's unique style of guitar playing, a technique referred to generally as the "Carter scratch." Essentially she would strike one string as the lead note with her thumb and brush the other strings with her index finger, also equipped with a finger pick. This became Maybelle Carter's trademark technique that guitar players would learn for generations to come. The style closely resembles black banjo playing, and it is very likely that she learned it from black musicians. Historians have documented that Maybelle's guitar style had been influenced by Leslie Riddles, who had also accompanied A.P. on his field trips.[8]

It turns out that the influence of black musical sources on the Carters was even more profound. Religious music, such as gospel songs and spirituals, comprised some 40 percent of the Carters' full repertoire. In turn, half of those songs originated from the music of black artists. Songs such as "Little Moses" and "When the World's on Fire" were either taken directly from black musicians or learned from their recordings. A number of blues songs rounded out their varied repertoire.[9]

Jimmie Rodgers, the Singing Brakeman

A second act from Ralph Peer's Bristol recording sessions led to a similar outcome. Singer Jimmie Rodgers hailed originally from Meridian, Mississippi, after which he relocated to the mountain town of Asheville, North Carolina, to find relief from tuberculosis.[10] His broad repertoire of songs represented a fusion of popular tunes, blues, and folk traditions. It was his particular talent for yodeling, however, that earned him additional fame, and the recordings at Bristol propelled his signature "blue yodel" into the national spotlight. As an ex-railroad worker from his Meridian days, he further became known for his prolific railroad songs, earning him the moniker of the "singing brakeman" as well as the "Blue Yodeler." His short but remarkable career in the early recording industry eventually led to his being dubbed the "Father of Country Music."

Both his adaptations of the blues and his yodeling could be clearly traced to black cultural influences. Yodeling had been common in African folk music as it was with European traditions, and examples of yodeling were documented among African American field hollers. The fact that Rodgers was raised in a predominantly black community explains why his later music exhibited such a marked influence.[11]

Jimmie Rodgers and The Carter Family are credited together as

America's first country music stars—both of which could be traced to Ralph Peer's Bristol recordings. For this reason, Bristol is considered by many as the birthplace of country music. Others disagree, however, given that earlier commercial recordings and talent-finding "field trips" had occurred several years earlier. The recording industry had thus already initiated its desperate attempt to avoid obsolescence at the hands of local radio stations.

Still, few doubt the historical significance of Bristol. The recordings preserved the regional music of nineteen different acts, and they managed to propel Jimmie Rodgers and the Carter Family to stardom well beyond the mountains. If commercial country music was not technically born at Bristol in 1927, it was certainly off and running.

The Valley Song

Along with "Keep on the Sunny Side," the so-called "valley song" of Collins' original trilogy is likewise derived from this first generation of country music. Readers of *The Hunger Games* become aware of the "valley song" during the cave scene, when Peeta recollects his early adoration for Katniss. He describes one day in music assembly when the teacher asked the students if anyone knew the valley song. Katniss' hand shot right up, after which she stood on a stool and sang it. According to Peeta, "every bird outside the windows fell silent" (*THG* 301).

We now know that Peeta's mention of the song served as an Easter egg, or clue about what readers would later learn within the prequel. The "valley song" of the Hunger Games series is based on an early country tune titled "Down in the Valley," though it is sometimes referred to as "Birmingham Jail." This is consequently yet another song from the early country music genre that Collins borrowed and adapted for her dystopian saga. Singing live and unaccompanied from the monkey cage in the Capitol Zoo, Lucy Gray is heard "singing sweet and clear through the night air" (*BSS* 69). The theme of the original "Down in the Valley" revolves around a rather forlorn male singer, incarcerated in a jail in Birmingham, Alabama. He beseeches whoever might be listening to "build me a mansion" so that he might see his "true love go by" on a passing train.

As rewritten for Lucy Gray's purposes, the singer's gender is flipped. She thus sings, "See him go by, love, see him go by," referring to the same passing train as that of the original song. It is a sentimental love song laced with sadness and tragic circumstance. In Lucy Gray's situation, the Birmingham Jail of the original song is replaced with the "Capitol jail" of the monkey cage. In this one song, therefore, we find the common Appalachian themes of railroad trains, love sickness, and the tragic tale of incarceration.

It further incorporates imagery of nature, with red roses, blue violets, and "birds in the heavens."

The original "Down in the Valley" is rooted in earlier folk song traditions. Like typical folk music passed down orally, the lyrics of this one have been altered many times over. Regardless of its varied wording, however, this is not one's idea of a snappy, upbeat number. That Lucy Gray "sounded so sad, so lost" while singing it within the prequel (*BSS* 70), is likely more due to the song's dreadfully slow pace and despondent theme. Lucy Gray finds herself no better than a caged animal awaiting an untimely death.

As for the historical origin of "Down in the Valley," one theory posits that the song can be traced to a prisoner in the Raleigh, North Carolina State Prison, in the form of a letter written to a girl in Alabama.[12] But there is an alternate, if similar claim that the song was written (or perhaps modified) by the early country music star and guitarist, Jimmie Tarlton. According to the song's Wikipedia entry—which unfortunately was not well referenced—Tarlton takes credit for writing the song's lyrics in 1925 as a prisoner in the Birmingham, Alabama, city jailhouse, purportedly for illegal moonshining. Such a scenario is certainly not out of the realm of possibility for that time and region.

Regardless of who actually wrote the song and in what jail, it is clear that the first popular, commercial version was recorded in 1927 by Jimmie Tarlton and his partner Tom Darby for Columbia Records. Even Tarlton and Darby occasionally swapped out various words and lines, sometimes singing "down in the levee" instead of "down in the valley." This change makes little geographic sense, but no matter. In another version by Lead Belly in the 1930s, "Birmingham jail" is replaced with "Shreveport jail." It is not too crazy to presume that singers substituted place names on a whim to elicit local sentiments of pride from the home crowd. As for Lucy Gray, her own alteration of the lyrics fits well into this common practice.

As for Jimmie Tarlton's own backstory, his upbringing in a musical household was rather common for rural families of the South, and within the Appalachians in particular. Raised in rural South Carolina, his father played a banjo and his mother was a singer. By age six, Jimmie was already playing the banjo and French harp, later taking up the guitar. He was performing in the Northeast and the Texas-Oklahoma region by his teens, and he eventually made his way to California. In 1927 he began a partnership with Tom Darby, the same year they recorded "Down in the Valley."

Of course, musicians are often networked in various ways, and Tarlton found himself collaborating at some point with country music star Jimmie Rodgers. As for "Down in the Valley," the song took on a life of its own after Tarlton and Darby made it commercially famous as a country music exemplar. While the basic lyrics and theme remained recognizable, numerous music stars have since produced their own versions and record-ings. Some standout examples include The Andrews Sisters (1944), Bing Crosby (1961), Connie Francis (1961), and Jerry Garcia and David Grisman on their more recent 1996 album, *Shady Grove*. The song has also appeared in various Hollywood films and television shows, including the film *Stir Crazy*, and the Academy Award-winning film, *Bound for Glory*, among numerous other cases.

Perhaps more amusing, the song further appeared in an episode ("Dark Page") of *Star Trek: The Next Generation*, when a projection of Deanna Troi's father sings the song. Somewhat eerily reminiscent of the *Hunger Games* trilogy, Troi mentions that as a baby she could never fall asleep without hearing the soothing tune. Perhaps it was a version of this song that somehow made it to the Capitol for Coriolanus to hear as a toddler?

One of the most common renditions of the song was made popular by the aforementioned country music star, Eddy Arnold, who enjoyed a career that spanned six decades and represented the so-called "Nashville Sound" of the late 1950s. He sold some 85 million records (wow!) and became a member of the Grand Ole Opry in 1943. His lyrics are remarkably similar to the Lucy Gray version of the "valley song."

Thus, "Down in the Valley" contributes handily to our Collins-inspired tour of first-generation country music from the early twentieth century. Beyond all this, the song appears to serve as one of numerous clues point-ing to the possible ancestry of one Katniss Everdeen, who as a child had clearly picked it up from her musically talented father. We will take up this line of conversation once again in Chapter 15.

Roses Are Red

One additional aspect of the "valley song" is worth noting here, namely its reference to the popular "Roses are Red" poem. Many of us likely recall some version of *Roses are red, violets are blue, honey is sweet and so are you*. In one of numerous childhood memories described within the pre-quel, Coriolanus does not remember the "valley song" itself, though he does recognize the words, "roses are red" and "violets are blue." He further recalls that the song of his childhood had included the phrase "loving him" (*BSS* 70). Within the last verse of her own version, Lucy Gray sings, "Roses are red, love; violets are blue." In comparison, Eddy Arnold's version main-tains the same theme, even with differing words: "Roses love sunshine, vio-lets love dew."

As for Coriolanus' reaction to Lucy Gray's "valley song," the prequel's narrator describes him as "transfixed by the music and the rush of memories that accompanied it." This association nudges him to contemplate the photo in the silver frame, which serves as a memento of his own mother and how she held him at about the age of two. The song further conjures his memory of the rose-scented powder that his mother had worn. This suggests the origin of his later obsession with roses and their symbolic connection to the days of his mother and home. Somehow Suzanne Collins successfully managed to build the "rose theme" into her saga through the incorporation of numerous elements within the story line: the "valley song," his mother's rose powder, his Grandma'am's rose garden, the traditional "Roses are Red" poem, and President Snow's attempts to torment Katniss with his own white roses. In all these ways, the symbolism of the rose is woven creatively throughout the saga, and it follows Coriolanus throughout his life—quite literally from birth to death.

Hillbilly Music

Before the term "country" became the accepted standard for the emerging genre, it had instead been widely referred to as "hillbilly music." Looking back, it is not a stretch to imagine that such a label might eventually ruffle some feathers, so to speak. The term was first used in 1925 to describe the commercially recorded music of the rural South, including that performed by Jimmie Rodgers and the Carter Family. The moment this descriptor emerged can be traced precisely to one of Ralph Peer's recording sessions, in this case with Al Hopkins' band. After recording several of the band's numbers, Peer suggested they decide on a name. Hopkins responded, "Call the band anything you want. We are nothing but a bunch of hillbillies from North Carolina and Virginia anyway."[13] Since they did not provide their own identity, Peer created one for them. From that point on the group was referred to as, well, The Hill Billies. With that decision, a pervasive and unrelenting national stereotype would be perpetuated by the recording industry.

For their part, The Hill Billies were a rousing success, with impressive record sales and tours around the vaudeville circuit. However, the group unwittingly promoted the hillbilly stereotype with their overalls and ragged hats, along with their performances of old-time music for urban audiences. From that point onward, such "old-time" mountain music became known as hillbilly music.[14] Although recording companies did not outwardly promote the "hillbilly" term, it became widely used at the grassroots level among "musicians, fans, critics, and detractors."[15]

As for Appalachian musicians of the time, they were often pressured by representatives of the radio and recording industries to conform to prescribed, mythical ideals. Southern musicians were directed to "keep it country," which included a preferred repertoire of old-time tunes and country-type clothing outfits. For decades into the present day, Appalachian musicians have thus played a role in promoting mountain stereotypes largely constructed by outsiders.[16]

On the other hand, hillbilly bands and musicians often took advantage of the romanticized mystique associated with the Appalachians. They consequently named their bands to reflect the imagery of local mountain places. Just a few of the well-known groups included Ernest Stoneman's Dixie Mountaineers, Mainer's Mountaineers, Cumberland Mountain Folk, Blue Ridge Entertainers, and the Clinch Mountain Clan. Though some of their songs were definitely written locally, much of the emerging hillbilly music was originating from outside the Appalachians.[17]

As for the growing music industry, its persistent marketing and advertising perpetuated an array of hillbilly stereotypes, the origins of which are described in more detail below. A false racial distinction was also unfolding. The records of white musicians were being marketed to white audiences, while those of the black community were marketed primarily to black audiences. This practice of racial separation obscured the more complex, intercultural mixing that had contributed to the development of old-time mountain music.[18]

The Hillbilly Stereotype

The term "hillbilly" was not always derogatory. It is likely the term emerged from the British roots of Appalachian culture, itself derived from the word "billy," which was British slang that meant "fellow" or "comrade." Quite logically, then, a hillbilly was a fellow from the hills.[19] Further, the term was not used exclusively to describe Appalachian residents. The first documented use of the term in print has been traced to 1900 in the *New York Journal*. For whatever reason, the writer described a "Hill-Billie" as a "free and untrammeled white citizen who lives in the hills ... has no means to speak of, dresses as he can, talks as he pleases, drinks whiskey when he gets it, and fires off his revolver as the fancy takes him."[20]

The term appeared again in 1902 within a travel narrative about the Ozark Mountains. Geologically speaking, the folded mountains of the Ozarks are an ancient extension of the Appalachian chain. In this case, the writer chided the Arkansas mountain residents for their dilapidated and unreliable railroad network. This was followed one year later with an entire book of jokes about the hapless Ozark railways, which ended up being a best-seller for the time. This very book was responsible for accelerating the hillbilly stereotype and the negative connotations associated with it, thereby promoting the myth of the "laziness and ineptitude of hillbillies."[21] It was the likes of this and future publications that legitimized the hillbilly stereotype as derogatory in the minds of an urban readership.

Two of the most popular and stereotypical images of Appalachian people, according to Rebecca Scott, are those of the hillbilly and the coal miner.[22] The national mindset since the late nineteenth century has viewed Appalachia as the American region left behind by modernity. Until recently Appalachian people have also been promoted as distinctively "Anglo-Saxon stock" within the comforting myth of a purely Anglo-Celtic region that time forgot. The hillbilly image ascribed to Appalachia's poorer white residents has thus endured despite persistent work to combat these negative stereotypes.

On the flip side, contrasting positive imagery has placed Appalachia on a sort-of mythical pedestal. There is an equally long tradition of "glorifying Appalachia as a bucolic landscape and white Appalachians as ideal rural citizens."[23] Thus the people of Appalachia have found themselves on the receiving end of either condescending disdain or romanticized idolatry. Either way, both extremes have led Americans to view Appalachia as "a place apart" or as a "persistent frontier in the nation's heartland."[24] It was this dichotomy of stereotypes through which Suzanne Collins presumably needed to tiptoe rather carefully.

The Grand Ole Opry

One way the industry promoted hillbilly music and its up-and-coming stars was through a new form of entertainment called the *radio barn dance*. These scripted events consisted of live hillbilly music performances broadcast by radio stations located primarily outside of Appalachia. These music radio shows became widely popular, especially in the Midwest and South. In one respect these "barn dances" brought joy to large audiences seeking a new form of entertainment. Unfortunately the practice further promoted a simplified, one-dimensional view of Appalachian music and culture, which "resulted in the firm entrenchment of the hillbilly image as an intractable stereotype."[25] Regardless, this is all part of the history of how the country music genre developed, and how it was promoted to an eager listening audience at the time.

The first notable barn dance can be dated to its premier broadcast from the Hotel Sherman in Chicago on April 19, 1924. Dubbed the *National Barn Dance*, the show was produced by WLS, a Chicago radio station which we might note was owned by the Sears-Roebuck Company. Reflecting the swagger of its corporate owner, the WLS call letters stood for "World's Largest Store."

The WLS show featured a variety of musical styles, including popular music of the time, rural folk music, and the first inklings of "hillbilly" music that would eventually be rebranded as "country." Perhaps as a marker of simpler times, the Barn Dance's director, George C. Biggar, recalled later that WLS had broadcast the show for nearly two years with no advertisers. In one sense the show served as a built-in advertisement for its corporate owner; after all, WLS was promoted unapologetically as the "Sears-Roebuck Station."[26]

Although profitable with numerous advertising clients by 1928, Sears sold the WLS station to *Prairie Farmer* magazine, whose management had promised to maintain the station's rural orientation. Eventually the National Barn Dance show moved to the Eighth Street Theater on South Wabash, which served as the show's home until 1957. Over the course of this lengthy period at Eighth Street, some three million people had paid admission.[27] The WLS show compiled its own impressive history until its final broadcast on April 30, 1960, though its own influence was felt far afield from its own home stage. In yet another clear case of imitation diffusion, the show inspired numerous spin-off programs which, in certain cases, realized even greater fame on their own.

One such spinoff was launched by George Hay, a former Chicago Barn Dance announcer and pioneering disc jockey. In 1925 he transferred from the Sears station to WSM Radio in Nashville to launch a similar show, simply dubbed the Barn Dance. Hay had already recognized the popularity of "old-time" music and brought the idea with him to Nashville.[28] He particularly believed that a mix of fiddle music and vocal numbers would assure his new home radio station a hit show.[29] Producers at WSM had also noted the success of the Chicago program and wanted to broadcast their own version to audiences outside the range of the Chicago radio signal.[30]

The new show was eventually renamed the Grand Ole Opry. Both the Nashville and Chicago programs aired for more than four straight hours every Saturday night and featured a variety of local folk music acts, fiddling, comedians, and up-and-coming hillbilly music performers. As many Americans might recall, the Grand Ole Opry took on a life and a level of fame all its own. The program quickly evolved from a regional radio broadcast featuring local amateur musicians to a live stage show featuring a mixture of professional acts and comedians.

Producers of these barn dance shows—including those of the Grand Ole Opry—further recognized America's growing sense of nostalgia for a pre-industrial past. They consequently learned to capitalize on this

American yearning for simpler times. For his part, George Hay fought tirelessly at the Opry to preserve the "informal, down-home atmosphere" of the shows and often admonished performers to keep their acts "down to earth."[31] He famously managed to keep drum sets off the stage until the 1940s. If string bands appeared without names, Hay promptly made up his own names that alluded to a rustic image, such as the Clod Hoppers and Fruit Jar Drinkers.[32] He and his colleagues thus consciously shaped the public presentation of these acts beyond their authentic identities.

Likewise, if music groups arrived with rather unappealing names, Hay and his associates simply changed them. For instance, "Dr. Humphrey Bate and His Augmented Orchestra" was instantly rebranded as "Dr. Bate's Possum Hunters." They often took group publicity photos placed strategically in cornfields or on the side of barns.[33] This practice mirrored Ralph Peer's efforts in the 1920s to rebrand various acts for his recordings. Neither George Hay nor John Lair—who ran the Opry at the time—claimed to ever have used the term "hillbilly," considering it derogatory. However, their concerted efforts to promote a distinct and exaggerated image of rural, country life helped to legitimize the hillbilly stereotype, along with an "imagined if humorous rustic conception of mountain folk and country musicians."[34]

For his part, John Lair played numerous positive roles in the country music industry, including the founding of Ohio's own Renfro Valley Barn Dance in 1937. On the flip side, he was also known for crass commercialism, showing little concern about blatantly misrepresenting old-time music, history, and culture.[35] For instance, Lair was responsible for naming banjo picker Lily May Ledford's old-time band the Coon Creek Girls. Although Ledford protested that this fictitious name had nothing to do with her home, Lair shrugged and claimed that the "audience out in radio land won't know the difference."[36]

Lair's efforts to construct an exaggerated image of rural life included his launch of the Ridge Runners as the first nationally known hillbilly band. His publicity photographs and comic sketches heavily promoted the hillbilly image that helped make the Ridge Runners famous. He further had banjo player and singer Linda Parker wear a frilly gingham dress onstage while playing the role of "sunbonnet girl," and he created other characters and imagery that arguably paved the way for the *L'il Abner* comic strip and for the hit TV show *The Beverly Hillbillies.*

Early hillbilly musicians relied primarily on old-time mountain folk music or gospel songs to build their repertoires. Prime exemplars of this early trend included Jimmie Rodgers and the Carter Family.[37] Perhaps one paradox of this early phase of country music was that the vast majority of people involved at that time were young, white Protestants, and most musicians were young men. This was in stark contrast to the multicultural origins of the music they were performing.

One important reason for this demographic trend is found in the tremendous out-migration from the region during the mid-twentieth century. The majority of listeners and musicians alike were in the process of relocating from impoverished Appalachian farms and rural towns to find industrial work in nearby cities. These migrants naturally remained in contact with old neighbors or family members back home.

Even in these expanding urban communities, it was rare to acquire a radio or a phonograph to listen to familiar music from home until the 1930s. If families wanted to participate socially in music, they had to sing it or play it themselves.[38] Thus, as the first commercial hillbilly musicians performed renditions of traditional music, they naturally found enthusiastic audiences within these urban immigrant communities feeling nostalgic for home. Some of the migrants to the Piedmont region even became professional hillbilly musicians themselves.

Hillbilly Bands and Instrumentation

The so-called hillbilly bands of this era were always composed of string instruments, though the instrumentation could vary widely. Many adopted the tradition of earlier mountain string bands, often including the fiddle, five-string banjo, and guitar. These three common instruments had already become the favorites of the urban middle class, prior to the advent of the hillbilly music craze.[39] Sometimes a mandolin would appear as well, though this Italian-born instrument had not yet been elevated to a lead role.

As for their vocal components, it was common to find brothers or cousins singing in the same band. Many of them had grown up with the same folk songs passed down through their families. One common form was known as the "brother duet," sung by two men, often kin. Religious quartets were likewise popular, and some of the more influential gospel singers could be either black or white.[40] The performance style of hillbilly groups usually involved themed costumes with matching outfits—perhaps not unlike that of the Covey, with bird feathers in their hats and all. The choice of dress reflected the image the band was trying to portray. Common examples were cowboy duds, farm clothes and hats or even expensive suits and ties typically worn by bankers.

The term "hillbilly music" remained in widespread if diminishing use into the 1940s. Billboard renamed its "hillbilly" category "folk songs and blues" in 1944, and by 1949 it eventually settled on the more favorable terms of "country" or "country and western." Western music had been developing in parallel fashion to the eastern hillbilly variety. This trend ultimately encouraged the industry to combine the terms "country" and "western" to describe the growing national craze.

Folk Music and Finnick's Wedding

If early hillbilly music had technology and commercial investment driving its success, the proponents of mountain folk music relied heavily on annual folk festivals to promote mutual kinship and enthusiasm.[41] These festivals played two simultaneous roles during these early decades. They helped to preserve and celebrate the tradition of old-time mountain music, while they secondarily promoted local economic growth. The business-oriented Chambers of Commerce within these communities often helped sponsor or promote these events.

The first folk festival of note was organized in 1928 by Bascom Lamar Lunsford in Asheville, North Carolina. The folk music component was one of several attractions found at Asheville's Rhododendron Festival. Lunsford's personal effort to preserve old ballads, instrumental numbers, and dances eventually carried over to festivals held elsewhere. And their organizers, audiences, and musicians often became downright combative against the intrusion of popular hillbilly music.[42] One of the most enduring legacies of Lunsford's festivals was group clogging, which reflected a diverse, multicultural blend of music and dance. Clogging essentially fused the traditions of folk music, stage and minstrel shows, and even Native American dance practices.

Returning to the world of *The Hunger Games*, one might interpret Finnick and Annie's wedding in *Mockingjay* as representing the type of folk music and dancing that were featured at such festivals. The local traditions of District 12—which carried over briefly to District 13—emulated Appalachian folk customs of dancing and fiddle tunes such as jigs and reels. Katniss even proudly teaches her footwork to her District 13 counterparts who had never witnessed such customs. The style of dancing might have even approximated the traditions of Appalachian clogging or flatfoot dancing which, as Tina Hanlon explains, "mountain people of all ages continue to enjoy in formal and informal settings."[43] These timeless customs stand in stark contrast to commercial country music and its rebranded images of Appalachian culture.

In hindsight, the efforts to collect and preserve old-world ballads and Appalachian folk songs was a mixed blessing. On the one hand, Cecil Sharp and his contemporaries contributed grandly to the literature and cumulative knowledge of local customs and folk ways. On the other hand, such efforts led to growing romanticism for "all things Appalachia" that tends to occur when places are "discovered" by outsiders. In the century that followed Cecil Sharp's own research, historians have documented no less than four distinct folk music revivals: those of the 1930s, the 1940s, the late 1950s and 60s aligned with the popularity of bluegrass music, and much more recently in the late 1990s and early 2000s.

According to Ted Olson and Kalra Ajay, Appalachian musicians have been portrayed generally as reflecting one of two possible extremes: the first as the exalted "folk" musician viewed as the keeper of a disappearing way of life, and the second as an unrefined "hillbilly" musician still living a backward lifestyle.[44] For her part, Suzanne Collins may have sought a middle ground with her own portrayal of Appalachian customs in District 12. She clearly borrows from the full array of central Appalachian music styles that have contributed to the region's identity since colonial times. Perhaps hers is a more accurate, blended portrayal of authentic Appalachian culture than either of these two extremes.

Stereotyping District 12

Collins appears to call attention to hillbilly stereotypes by placing them front and center within her world of Panem. The Capitol's perception of District people can be closely approximated to America's persistent view of mountain hillbillies. Until roughly the Civil War, the Appalachian way of life and rural economy were quite similar to that of the rest of America. The majority of Americans did not yet live in cities, and the pre-industrial economy was focused on small-farm agriculture—essentially producing for local, small-town markets. This lifestyle largely described agrarian communities both within and beyond the mountains. As the Industrial Revolution encouraged urban development and employment in the factories after the 1870s, farm employment continuously dropped, and the distinction between "modern" urban America and rural Appalachia became more pronounced.

For its part, the Appalachian economy held its own throughout the early twentieth century. The region persisted largely on a self-sufficient agricultural system and numerous small-scale industries. This is the type of subsistence lifestyle that Katniss and Gale—and the Covey—were desperately attempting to achieve under the watchful eyes of the Capitol. Lucy Gray and her Covey counterparts looked forward to "raising a herd," for instance, and both Maude Ivory and Primrose Everdeen managed their own goats—albeit with some helpful assistance. Further, their combined hunting and gathering activities reflected a yearning to escape oppression and move toward self-sufficiency. Katniss and Gale learned how to sell their small surpluses to the local black market known as the Hob as well as throughout the community at large. This is precisely how small-town, agrarian communities traded goods and services—but legally. Had the oppressive hand of the Capitol allowed such activities to persist and thrive in places like District 12, there is no doubt that Katniss, Gale, Lucy Gray and their respective families would have been well on their way to a lifestyle familiar to real Appalachian communities.

Unfortunately these positive, local economic activities have been interpreted by many outside the region as backward and stuck in the past. Such small-scale family farms are also commonly perceived as synonymous with rural poverty, daily misery, and economic stagnation. As Rebecca Scott poignantly explains, "Well water, outhouses, homespun cloth, newspaper-covered cabin walls, and other 'old-timey' artifacts of Appalachian material culture bear the stigma" of a rural America behind the times.[45] Such perceptions signal an ongoing urban-rural divide. Such misunderstanding was adroitly demonstrated by a misinformed Coriolanus Snow within the prequel.

The observations of social reformer Ellen Churchill Semple in 1901 exemplify this misunderstanding—and condescension—of rural mountain life. Of the people she encountered there, Semple observed that their "manners are gentle, gracious, and unembarrassed, so that in talking with them, one forgets their bare feet, ragged clothes, and crass ignorance, and in his heart bows anew to the inextinguishable excellence of the Anglo-Saxon race."[46] As we interpret her writing a century later, she was perceiving Appalachian residents as a distinct form of "Other," while oversimplifying their ethnic identity.

Semple further implied that the Appalachians could not afford sugar. She noted that they relied on more natural, "backwoods substitutes" including honey, sugar maple, and sorghum molasses. While an accurate observation, she and her contemporaries naturally presumed that sugar would be preferred due to its status as the accepted global commodity. More accurately, however, such natural "non-market" products as honey and maple syrup were the original sweeteners of the temperate zones, and they had played a significant role in mountain food ways for generations.[47]

Within her District 12, Suzanne Collins emulates local, non-market economic activities that relied on similar natural forest products. Katniss, Gale, and their families took advantage of gathering natural sweeteners. Such knowledge of local resources even led to Katniss' life-saving use of the spile during the 75th Games. With one paragraph in *Catching Fire*, Collins integrates traditional Appalachian lifestyles with the vital teachings of

Katniss' father. As Katniss attempts to identify the strange object sent into the arena by Haymitch, she explains that she has indeed seen one of these in the past. She recollects a cold, windy day when she was accompanying her father in the woods. He had driven a similar object into the side of a maple tree, allowing its sap to flow into a bucket below. Her father apparently had accumulated a handful of such spiles, though she did not know what happened to them (*CF* 294). Had her father not at least shown her this local skill, Haymitch's hard-fought effort to send a spile into the arena may have been for naught.

Collins continues her educational tour of Appalachian culture throughout the prequel. Not unlike Semple's own viewpoint from the early twentieth century, residents of the Capitol perceive the District 12 Appalachian people as a rural, backwoods "Other." Coriolanus and his peers reveal their elitist disgust for these uncivilized mountain people, mirroring Effie Trinket and her Capitol counterparts within the original series. Like Semple, Coriolanus expresses surprise at the unexpected upscale decency and manners demonstrated by the Covey, as this behavior did not fit his conception of District 12 norms. He considered it "funny" how such "society talk" came so naturally to the members of the Covey (*BSS* 420). It would not be out of line to view this comment as one of Collins' Easter eggs that points to a future novel. Such "society talk" could ultimately hold a backstory of its own that has yet to be revealed.

Similarly, Coriolanus makes an admirable effort to convince the Capitol viewership that Lucy Gray is not really "District." By highlighting her good-mannered Capitol behaviors, Coriolanus hopes to win Lucy Gray more sponsors. This strategy is therefore reliant on disassociating her from the rampant stereotypes aimed toward the outlying districts.

Likewise, Collins makes it painfully clear how Capitol residents perceive district people. For his part, Coriolanus attempts to rationalize Lucy Gray's social status based on his own Capitol worldview. That is, he considers Lucy Gray to be "his tribute," and still a second-class citizen not of the Capitol. She is human, he admits, "but bestial" and certainly "not evolved." She is one of a "shapeless mass of unfortunate, barbaric creatures" that hovers on the periphery of Coriolanus' consciousness (*BSS* 194).

This passage is further noteworthy because of Collins' skillful play on words. Just as these "barbaric creatures" hover on the "periphery" of Coriolanus' own consciousness, so too did the "Barbarian" tribal peoples exist on the outer periphery of the Roman Empire or—in this case—the Capitol.

Essentially all district residents suffered from a self-reinforcing pattern of marginalization at the hands of the urbanized Capitol: first from the direct oppression forced upon them by the authoritarian control over resources; and second by sentiments of disgust and condescension directed toward these disadvantaged people. Never mind that it was the Capitol's very same draconian policies that kept them impoverished in the first place.

The Beverly Hillbillies

Some readers might recall one of the more controversial if beloved television shows riddled with Appalachian stereotypes, *The Beverly Hillbillies*. Like Collins, who successfully weaves both positive and negative stereotypes throughout her stories, the show's portrayal of rural Appalachians were not always derogatory. The show itself ran for nearly a decade, from 1962 to 1971 and has been available as "re-runs" through syndication for many years since.

The family featured on the show was that of the Clampetts, branded as hillbillies and led by their affable father, Jed Clampett. The show's catchy theme song, "The Ballad of Jed Clampett," explains the story of the family, thereby linking the Anglo-Celtic ballad tradition with hillbilly imagery. The ballad basically explains that Jed is an impoverished mountaineer struggling to keep his family fed. He accidentally strikes oil and becomes instantly wealthy. Now suddenly out of place in their mountain home, the family is encouraged to relocate to the more prosperous California, which—for the Clampetts—means none other than Beverly Hills. [48]

As Rebecca Scott explains, *The Beverly Hillbillies* projected a presumed backwardness of the family and their mountain home through their stereotypical speech, clothing, and even their vehicle—none of which was changed after they moved west. Jed wore a rope for his belt, and Granny dressed in nineteenth-century garb. However, Rebecca Scott claims that very few negative stereotypes are on display throughout the show. Rather, the family actually brings a touch of "native dignity" to the otherwise snobbish Beverly Hills lifestyle (perhaps also a stereotype). They are "kind-hearted, generous, and good-natured," and they "stand for what is best about rural (albeit white) America."[49]

Others paint the TV show in a more negative light. Ted Olson and Karla Ajay contend that the overall influence of stereotypical shows including *Hee Haw* and *The Beverly Hillbillies* has been a demeaning one.[50] Similarly, in speaking of the widely popular cartoon *L'il Abner* along with *The Beverly Hillbillies*, biographer Eugene Chadbourne believes that neither of these productions helped improve the perception of Appalachia to outsiders.[51] Perhaps the important point to make is that stereotyping can be positive or negative, though both situations risk oversimplifying a complex set of cultural traits. It is this type of reductive, binary thinking that Collins practically urges us to reconsider while moving through her novels.

The issue of exploiting Appalachian culture for the entertainment of television audiences resurfaced around 2003. The CBS television network had been planning a new reality TV show called *The Real Beverly Hillbillies*, at least until the United Mine Workers and other advocacy groups got wind of it. These organizations unified in protest against the show's intention to place a real Appalachian family in a Hollywood mansion.[52] The network ultimately dropped its plans for the show. Not to be outdone, however, CBS turned to the Amish for a similar reality show because, in the words of a CBS chairman, "they don't have quite as good a lobbying effort."[53] Is it any wonder that, only five years later, Suzanne Collins would release her first Hunger Games novel centered around an exaggerated reality TV show, focused on the wholesale commodification of rural populations for the enjoyment of the Capitol? From her perspective during the early twenty-first century, she did not have to venture far to find inspiration for her dystopian tale.

12

Bluegrass and the Covey

For music enthusiasts it was an unexpected treat to be introduced to the Covey in the prequel. Though readers encounter Lucy Gray and some of her repertoire earlier in the story, it is in the novel's third part where Collins goes "full Covey." Readers are thereby offered a front-row seat to one of Appalachia's most enduring cultural legacies. It turns out that the Covey constitutes District 12's very own bluegrass band. Just as some 200 peacekeepers and local residents enjoyed a raucous Saturday night concert at the Hob, readers probably also appreciated a breather from the otherwise disturbing Hunger Games tale to unwind and get our toes tapping. Even Coriolanus could not resist the jovial atmosphere as the Covey took the stage. He not only found his own hands joining in, but then also noticed his heel tapping to the beat with the start of the Covey's first number. Imagine—the future President Snow at a Hob concert!

True to her style, Collins never directly mentions the Covey's musical genre, though she does provide a litany of clues and descriptions to lead us in the correct direction. As we saw in prior chapters, Collins included a sampling of songs that had gained national acclaim prior to World War II and generally represented the early country (or hillbilly) genre. She further integrates the tradition of Anglo-Celtic ballads that became rooted in central Appalachia during colonial times. What we find in the Covey, however, is the epitome of an early bluegrass ensemble from the 1940s. For those not majoring in music history, it is important to make the distinction between genuine bluegrass and its "cousin" known more broadly as country music. While they do exhibit some similar characteristics, bluegrass is defined by its own distinctive style. Some music historians treat bluegrass as a sub-genre under the country music umbrella. Either way, the distinctive characteristics of bluegrass music are the subjects of this chapter. For its part, the Covey band provides a virtual clinic on bluegrass instrumentation and vocal styling.

Bluegrass Instrumentation

Bluegrass music was an outgrowth of earlier country music and the Appalachian string band. With geographical roots that are both Southern and rural, bluegrass is first distinguished through its rather standard instrumental blend. The core of a typical bluegrass band usually features a handful of distinct yet complimentary "acoustic" stringed instruments— that is, those whose sounds are not enhanced or modified with electronic amplification. For this reason, an electric guitar would not qualify for the "traditional bluegrass" genre.

Five acoustic instruments are most typically associated with bluegrass bands, namely the mandolin, guitar, fiddle, five-string banjo, and upright bass.[1] Aside from occasional variations, this mix constitutes a standard bluegrass ensemble. That said, such groups can include from four to seven musicians, with a core of instrumentation that most often features the acoustic guitar, upright bass, and banjo. Even these instruments are not mandatory, however, given that the fiddle, mandolin, and resonator guitar (dobro) are common as well.[2]

The Covey fits precisely within this range of bluegrass standards, as we quickly learn when Maude Ivory introduces its membership. Namely, Tam Amber arrives on stage first with his A-style (tear-drop shaped) mandolin, followed sequentially by Clerk Carmine on fiddle, Barb Azure on base, and none other than Lucy Gray Baird with her guitar. We don't know if Maude Ivory plays an instrument other than a simple drum at this point, as she seems to focus on vocal performance at her young age. We know that Lucy Gray planned to leave her guitar to Maude Ivory prior to running away with Coriolanus. Beyond this description of the Covey, there is no indication of additional current instruments, whether percussion, brass, or the use of amplification. It follows that theirs is a pretty standard bluegrass ensemble.

The exclusive use of acoustic string instruments in bluegrass music is likely due to an accident of geography more than anything else. Historian Neil Rosenberg points out that many of the early bluegrass musicians— living in the poorer rural communities of Appalachia or elsewhere—had grown up without electricity.[3] Their playing of acoustic instruments came out of a necessity more than choice. This fact, along with the cultural proclivity for traditional folk instruments including the fiddle, mandolin, guitar, and banjo, likely encouraged Appalachian residents to favor one of these instruments over others.

District 12 provided similar conditions with respect to its unreliable electricity—an ongoing situation throughout all four Hunger Games novels. Within the prequel we are treated to a rather humorous if telling description by Coriolanus as he scans the makeshift Covey performance stage for the first time. As he stakes out his own obscure seat near the back of the Hob, his attention shifts to the stage. Someone then flips a switch to turn on a "hodgepodge of lights strung together by an ancient cable and several suspicious-looking extension cords" (*BSS* 360). In response, Coriolanus naturally—and humorously—scans the room for the nearest fire exit in a clear reference to his own urban upbringing. Nobody else there seems to blink an eye, as they live with such conditions every day.

Beyond the minimalist electrical power necessary for the standing mic and lights, the Hob's rudimentary outfit would not likely support more powerful amplifiers. It stands to reason that the Covey members were likewise raised in similar conditions without much electricity before "taking a wrong turn" and settling in District 12. They had consequently learned their musical skills and chosen their instruments much as Appalachian people had done—handed down and taught through direct contact with family members.

This is not to say that this particular mix of acoustic instrumentation—part of the bluegrass "recipe"—could not vary from one group to another. Slight deviations could occur given the unique makeup and skills of a particular group, while still maintaining the standard bluegrass approach. For instance, one could on occasion find a Jew's harp, harmonica (mouth harp), or resonator guitar (sometimes referred to as a *dobro*) contributing to a bluegrass band. In more contemporary groups, one might find twin fiddles or twin banjos, and sometimes upwards of six to ten musicians. Ricky Skaggs and his Kentucky Thunder come to mind as one contemporary case in point.[4] It is also not uncommon for band members to demonstrate proficiency on more than one instrument. Musicians could trade off from one instrument to another as necessitated by a particular song, or number.

Such instrumental variety is found within the Covey as well. This is perhaps expected, as various tragedies and life circumstances have forced its membership to change through time. What is emphatically not represented on the Covey's stage, however, is the banjo, which continues to perplex some readers, including this one. Why Collins would not include perhaps the most standard of bluegrass instruments remains a mystery. Still, her choice is not unreasonable for a traditional bluegrass band of the World War II era, as we will discuss further below. Collins may simply be recognizing the diversity from one bluegrass group to another, especially in rather isolated, rural mountain areas such as District 12. Perhaps the Covey somehow lost its former banjo player to tragic or other circumstances and no one has picked up the slack. Still other fans and observers have considered the possibility that Collins is shying away from the banjo's complicated racial past, though it is admittedly difficult to imagine Collins shying away from anything.

Aside from all this speculation, the most logical explanation for omitting the banjo likely involves historical precedent. Just as Collins pulls from a veritable "highlights reel" of Appalachian music history, she is likely doing the same with respect to bluegrass music. As my own breadcrumb for now, we will explore later how the Covey's instrumentation precisely matches that of America's founding bluegrass band, that of Bill Monroe and the Blue Grass Boys. Monroe's original ensemble utilized the same instrumentation as the Covey for approximately three years, from 1939 to 1942, while the bluegrass sub-genre continued to develop into its own distinctive sound. I will thus make a rather lengthy case in Chapter 13 that Collins most likely decided to reflect this very legacy of Bill Monroe—the "Father of bluegrass music."

The Curious Role of Billy Taupe

Banjo or not, Collins drops clues regarding another instrument that once performed with the Covey. Specifically, the case of Billy Taupe—Clerk Carmine's trouble-prone brother—provides an excellent example of how bluegrass band membership can be fluid, adjusting out of necessity as new circumstances present themselves. Not only is Billy Taupe's name representative of the Covey lexicon—his first name for a ballad, second for a color— but he also seems to walk around randomly carrying his instrument. At the end of their Hob performance, it is a somewhat inebriated Billy Taupe who approaches the stage to confront Lucy Gray and all of the Covey. As the narrator states, "Over one shoulder hung a boxy instrument with part of a piano keyboard along one side" (*BSS* 368).

Later in the story, the bulky instrument appears once again after Coriolanus and the Peacekeepers take Mayfair home. As Coriolanus departs with his peers to return to base, he is distracted by the sound of a "soft, mechanical wheeze." A light from the house reveals Billy holding his instrument, "the source of the wheeze, against his chest" (*BSS* 373). Given these descriptions, Billy's instrument is most certainly the accordion. And part of him already misses not playing with his Covey counterparts. The fact that Billy is sighted carrying the bulky, wheezing instrument around with him—those things are not lightweight by any means—indicates his strong identity with both his instrument and with the Covey in general.

While confronting the Covey at the end of their concert, Billy Taupe vainly suggests that the group won't be the same without him. As a true musician might argue, he claims, "You're all sounding thin. You're sounding thin," as one hand slaps his instrument (*BSS* 369). Like traditional bluegrass groups, the Covey's instrumentation and membership can change and adapt as necessary. Perhaps in this way Collins has provided us with a more realistic scenario, one that is more believable than a bluegrass ensemble that simply contains the five standard instruments. Further, is it not in Collins' style to make us guess and wonder a little bit?

In his detailed study of bluegrass music during the 1960s, Mayne Smith defined the typical bluegrass sound as requiring some combination of six instruments—though not all were required to exist within an ensemble simultaneously.[5] They included the five-string banjo, mandolin, Spanish guitar (with steel strings), fiddle, upright string base, and steel guitar. This latter instrument has been derided by purists as not being worthy of bluegrass membership, since it was not employed by the founding bluegrass band of Bill Monroe and the Blue Grass Boys.[6]

Since then, the steel guitar has become rather common among "progressive" bluegrass bands up through the present day. In bluegrass circles the controversial instrument is known commonly as a *dobro* or resonator guitar, so named for a specific brand manufactured by the three Dopera brothers during the 1930s. The two essential instruments to the bluegrass style, however, were the Spanish guitar and banjo, though at least one of the other four essential instruments must be added to consider the sound distinctly bluegrass.

Beyond this ensemble core, various supplemental instruments can make an appearance. "On rare occasion," allows Smith, "the autoharp, mouth harp, Jew's harp, accordion, and electric organ have also been used."[7] One might recognize the "mouth harp" by its more popular name, the *harmonica*. Such additions were most often found in recording studios for their commercial production. However, a few performance-based groups—like that of the Covey—also occasionally made use of them.

It does seem clear that the Covey had included Billy Taupe's accordion up until the tenth Games. Still, his instrument is not an accepted standard instrument of a bluegrass ensemble, so perhaps it was symbolic that Billy Taupe was left on the outside looking in—accordion and all. The occasional addition of these supportive instruments does not alter the core ensemble, nor their interactions within the group. As Smith pointedly concludes, "it is addition without integration."[8] This seems to describe Billy Taupe's past role with the Covey quite handily, indicating that the Covey will survive quite well without him. He is now superfluous and not a true part of his former Covey family. His instrument therefore serves as a reliable metaphor for his own outsider status.

Community and Teamwork

Beyond the typical recipe of instruments, the bluegrass style is defined by the teamwork, or the community aspect, of a band's members. While one individual may lead the group in various ways, nearly all members take their respective turns in the spotlight during a performance. Every member and instrument is crucial to the overall sound and progress of a song or number. For instance, musicians might "take a break" between a song's choruses or verses, allowing their cohorts to demonstrate unique singing or instrumental skills. Thus, quite unlike the standard lead singer and guitar within a country band, bluegrass players rotate, swap leads, and play or sing occasional solos or duets before relinquishing the mic to others. As stated by author Stephanie Ledgin, "The bottom line is interaction, and a successful bluegrass group demonstrates great teamwork."[9]

What does this mean for the guitar, which often enjoys a lead role in a country band? A bluegrass guitar is often relegated to the background as a rhythm instrument, though it can occasionally take its turn at the mic. More often than not, it is the banjo, fiddle, or mandolin that takes center stage. In a sense, the instruments—and the musicians who play them—must demonstrate a degree of egalitarianism, or equality, which does not entirely privilege the role of one instrument above the others. While the fiddle, banjo, mandolin, and dobro are more commonly employed as lead instruments that carry the melody or lead improvisation, all instruments within a bluegrass ensemble enjoy the opportunity to take center stage.

The guitar was rarely used as a lead instrument until the 1960s, with the development of the flat pick—as opposed to triangular ones more commonly used with string instruments. The individual most responsible for elevating the guitar to lead status in early bluegrass music was one Arthel "Doc" Watson who hailed from the Appalachian community of Deep Gap, North Carolina. It was Clyde Moody, however, also from North Carolina, who took this one step further by demonstrating a "bluesy-style" guitar playing style with picks for both the thumb and index finger. Moody promoted the flat-picking technique originally perfected by Watson and introduced it to regional and national audiences.[10] It may not surprise us, therefore, should we find Lucy Gray armed with one or more flat picks in her hand. Although emerging several centuries later, Lucy Gray would likely bow a curtsy of appreciation for the legacy of "Doc" Watson who likely enabled her own guitar playing style to exist.

When Lucy Gray is not playing lead guitar, her role occasionally takes a back seat to fellow Covey members. Her own guitar spends quality time as a rhythm instrument backing up other lead musicians. Such is the case when she fades to the background a bit to allow Maude Ivory to take the spotlight, or for Tam Amber to showcase his own technique. This more egalitarian musical approach serves to level the playing field, so to speak, which is a fundamental contrast to standard country-western musicians and groups.

If any bluegrass band demonstrates the virtues of community and teamwork, it is the Covey. Its members form a tight, close-knit and inter-dependent community off the stage as much as on. Beyond the personal teenage drama associated with Billy Taupe, the Covey members form a mutually supportive community on their own, having survived tragedy and various traumatic events with the deaths of Lucy Gray's parents and other adult figures. They are but mere children, with a 16 year old bravely pressing onwards and protecting their small cohort as well as their way of life. Dean Highbottom's observation within the prequel rings true, stating that Lucy Gray was "sixteen going on thirty-five, and a hard thirty-five at that" (*BSS* 325). Despite her own youthful age, it was now Lucy Gray's responsibility to protect the younger Covey, and out of necessity she had matured more quickly into adulthood to do so.

The Business of Playing Music

This community-style dedication to one another is apparent at the very beginning of a standard Covey performance. On stage, a spritely Maude Ivory introduces every member of the Covey, and each steps into the center to recognize the crowd. The team is being introduced, one by one with each musician's distinct identity. The music then begins immediately upon their arrival on stage. Both practices here represent quintessential bluegrass protocols for opening a performance. Audiences and musicians alike expect the leader to introduce each musician individually. The music then begins without delay, and with no additional routines or gimmicks. The songs then transition seamlessly from one number to another. As Mayne Smith concludes about the standard bluegrass experience, "The band's business is clearly to play music."[11] The playfulness of the Covey's audience aside, attendees are there to enjoy the music, not to dance.

Like members of the Covey, bluegrass musicians are there first and foremost to demonstrate their "virtuosity"—that is, their combined technical and artistic skills as musicians. The combined bluegrass focus on demonstrating technique (virtuosity) and integration with the larger ensemble (community) is rare among other American folk styles. Likewise, rural dance bands rarely exhibit the bluegrass propensity of harmonized singing, upbeat tempos and rhythms, and creative song arrangements that bluegrass bands make standard fare.

Perhaps the Covey's Tam Amber demonstrates this focus on music and virtuosity the best. Of course, he plays the mandolin—considered a lead instrument in a standard bluegrass ensemble. But beyond his prominent musical role Tam is a boy of few words, something evident during his first introduction on stage. As Maude Ivory introduces him, Tam "walked straight to Maude Ivory's side, not acknowledging the audience in any way, his fingers moving easily over the strings" (*BSS* 361). Later when Coriolanus and Sejanus are visiting the Covey's home, Maude Ivory explains more about Tam's background, describing him as a "lost soul," further declaring that Tam is "Not much of a talker." Clearly, Tam Amber would fit in well with any serious bluegrass outfit, as there is no expectation of demonstrating showmanship during a performance. While more extroverted personalities are also found within the Covey, this is not a prerequisite when the musical performance is the first and foremost order of the day.

Breaks and Breakdowns

As the group's leader, Lucy Gray opens the prequel's first performance with an older song while the rest of the Covey are "gathered in a close half circle around the mic" (*BSS* 362). This was standard behavior for bluegrass performers into the late twentieth century, utilizing the single mic for vocal numbers with two, three, or even four-part harmonies. Because these bands were typically acoustic with no electronic amplifiers, the mic actually played a pivotal role in the group's performance routine and sound projection. While electronically enhanced instruments were—and still are—frowned upon, a lone mic on stage was not only acceptable but actually served as a minimalist though crucial "sound reinforcement system" to make instruments and singers more audible to larger audiences.[12] In fact, the audience tended to demand this practice, as the more avid listeners and fans were eager to pick out every instrument and vocal performer. As Mayne Smith described in the 1960s, an important bluegrass skill for any serious musician was the ability to "maintain the proper relationship, spatially and thus aurally, with the rest of the band and the microphone."[13]

In more recent decades the single lone mic has often, but not always, given way to more sophisticated sound systems for professional and local performances alike. Present-day performances tend to feature a separate mic for each musician. One can still witness this learned practice, however, as bluegrass musicians will still effectively move in toward the mic and back out again to either emphasize or reduce their sound as the tune requires.

It is almost as if the mic plays the role of a non-human performer itself. The Covey clearly realize and practice this bluegrass stylistic approach.

During their first Hob performance within the prequel, for instance, Lucy Gray sings a few verses of their first number, titled "That Thing I Love With." She then relinquishes the mic to Clerk Carmine, who comes forward to demonstrate his fancy fiddling skills. He then spends his own time in the spotlight "embellishing the melody"—that is, the main tune of the song—through what was likely his own improvisation, "while the others backed him up" (*BSS* 363).

What Clerk Carmine demonstrates here is known as a *break*—and not the "taking a rest" kind. Rather, this is a term derived from early bluegrass musicians to describe a distinctive performance approach. Generally, a "break" occurs when one band member takes the lead for one segment—or "lick"—of an instrumental number to demonstrate a musical skill or improvisation. Band members thus take turns playing the lead, often in between verses of a vocal number. Essentially, a *break* can therefore be defined as a brief instrumental solo integrated within a longer number, often playing some variation on the song's melody. Clerk Carmine was thus performing his own break, in between Lucy Gray's verses. This is not standard practice in mainstream country music, in which one singer and instrument typically remain at the mic to be featured throughout the song.

In bluegrass, this concept of a break can be taken one step further. Since some bluegrass numbers are entirely instrumental with no vocal component, the band can insert a whole string of breaks in a row. In such a case, one musician simply follows another in succession. Such instrumental tunes are called *breakdowns*, essentially created by stringing a series of breaks together. Actual examples of this practice include "Foggy Mountain Breakdown" and "Earl's Breakdown"—both composed by the famous banjo player Earl Scruggs. The breakdown was an innovation that broke tradition from the more standard, unified approach of old-time string music.

It was during this time of the Covey's first performance when Coriolanus found himself absolutely star-struck with a visibly happy Lucy Gray, even if also steeped in jealousy. Eventually Clerk Carmine finishes his musical break, acknowledges the crowd's applause, and fades to the background as Lucy Gray takes over to sing some additional verses. This integration of the ensemble's members, habitual turn-taking, and changing roles of the instruments are all behaviors that distinguish groups like the Covey from nearly all earlier string bands and country groups.

Beyond this, Collins provides additional descriptions of the Covey's style. The band demonstrates a diverse repertoire with a mix of vocal and instrumental tunes. This describes one of the most identifiable characteristics of a bluegrass performance, that of including an eclectic mixture of vocal numbers, full instrumentals (without singing), and combinations of vocal solos, duets, and even *a cappella* numbers in which one or more musicians sing without instrumental backup.

This is likely why Lucy Gray feels quite comfortable singing solo without instrumentation, both on stage at the District 12 reaping, in the Capitol Zoo as a prisoner, and on the interview stage. She is already accustomed to performing for her raucous District 12 audiences, and at age 16 no less! It is therefore not a giant leap for her—mentally, that is—to confidently jump up on stage or into the lens of a Capitol TV camera. The same can be said for the gregarious Maude Ivory, who during the prequel's first performance "piped out a darkly funny song about a miner's daughter who drowned," and invited the audience to join in. The fact that many of them did just that, despite various levels of inebriation, suggests that the song had been sung before, and that many were already familiar with it (*BSS* 364). This is the type of musical variety of vocal and instrumental repertoire that one would experience at a rather typical bluegrass event. Combined with occasional instrumental breaks and improvisations, it would be difficult to find a more colorful and diverse repertoire of music than that found within the Covey's bluegrass outfit.

Bluegrass Vocals and the "High, Lonesome Sound"

The distinctiveness of bluegrass music is also found in its unique vocal traditions. This puzzled Coriolanus to no end, admitting that he failed to comprehend all the words or the dialect being sung. It was during these more unintelligible numbers when the Covey "seemed to turn in on themselves, swaying and building complicated harmonies with their voices" (*BSS* 365). This harmonizing style became a quintessential feature of bluegrass vocals. While songs featuring solos and duets were common, it was also characteristic to include three or four harmonizing vocal parts—that is, trios or quartets—in certain numbers. This practice was clearly adopted by the Covey members and their "complicated harmonies," something much less common in traditional country-western music.[14]

For his part, Coriolanus did not find such a high-pitched, harmonizing style overly appealing. One source describes the style as "vocal harmonies featuring various parts, including a dissonant sound in the highest voice, laying an emphasis on traditional songs with sentimental themes." Such an approach is often characterized in bluegrass as a "high, lonesome sound."[15] Early country music star Jimmie Rodgers is often credited for introducing this sometimes-shrill style. Songs often feature lead tenor vocals which "often jump registers to reach sometimes ear-piercing falsetto."[16]

It is further possible that Katniss' father had sung in this high-pitched, tenor style. As Katniss nostalgically recalls, "when my father sang, all the birds in the area would fall silent and listen." She further describes his beautiful voice as "high and clear and so full of life" (*THG* 43). Might this be a coded statement pointing to a family connection between Katniss and the Covey? And more specifically, to the Covey's bluegrass sound from six decades earlier?

Likewise, the Covey seems to thrive on such vocal numbers. At one point we find poor Coriolanus having to endure three such songs before he realizes they remind him of mockingjays (*BSS* 365). Their songs likely demonstrate the higher pitch and emphasis of mountain dialects and vowel sounds expected in bluegrass vocals. For music aficionados, it is instructive that parts of bluegrass songs can reach a full octave or more above middle C, and music keys are chosen to push voice pitches as high as possible. One might even sympathize with Coriolanus and imagine him wincing through such numbers. Indeed, such a "high lonesome" sound can be an acquired taste. Fortunately for him, most of the Covey's repertoire consists of newer songs that aligned better with his own tastes (*BSS* 365). By having Coriolanus in the audience providing this silent critique of various Covey numbers, Collins subtly demonstrates the wide array of stylistic options—both vocal and instrumental—available to a typical bluegrass band.

Further, there is no evidence of written music guiding the Covey, either on or off the stage. In contrast, the group's collection of instruments—especially the string bass—are regularly described as leaning against a wall in their own home, for instance, or in the garage behind the Hob. But there is no printed music, or at least no mention of it. Rather, they likely memorize their own musical parts and can improvise while taking turns at the mic. This reflects yet another important trait of the genre. As bluegrass music proliferated during its first decades, it was relatively rare for musicians to learn through formal teaching and printed musical scores. This likely remained true to some extent up through the present day. Earlier generations of professional bluegrass musicians had usually learned their music aurally—by listening to their predecessors, whether they be family members, earlier mountain string bands, or even radio broadcasts of the time. This characteristic is uncommon with pop and country-western music genres. Rather, these musicians typically rely at some point on written lyrics and musical scores.

Folk Songs and Ballads in Bluegrass

The subject matter of early bluegrass lyrics depended heavily on traditional folk songs and ballads. This is likely a central reason why Collins features the bluegrass genre within her prequel. Similar life situations and topics found in Appalachian folk music provided the material for the newfangled bluegrass bands of the 1940s and 1950s. The timeless ballad themes of love, death, religious experiences, sorrow or anger over a lost romance, and tearful nostalgia for the past all remained prominent. By the 1960s such topics became more common for bluegrass bands than in any other music style of the time.[17] In a somewhat morbid sense, one of the most popular topics of ballad lyrics consisted of violent death and its related topics of imprisonment, executions, suicide, and romantic tragedies of murder. Such themes harkened back to the murder ballads of the nineteenth century, like those discussed earlier.

This array of topics is featured heavily within the Covey's own repertoire, given the group's wide variety of folk and country-style numbers. "The Hanging Tree" is a prominent case, of course, as are numerous mournful laments of Lucy Gray's songs. Their themes often reflect a former relationship with Billy Taupe—regardless of what Coriolanus might have preferred. Her heart had been broken; she was angry, resentful, resolute, and determined to carry on—depending upon the particular song. She had logically first arrived in the Capitol fresh from her own life story, something the youthful Coriolanus had trouble accepting.

According to Mayne Smith, approximately one out of five bluegrass songs by the 1960s was derived somehow from Anglo-American folk traditions. These included standard bluegrass ballads, along with a high proportion of instrumental numbers and traditional "lyric" songs. This is because early bluegrass musicians learned of traditional "broadside" ballads and other songs from family members or musicians who came before them. Of course, bluegrass musicians adapted earlier tunes for their own uses, and modified the traditional lyrics to suit more contemporary situations. Lucy Gray demonstrates such creative adaptation quite well, as she and the Covey perform a wide variety of traditional songs and ballads handed down through generations.

Their repertoire is rounded out with an assortment of newer, more personally meaningful numbers. Some of these tunes are even modified or composed on the spot. Upon singing her own "Ballad of Lucy Gray Baird," for instance—discussed earlier in Chapter 9—Lucy Gray explains later that she had made up the ballad's last stanza only a few hours earlier (*BSS* 173). This is common practice for modifying music and lyrics passed down through the generations.

Folk Music with Overdrive

One character in the prequel is particularly intriguing, namely Tam Amber. We are told that the young performer had "proved something of a standout" on his mandolin (*BSS* 364). He is further described as "riveting the crowd with his lightning-fast fingering." This speaks to yet another common bluegrass trait—that of musicians standing stone-faced in deep concentration while playing as fast as humanly possible. For bluegrass enthusiasts, Tam Amber's feverishly quick pace represents a quintessential trait of the genre. Overall, the music of a typical bluegrass outfit is played considerably faster than any other style of country music.[18] This is precisely why folklorist Alan Lomax fittingly described bluegrass as "folk music with overdrive."[19]

From a more technical perspective, Charles Perryman explains that the impression of speed is further enhanced through the use of "accented upbeats, off-beat melodic phrasing, and changes in pitch to accent the rhythm."[20] Beyond these approaches, bluegrass banjo players will pick a steady stream of fast sixteenth notes (four notes to every quarter note played by the bass), even at incredibly up-tempo speeds. It is this fast-paced, catchy style of music that the Covey performs at the Hob and again later at the Peacekeeper base. Following their introduction by Maude Ivory, Lucy Gray leads with their first number, described as "bright and upbeat." This is when a doubtful Coriolanus could not help but feel his own heel tap out the beat (*BSS* 362).

Such lively, upbeat music is the polar opposite of Lucy Gray's slower-paced, sometimes sorrowful ballads and country songs. It will be interesting to learn how this array of music styles is eventually interpreted for the prequel's promised feature film, currently in production by *Lionsgate* as of this writing. The extent to which the film showcases the Covey's performances and stylistic traits remains to be seen. Should the Covey and its various stage shows be relegated to the background of the story line, then music fans may experience a rather disappointing two hours. On the other hand, if the Covey is provided enough "on-screen" appearances with a contributing role and follow-up soundtrack, it would not be unreasonable to see the film spawn yet one more bluegrass craze—along with the predictable if short-lived run on beginner mandolins and lesson books.

Now that we have explored the Covey as the bona-fide bluegrass band of District 12, the chapters that follow dive further into the historical and geographical context that led to the development of bluegrass music. Before we can adequately "place" the Covey within this historical timeline, it is necessary to understand the backstory of bluegrass music and its history of development.

13

Building a Bluegrass Sound

Something new and exciting was transpiring at the Grand Ole Opry in October 1939. Bill Monroe and his recently formed string band, the Blue Grass Boys, took the stage to audition for what they hoped would become a more permanent performance role within the Nashville show. One song they performed for their audition was "Mule Skinner Blues," a version of an earlier "blue yodel" song originally performed by hillbilly music star, Jimmie Rodgers. As the group launched into the number, attendees of the audition immediately knew something was different. Monroe and his peers were playing the song at a tempo much faster than usual, and in a higher key. The group also infused the song with what Monroe would eventually call the "bluegrass beat." Cleo Davis, guitar player and the first to be hired into the band, recalled how their rendition absolutely stunned other musicians who were waiting in the wings.

Asked to recall that memorable audition fifty years later in 1989, Monroe—later dubbed the "Father of bluegrass music"—explained that they had arrived at the Opry on a Monday in 1939 to audition. They first ran into Harry and David Stone and some others, who were just heading out to get some coffee. Monroe managed to inform them of his group's intent to audition. Bill Monroe continues the story: "'I told them I wanted to have an audition.' They said, 'Well, you're supposed to be here on Wednesday, but we'll be right back and listen to you.' So they came back, and we went over about three or four songs, and they said, 'You can go to work this Saturday night, and if you ever leave here you'll have to fire yourself.'"[1] In this way, the group was hired on the spot for a long-term stint with the Grand Ole Opry that would continue for decades thereafter.

Monroe would also recall later that "Mule Skinner Blues" was the first song to ever receive an encore upon its premier performance at the Opry.[2] For many scholars, it was this very song and performance that ushered in a new and distinct sub-genre of country (formerly hillbilly) music that came to be known much later as *bluegrass*.

As with most events in history, this one was more complicated than

might appear on the surface. In fact, on that night of the public premier—
which some claim as the initial launch of the bluegrass sound—neither the
term, "bluegrass" nor the concept of bluegrass music had yet been invented.
Nor could the origins of their four-member band be considered entirely
Appalachian in its origin. Bill Monroe had already earned renown as a hillbilly music star, and—until that first night at the Opry—his had been a
rather typical string band of the time. The term "bluegrass" to describe this
distinct genre of music would not appear in print until much later, in 1957.
One might ponder, then, what of the band's iconic name? Quite simply,
Bill Monroe had grown up in western Kentucky, not in the Appalachians.
He simply named the Blue Grass Boys after the existing nick name for his
home state of Kentucky, the "Blue Grass State."

Uncle Pen

As for Monroe's (Bill's) early life, he grew up on a farm near the
west-central Kentucky town of Rosine. Born in 1911, William (Bill) Smith
Monroe had been the youngest of eight children and was a combination of
English and Scottish descent. Both of his parents had died before his seventeenth birthday, and his brothers and sisters moved away as he progressed
through his own childhood and adolescence. Various aunts and uncles took
him in, until he finally settled with his Uncle Pendleton (Pen) Vandiver. It
turns out that "Uncle Pen" was already a locally renowned fiddler, a fact that
would transform Bill's budding life and the future of the bluegrass sound.

Before landing on Uncle Pen's doorstep, young Bill was raised into an
otherwise typical farm family of the early twentieth century. However, the
family harbored an impressive array of musical skills. Bill's father was well
known around Rosine as a step-dancer, and his mother sang and played
several instruments. Two of Bill's older brothers, Harry and Birch, played
the fiddle, while his brother Charlie and sister Bertha played the guitar.[3]

As one might expect, Bill was pulled into his family's musical hearth
early on, and he first picked up the mandolin at age ten. Circling back to
the Hunger Games, one could posit that Bill effectively became the "Tam
Amber" of his own Covey-like family. More curiously, both Tam Amber
and Bill Monroe had been orphaned, and—also like Tam—Bill would go on
to arguably become one of the "finest pickers alive"—to use the praisewor-
thy words of one Maude Ivory. Moreover, both would become renowned
for their extremely fast playing of the mandolin. For these reasons, while
Tam Amber's first name is likely linked to Child Ballad 39 as discussed earlier, it would not be a surprise to find that Collins considered Bill Monroe
as an inspiration when developing Tam Amber's own fictional background.

Back to reality, it was Bill's formative years with Uncle Pen that heavily shaped his musical skills and style. Aside from personal interviews with Monroe later in life, little is actually known about the mysterious Uncle Pen. His own family had passed away earlier, however, which led him to become something of a wandering soul.[4] Pen had even come to live with the Monroes when he was not traveling elsewhere to trade livestock and other goods. Most notably, Uncle Pen took Bill under his wings as a budding musician for several years when the two of them lived under the same roof.

Pen's own renowned fiddling made a significant impression on young Bill. At the formative age of twelve, Bill accompanied his uncle on guitar at local dances where he was brought onto the public stage for the first time as a regular performer. Later in life, when Bill coached his new fiddlers of the Blue Grass Boys, he recalled the exact phrasing and notes of the melodies derived from Pen's fiddle playing—perhaps not unlike the auditory skills of Maude Ivory. The style of Pen's dance music therefore contributed directly to "part of the rhythmic backbone of bluegrass."[5]

In honor of the role Pen played in Bill's own development, Bill wrote a bluegrass-style tribute to his uncle, modestly titled "Uncle Pen." The catchy tune continues to be performed widely, capturing the legacy of Pen's own dance music and fiddle playing.[6] Examples are rather prolific on YouTube and on numerous bluegrass albums.

The Role of Arnold Shultz

During his time with Uncle Pen, Bill met Arnold Shultz, a local black guitarist and fiddler who specialized in the decidedly African American style of the blues. It might be noted that he also earned his living as a coal miner. Despite Shultz's own role in shaping Bill's musical style and the bluegrass sound, Shultz had been all but ignored by scholars and others. Only in recent decades has his own role been clarified and given its due place in bluegrass history.

Bill's first encounter with Shultz was at a square dance in Rosine. Shultz had his own string band, which featured the fiddle, banjo, and guitar. While the guitar was Shultz's main instrument, he also occasionally played the fiddle. His father had been born a slave, though his mother was born a free woman. Like typical folk traditions and culture ways, Shultz absorbed his musical skills at home, and members of his own family played for regional events like brush dances and taffy pulls. By his teen years, however, he labored as a coal miner in western Kentucky when he wasn't performing. While he could be found playing with white musicians as well as with members of his own family, he adopted numerous black folk traditions including blues, rags, gospel music and various guitar styles.[7]

Charles Perryman points out that although racial segregation "certainly existed in this part of Kentucky, musicians often crossed these barriers."[8] Shultz's style also leaned toward jazz, which arguably influenced Bill's early music education as much as that of Uncle Pen. Shultz's own influence on Bill's playing remained evident throughout Bill's later career and was clearly present within the "soulful vocalizations and syncopated delivery" of his bluegrass style.[9] Bill has openly credited Shultz with exposing him to blues music and for Shultz's significant influence on bluegrass. He also recalls being influenced by Shultz's guitar playing, including various melodic licks as well as his style for backing up fiddle tunes. On one memorable and formative night—which Bill would fondly recall—he had stayed up all night to perform with Shultz at a dance until they saw the sunrise the next morning.[10] In this way young Bill had already been learning and practicing a variety of musical styles that represented both white and black cultural traditions.

Bill's multicultural exposure mirrors the evolution of bluegrass music, as the form "did not develop from a single strain of music or a homogenous group of people."[11] Rather, bluegrass in general and Bill Monroe's training in particular were shaped by a fusion of multicultural traditions that had developed beforehand. In turn, these very traditions had been passed down to these younger, innovative musicians. By the time bluegrass appeared on the national stage in the 1940s, it bore the legacy of this continued intermixing of black and white musical approaches.

The Monroe Brothers

As Bill Monroe transitioned into an eighteen year old, it was time for him to seek more permanent employment. This involved uprooting his life and moving to an urban area as did many other rural out-migrants of the early twentieth century. To boost his chances, Bill reasonably chose to live with his brothers, Birch and Charlie, who had already relocated to Whiting, Indiana. They all ended up working at the Sinclair Oil Company, where Bill experienced his first taste of industrial work. During off hours, the three brothers formed their own band and occasionally played at smaller events such as house parties—something characteristic for such family bands, and not unlike District 12's own Covey.

This experience then led to further opportunities, as the brothers found themselves in the emerging realm of radio broadcasting. As discussed earlier, the WLS Chicago station aired an old-time music show every Saturday night called *Barn Dance*, and the brothers were eventually hired for the station's traveling road show. This was Bill's first experience in the life of a full-time, traveling musician. Perhaps not surprisingly, he found it much more preferable to his work at Sinclair. In 1932 they joined a barn-dance touring show sponsored by Texas Crystals. Birch preferred not to travel, so Bill and Charlie struck out as a new duo, dubbed the *Monroe Brothers*.[12] This exciting new gig took them to North and South Carolina and as far west as Iowa and Nebraska, where they performed live on local radio stations between 1934 and 1936.

Finally in 1936 the brothers landed their first-ever recording session for the Bluebird label, performing the single "What Would You Give in Exchange for your Soul?" The song would go on to become the Monroe Brothers' biggest hit.[13] With this early success under their belts, the brothers had now become full-time professional musicians and hillbilly music stars. They became particularly popular between 1935 and 1939 in the southern Appalachians and within the Piedmont region. Their timing was perfect, as they effectively tapped into the emerging commercial genre of hillbilly (country) music discussed earlier.

The story of how the otherwise obscure mandolin became Bill's primary instrument is an intriguing one. Bill had originally expressed his preference for playing the fiddle or guitar instead, because he had understandably desired to replicate the talents of Uncle Pen or Arnold Shultz. Unfortunately, both of those instruments had already been claimed by his older brothers. Consequently, as the smallest and youngest, Bill took up the mandolin as a last resort. This outcome proved to be an auspicious one for his future career. Since he was essentially "stuck with the mandolin," he embraced a personal resolve to master the instrument in his own style.[14]

Enthusiasts of Tam Amber and his mandolin therefore have Bill Monroe to thank for elevating the smallish instrument to the national stage. In developing a personal style with the instrument, Bill revolutionized his own mandolin playing technique. One of his specific aims was to adapt the mandolin to the fiddle techniques and folk songs of his Uncle Pen. Also armed with a distinct blues style largely adopted from Arnold Shultz, Bill molded the mandolin to his own playing tastes and goals. He further created a new lead role for the instrument within his own band and—later—within future country and bluegrass circles. Until Monroe began to showcase the mandolin with his exceptionally fast playing style, the instrument had usually taken a back seat to the fiddle and vocals. It also did not enjoy a lead role in country music until the 1930s.[15]

Promoted as the Monroe Brothers, Bill and Charlie began to separate themselves from the pack as they gained more attention. They consistently sang at higher pitches and played faster than their peers. Like other "brother acts" of the time, Bill and Charlie primarily sang combinations of sentimental songs in two-part harmonies. However, Bill developed his own "rapid-fire" style with his mandolin that brought a "power and urgency" to his music. According to Doug Green from the Country Music Foundation, Bill Monroe "drew his inner fire and turmoil into his music, expressing it with his mandolin."[16] Despite competition from an array of brother duos and string bands performing throughout the South, it was their act which consistently stood out. Charlie's use of snappy bass lines on his guitar and Bill's dexterous mandolin style made their music unique and attracted an impressive fan base for the time. Further setting them apart from other string bands was their incorporation of the blues style and the "lonesome qualities" of their distinct sound.[17]

Although Bill's exceptional mandolin playing earned special acclaim on the hillbilly performing circuit, he still found his primary instrument taking a back seat to the fiddle and vocal numbers. Not at all satisfied, Bill was determined to hoist the mandolin to the status of lead instrument.[18] He also came to favor a distinct style of mandolin, namely the Gibson F5 model, which "gave the instrument enough resonance to hold its own in southern string bands" without being relegated to the background.[19] Having endured decades of diminishing popularity through the early twentieth century, the mandolin was thus poised for a comeback—thanks in large part to Bill Monroe. It is not unreasonable to suggest that the Covey's own Tam Amber and his lightning-fast playing served as a nod to the very Father of bluegrass himself.

Creating the Blue Grass Boys

The origin of Monroe's famed group was a story of successive, gradual events. At the height of the Monroe Brothers' success as hillbilly music stars, sibling rivalry took its toll. Bill and Charlie parted ways in 1938 (nobody seems to know exactly why), and Charlie soon formed his own group, the Kentucky Partners. Charlie found it easier to begin his own band due to his prominent role as lead singer; he could thus easily replace his brother with other instrumentalists. On the other hand, Bill needed to attract a new lead singer, on top of needing a guitarist to replace Charlie.[20] After several months of fits and starts, he finally emerged with his own hard-earned group in 1939. Bill's first hire was Cleo Davis, mentioned earlier, who soaked in everything Bill could offer about playing the guitar. The new duo was soon hired at WWNC radio station in Asheville, North Carolina, where they played for a program called "Mountain Music Time."

Monroe and Davis worked to expand upon the original repertoire of the Monroe Brothers, and they eventually hired two new musicians: Art Wooten and Tommy Millard. Wooten's fiddle playing provided a connection back to Bill's memories of Uncle Pen and the old-time music they once performed. Millard was hired specifically as the band's MC and resident comedian. He also brought with him a host of talents, not the least being his ability to play folk-type instruments including the spoons, bones, and the jug—revealing his own roots in African American music traditions. Millard further provided a link to earlier minstrel shows which, as Perryman points out, "despite its racist and stereotypical elements, was itself a link to the rural black music which Monroe had experienced as a boy."[21]

Millard was later credited with being one of the first blackface comedians to transition to less racially offensive acts, such as rube comics. After performing one of his regular blackface skits during his younger years, Millard recalled that a black preacher had called up to complain about the racial overtones. This incident in particular encouraged Millard to give up his blackface routine altogether, realizing that times were changing.[22] Upon moving later to Asheville, North Carolina, he eventually met up with Bill Monroe—who had just recently parted with Charlie. This is how Millard was ultimately hired to play the role of MC and comedian for the newly formed Blue Grass Boys.

With this founding group of four musicians, Monroe began to promote their band's new identity. Although not yet described as a distinct "bluegrass" style, the group ventured into new territory and continued to build on the innovations of its forerunner, the Monroe Brothers. During this early period the Blue Grass Boys started to perform live for small audiences in the region, usually numbering no more than 50 to 70 people.[23]

After three months in Asheville they moved to Greenville, South Carolina, and added one more quintessential piece to their ensemble. A string bass player, Walter "Amos" Garren was hired to replace Tommy Millard, who by this time was tiring of road travel and decided to move back to Asheville to help raise a newborn. This latest hire marked another innovative turn for Monroe. It was still uncommon to include a bass within a mountain string band, and the bulky instrument could be found in only a handful of groups during the 1930s. For Monroe, Garren's base strategically provided a "more solid rhythmic foundation" and played a critical role in defining the band's distinctive sound.[24]

It was this early version of the Blue Grass Boys that arrived for its audition at the Grand Ole Opry in October 1939. This edition of the band included Bill Monroe (mandolin), Cleo Davis (guitar), Art Wooten (fiddle), and Amos Garren (string bass). Hunger Games enthusiasts may notice something familiar here, namely the precise instrumentation of the Covey. For his part, Monroe maintained this same instrumental mix for approximately three years, from its inception in 1939 until he added his first banjo player in 1942. Let's look more closely at how the Covey's membership during time of the prequel intersects with this early version of the Blue Grass Boys.

Placing the Covey in Appalachian Music History

In one sense, the Covey band represents three distinct developmental periods of Appalachian music history. On the one hand, Katniss, Lucy Gray and her "little birds" become well known for their lone, female vocals sung in the form of traditional Anglo-Celtic ballads. But their repertoire expands to include songs reflecting early phases of hillbilly and country music—most notably their adaptations of "Down in the Valley" and "Keep on the Sunny Side."

As detailed earlier, however, the Covey is no typical country band. Such an outfit would normally be defined by a single lead singer and a small set of backup musicians. We would further add a drum set, remove the mandolin and bass, and emphasize the guitar. Rather, what we have performing at various District 12 venues is a quite standard, traditional bluegrass ensemble that has its roots in the mountain string bands of the early twentieth century. Given the Covey's mannerisms, behaviors, and musical performances as detailed in her prequel, Collins has effectively channeled Bill Monroe's founding group as it existed between 1939 and 1942—pre-banjo. These three formative years of the Blue Grass Boys represent the closest approximation to the Covey as we see them within Collins' prequel.

In the world of Panem, the Covey membership converges with the foundational Blue Grass Boys for only one summer—namely, that which follows the tenth annual Hunger Games. By the time Lucy Gray attempts to run away with Coriolanus, the Covey members begin to diverge from the Bill Monroe model. Lucy Gray goes missing for some as-yet unknown period of time, and Covey-style performances are summarily banned at the Hob. In turn, the Blue Grass Boys would likewise diverge from the Covey in 1942. This is when Monroe added his first banjo player. Soon thereafter various members of the Blue Grass Boys would launch spinoff groups of their own.

It may be appropriate to invoke *Occam's razor* at this point, which essentially states that the simplest explanation for a puzzling mystery is most likely the right one. The mystery in question here is why Suzanne Collins created a full-fledged bluegrass band in the form of the Covey but did not include a banjo. Aside from all the speculation surrounding this issue, it may very well be that Collins desired to emulate—and honor—what many consider to be the first-ever bluegrass band, that of Bill Monroe and the Blue Grass Boys. What are the odds that her own District 12 band happened to include a mandolin, guitar, fiddle, and bass, just like that of America's founding bluegrass group? Indeed, the odds are ever in her favor. Quite simply, the Covey membership constitutes the earliest Blue Grass Boys, reincarnate.

Tam Amber's Mandolin

Fans and other enthusiasts of the Hunger Games would not be off base for asking, "What exactly is a mandolin, and why is it showing up in the prequel, of all places?" I confess to having thought similarly. This question invites us to explore some history that has likely remained rather obscure in America. Part of that history involves Bill Monroe as discussed above, who essentially saved the instrument from a continued descent into obscurity. He had effectively normalized the role of the little eight-string instrument within the emerging bluegrass genre. Given Suzanne Collins' decision to include her own bluegrass outfit into the prequel, the mandolin unquestionably comes with it.

As is true with many musical instruments, the mandolin comes in a variety of possible shapes and sizes. Collins provides one important clue with respect to the style of mandolin played by Tam Amber. As the "tall, rawboned young man" was introduced by Maude Ivory, he emerges from behind the curtain "strumming an instrument similar to a guitar but with a body more like a teardrop." This is one of the instrument's several distinct forms, known as an A-style mandolin. It should be noted that the F-style mandolin, like that adopted by Bill Monroe and many professional musicians, exhibits a more guitar-like appearance with a characteristic wooden scroll on top. This feature is merely aesthetic, however. For most intents and purposes, both the A-style and F-style mandolins are essentially interchangeable and provide a similar sound. That Tam Amber was provided with the tear-drop A-style version probably makes sense, as these are more typically adopted by beginners and young people. Many life-long and professional musicians trend toward the more intricately designed F-style instrument.

The earlier development of the mandolin dates back to the eighteenth-century Italian peninsula. As a member of the lute family of instruments, the mandolin came with a number of diverse shapes and construction approaches by the mid-nineteenth century. The mandolins we recognize today were first developed in different places on the Italian peninsula during the 1700s. It is instructive to note that today's Italy was not unified into its modern nation-state until after 1861. To consider these earlier mandolins "Italian," therefore is not entirely accurate. Rather, the instrument developed in several distinct regions of the Peninsula.

The more recent Neapolitan, bowl-backed instrument was developed in Naples around the 1830s. A second similar, though still distinct variety was produced in Rome by the De Santi family.[25] It follows that by the 1840s there were two prominent mandolin styles—those originating either in Naples or Rome.

Consequently, we can consider the Italian peninsula as the *cultural hearth*, or place of origin, for the modern mandolin. The popular instrument was causing somewhat of a craze within performing groups across Europe during the latter part of the nineteenth century. At the same time, the Industrial Revolution in Europe was disrupting the continent, especially wreaking havoc on family farms and their small-scale agriculture. As with America in previous decades, urban populations grew quickly, and factories hired evermore laborers in Italy and Eastern Europe. Overall, this industrializing process provided new jobs and opportunities, but it also caused massive displacement and impoverishment for those who no longer worked the land.

Between the 1880s and early 1900s, the resulting wave of immigrants from these parts of Europe arrived in America. In a classic case of migration diffusion, enough of these immigrants brought their mandolins and playing skills along with them. These newcomers sparked a fad especially for the Neapolitan, bowl-backed mandolin. A wave of Italian mandolin musicians and teachers fanned across both the United States and Europe during these decades and ushered in what historians consider the "Golden Age" of the mandolin. Entire mandolin orchestras were organized, and the quality of mandolin production improved markedly.

From a geographical perspective, the mandolin enjoyed two mutually reinforcing influences from the Industrial Revolution. First, untold numbers of mandolin-playing immigrants were arriving in the United States, looking to start a new life after being displaced from their farms. At the same time, industrialization in America allowed for mass production of the instrument and its component parts, which could now be produced quickly and efficiently in specialized factories. By 1900 mandolin ensembles were performing regularly on the vaudeville circuit, and schools and colleges were forming mandolin orchestras. For its part, the mandolin gained popularity quickly and became "something of a phenomenon."[26]

The mandolin first earned prominence within wealthier urban areas— as most cultural innovations do. It then eventually diffused down into more rural communities within and around the Appalachians. This process was enabled primarily by the influential mail-order catalogs of Sears-Roebuck and Montgomery Ward—which essentially served as the veritable "Amazon" retailers of their day. They promoted the sale and delivery of the popular instruments in urban and rural areas alike, including deep within some of the more isolated mountain places. For its part, Montgomery Ward's catalog admitted to being stunned with the "phenomenal growth in our Mandolin trade." In 1900 the Lyon & Healy company proudly claimed, "At any time you can find in our factory upwards of 10,000 mandolins in various stages of construction."[27] This scale of mass production was only possible with the standardized factory machinery provided by the booming industrial revolution.

Aside from mail-order catalogs, rural mountain communities might have first encountered the mandolin through published instruction books, door-to-door salesmen, or traveling performances that attracted members of smaller communities to hear their distinctive sound. This is how the Italian-born mandolin ultimately reached Appalachia and intersected with the region's ongoing folk song traditions and mountain string bands.

The craze was not to last forever. By World War II, American demand for mandolin instruments and music had dropped considerably, and—to use a popular pun—became somewhat of a "second fiddle" to other acoustic instruments. While mandolins were still found performing in some old-time string bands, it became more of an accompanying instrument rather than one that was regularly featured.

And then someone named Bill Monroe came along and breathed new life into the instrument. Of course, some eighty years later an author named Suzanne Collins would rediscover the mandolin as a key component of her own bluegrass band, perhaps honoring Monroe and his Blue Grass Boys within the fictitious world of Panem.

14

A National Audience

How did the bluegrass genre evolve following its first three formative years? Starting in 1942, Bill Monroe began a trend of occasionally varying the group's instrumental makeup. As discussed earlier, it was always possible to experiment with alternative sounds by swapping out various instruments. The first significant addition to Monroe's group actually turned out to be a trend-setter with respect to the emerging bluegrass sound. This came with the hiring of banjo player David Akeman—fondly known as "Stringbean"—who served as the group's fifth primary instrumentalist from 1942 to 1945. Many scholars and musicians consider this rendition of Monroe's group to set the standard for true bluegrass instrumentation, including the mandolin, banjo, fiddle, guitar, and bass. From this point onward, the banjo would forever be closely associated with bluegrass music.

Monroe further supplemented his band with non-standard instruments—though often temporarily—over the next few years. Curley Bradshaw appeared with the group in 1944–45 playing both the guitar and harmonica, and Sally Ann Forrester was added with her accordion between 1943 and 1946.[1] Thus, even during Monroe's trend-setting early years, his group at least legitimized the accordion as a worthy, if non-essential, addition. And while the primary membership of the Blue Grass "Boys" was decidedly male, occasional women were sometimes added to the mix. Bessie Lee Mauldin filled the standard post of string bass for eleven years, from 1953 to 1964, following Sally Ann Forrester's stint with her accordion during the 1940s.

Despite the clear contributions of Bill Monroe and the Blue Grass Boys to this new musical genre, it is important to consider the numerous factors that enabled their ascent. While some believe that Monroe's heart-stopping performance of "Mule Skinner Blues" in 1939 represented the precise jump to bluegrass style, others are less convinced. Some scholars argue that bluegrass matured only with the group's addition of Earl Scruggs and his banjo between 1945 and 1948, as we will explore below.

Scruggs Style

According to Mayne Smith, it was the 1945 edition of the Blue Grass Boys that finally assembled all of the key traits of the bluegrass style. The "new and crucial element" was the arrival of Earl Scruggs, hailing from Shelby, North Carolina, with little professional experience at the time.[2] During his developmental time with Monroe's band, Scruggs perfected an intricate, three-fingered banjo picking technique that allowed him to play the instrument decidedly faster and with more clarity and flexibility than most who preceded him.

Scruggs was not the first to invent the three-fingered roll; numerous others of diverse ethnic backgrounds had demonstrated success with the approach back through the nineteenth century. Historians have actually identified the immediate predecessors to Scruggs, namely Snuffy Jenkins and Smith Hammett from the Shelby, North Carolina, area. Their own picking style was passed down to Earl Scruggs, who then perfected the intricate approach and introduced it to regional and national audiences.[3]

By the time the 21-year-old Scruggs took the stage for the first time with Monroe in 1945, he had already been playing "Scruggs Style" for eleven years. He had triumphantly conquered his three-fingered picking roll as a mere child. Looking back to his earlier years, Scruggs recalled that around age ten he "had been into a fuss" with his brother one day, after which he retreated to his room to pout. He picked up his banjo to calm himself down and soon realized he was picking with three fingers while playing the popular bluegrass tune "Reuben." Upon his delightful discovery, young Earl ran out of the room to his brother, shouting, "I've got it, I've got it!"[4] His three-finger roll became the defining feature of his technique, one that launched and sustained his career for life.

In a tribute to Scruggs in the *New Yorker* following his death in 2012, Steve Martin (yes, the comedian-actor and former *Saturday Night Live* star) wrote: "Before [Scruggs], no one had ever played the banjo like he did. After him, everyone played the banjo like he did, or at least tried." And during his first stage performance with Monroe, when he "played banjo the way no one had ever heard before, the audience responded with shouts, whoops, and ovations."[5] Scruggs also elevated the banjo that night to a serious solo instrument, rather than one played mostly by comedians. About Scrugg's debut, Uncle Dave Macon—an Opry regular who was watching from the wings—is reputed to have said, "The boy can play the banjo, but he ain't one damned bit funny."[6]

It would be reasonable to consider Monroe's band of 1939–1945 as a significant transitional phase between the earlier mountain string bands and the fully developed bluegrass ensembles that emerged following World War II. Charles Perryman, in his more recent analysis of bluegrass history, appears to agree with this perspective. He describes Monroe's band during the War years of 1941–45 (pre–Scruggs) as still a "typical hillbilly ensemble," which relied on a more uniform and homogenous sound than later bluegrass bands would employ.[7] Monroe's lead singing is the only thing heard in the foreground of the ensemble, essentially making it a "hillbilly band with a lead singer." This was not much different than other early country bands of the time, albeit with Monroe's distinctively fast-paced style and bluegrass instrumentation.

Only after the addition of Scruggs in 1945 did the Blue Grass Boys "become bluegrass." Scholars consider Monroe's band during the Scruggs years—that of 1945–48—to be his best, and the first to create the full bluegrass sound.[8] That band's roster of musicians included Bill Monroe (mandolin), Chubby Wise (fiddle), Cedric Rainwater (bass), Lester Flatt (guitar), and Earl Scruggs (banjo). In his own historical study of bluegrass music, Mayne Smith found that every bluegrass band thereafter would include a Scruggs-style banjo or some version of it.[9]

By early 1948 these five trend-setting bluegrass musicians played their last shows together. The first to leave the group was Chubby Wise, followed by Lester Flatt and Earl Scruggs himself. There is apparently no surviving account of why they all left Monroe around that time, though Monroe had shrugged it off as "normal band turnover." In reality, he was "clearly angered" by their departure and remained bitter for quite some time before making amends years later.[10] In some respect the "turnover" argument was true. Monroe's band represented a sort-of "revolving door" of musicians coming and going over the years, essentially providing a veritable "school" for future bluegrass performers.

The departure of Flatt and Scruggs produced a historical jump of its own for the development of the bluegrass sound. The duo formed their own spinoff group in 1948, dubbed the Foggy Mountain Boys—once again associating the Appalachians with the bluegrass style. Earl Scruggs naturally became the showpiece of their identity, showcasing his newfangled three-finger banjo picking style. Much like Monroe had accomplished, this new band generated its own widespread following and ultimately became one of the nation's most popular groups.

While Earl Scruggs is not the primary focus of this book, it would be negligent to discuss the historical development of bluegrass without considering his substantial contribution. Scruggs remained active throughout a lengthy career which had begun with Monroe and ended only recently with his death in 2012. One can find numerous inspirational and toe-tapping videos of his performances on YouTube as a featured performer with the likes of country music and bluegrass greats Ricky Skaggs, Doc Watson, Travis Tritt, Vince Gill, Patty Loveless, Alison Krauss and many others. Fans of the memorable and trendsetting 1967 film *Bonnie and Clyde* are likely familiar with its feature hit, "Foggy Mountain Breakdown." This is an Earl Scruggs tune, still widely performed by professionals and amateurs alike.

With the song's featured inclusion in *Bonnie and Clyde*, a whole new generation was introduced to Earl Scruggs and bluegrass music in general. Beyond this, Flatt and Scruggs were also responsible for another big hit that pulled bluegrass even further into the mainstream: "The Ballad of Jed Clampett," discussed earlier. This was the theme song for the aforementioned TV sitcom, *The Beverly Hillbillies*. The song was Scrugg's first to reach number one on the Billboard charts.

The Stanley Brothers

One more "branch" of the early bluegrass tree deserves mention. Thus far we have touched on two distinct though related styles of traditional bluegrass—those of Bill Monroe, and Flatt and Scruggs. A third, derivative style can be described as the "powerful, raw sounds" of the Stanley Brothers.[11] As another pair of brothers, Ralph and Carter Stanley were World War II veterans who aimed to launch their own country music careers. Ralph was a baritone singer and played a two-finger banjo style, while Carter could sing lead and play the guitar in a style similar to that of Lester Flatt. To augment their own sound, they also hired mandolin and fiddle players for a new band they called the Clinch Mountain Boys, named for their home region in Virginia.

Their aspirations for future stardom hit pay dirt with the coincidental creation of a new Bristol, Tennessee, radio station, WCYB. Though the station was only one of many to proliferate after the War, the Stanley Brothers had played for WCYB since it first went on the air.[12] They further played professionally in 1946 for a Norton, Virginia, radio station. By 1948 the group was closely emulating the innovative sounds of the Blue Grass Boys. Ralph had also learned banjo technique from Earl Scruggs and had begun to emulate his three-finger style. Bill Monroe actually befriended the Stanley Brothers, and Carter briefly played guitar for Monroe in 1951.[13] As with all close-knit communities of musicians, they tended to learn from one another and networked in various ways.

The Stanley Brothers earned a commanding popularity within the broadcast range of WCYB, and they played to sold-out audiences and made personal appearances in the region. Eventually their music was recorded as well, at first through the independent label of Rich–R–Tone. When interviewed years later by Stephanie Ledgin, Ralph was asked to reflect on how his style differed from those of Monroe's Blue Grass Boys and Flatt and Scruggs. He replied, "I think mine goes back a little bit farther in what I call a mountain style or traditional bluegrass. Bill Monroe and Flatt and Scruggs were traditional bluegrass, but they were just a little bit slicker and a little bit more polished than what I do. I just do it straight from the heart, right out of the mountains."[14]

Over the years they earned the public perception of how a mountain band "should" sound. They were further noteworthy for their distinctive bluegrass blend of high, lonesome vocal harmonies, "hard-driving" rhythms, and a veritable cornucopia of old-time mountain songs. As music historian Bill Malone offers, the Stanley Brothers "conjured up visions and sounds of deep rolling hills, isolated mountain glens, lonesome rivers, little country churchyards, broken family circles, and the undying love of Mama and Daddy."[15] Geographers might interpret this "conjuring" as promoting a distinctive sense of place. The Brothers highlighted and awakened in their listeners a deep emotional affection for the Appalachian Mountains.

After his brother Carter died young in 1966, Ralph made a comeback and continued to record and perform widely with the Clinch Mountain Boys until around 2013, capping off a remarkable career of his own. Ralph's fortunes blossomed once again in 2000 with his role in the soundtrack for the acclaimed film *O Brother, Where Art Thou?* which featured his song "Man of Constant Sorrow" among others. Strangely, the soundtrack's enormous popularity led to another revival of interest in bluegrass, as numerous music journalists declared the soundtrack a "triumph for bluegrass music."[16]

This would be truly impressive had there actually been one identifiable bluegrass song on the entire album. Journalists were probably deceived because so many bluegrass musicians performed for the soundtrack, including the famed Ralph Stanley. The truth, however, is that both the movie's producers and musicians were attempting to emulate a Depression-era, 1930s heritage of the rural Mississippi Delta that really had nothing to do with the Appalachians. Only the award-winning song "Man of Constant Sorrow" could be classified as "mountain." The rest of the soundtrack evoked more of a generalized rural South.[17] Nonetheless, the film and music fanned the flames of enthusiasm once again for Ralph Stanley and bluegrass music in general as we moved into the twenty-first century. Might Suzanne Collins and her Covey be unwittingly preparing us for the next bluegrass revival? Perhaps this time the soundtrack will include authentic bluegrass music.

A Bluegrass Culture Hearth

Just when did bluegrass become "bluegrass"? It is a curious thing to note that none of the three legendary bands discussed earlier had described their music as "bluegrass" as late as the 1940s. Rather, they still identified as country musicians. Although the 1945 version of the Blue Grass Boys is widely considered the first true bluegrass band, the "naming of the child," to use Ledgin's words, did not occur for another 12 years—at least in print.[18] The first use of the term "bluegrass" appeared in the liner notes of the first-ever bluegrass album, *American Banjo: Scruggs Style*, released in 1957. Of course, fans and radio stations alike were already referring to Monroe's band and its style as "bluegrass." The term was primarily favored by listeners who preferred the sounds of acoustic string ensembles rather than the more contemporary electric sounds of country music. Paradoxically, the musicians themselves were originally hesitant to adopt the "bluegrass" term, apparently believing that it might place boundaries around their own artistic identities.[19]

The term "bluegrass" made its second printed appearance within the title of a new album released in 1959: *Mountain Music, Bluegrass Style*. This is the first time that "bluegrass" and "mountain" appeared together in print, thereby linking the music style with the Appalachians.[20] By the mid–1960s more than 300 Southern musicians had been regularly performing bluegrass music with some 60 professional or semi-professional bluegrass bands.[21] They had finally recognized the usefulness of this new identity to differentiate their own style from other strains of "hillbilly" music, including country-western, western swing, and rockabilly.

The emerging association of bluegrass music with the Appalachians was cemented further through its expanding repertoire of songs. While Bill Monroe and other early bluegrass musicians were not necessarily "from" the Appalachians, the music sounded familiar and evoked "a certain sentimentality" that resonated with mountain populations.[22] At the time of Monroe's acclaimed debut at the Grand Ole Opry in 1939, much of the music heard on the radio was of the country-western variety by artists the likes of Gene Autry, Roy Acuff, Ernest Tubb, and Bob Wills. For those not enthralled with either "country" or "western" music, there was little of the traditional "mountain music" to be found. By then such old-time music was all but obsolete and was rarely played by professional radio stations or musicians.

Then Bill Monroe and the Blue Grass Boys came along. In a simplified sense, Monroe took traditional mountain music, sped it up, added the mandolin and bass, and adapted it for the concert stage. While traditional mountain string bands had performed for house parties and local dances, the new style dubbed "bluegrass" was instead designed for the stage. Thus, when Appalachian families tuned in to their local radio shows and heard the innovative sounds of Monroe and his contemporaries, "they no doubt heard the familiar sound of the square dance band or a string band playing for a party at the home place."[23] The music style, songs, and lyrics spoke to the emotional sentiments of home, appealing quite easily to the strong place attachments of eager listeners.

By the 1960s bluegrass music had become closely identified with the central and southern Appalachians, even while spreading to a national audience. The snappy, innovative music provided an outlet of expression, or "sense of place consciousness" for the mountains.[24] According to Mayne Smith in 1965, more than 95 percent of professional bluegrass musicians were Southerners like Bill Monroe, and about 80 percent were "Appalachian-bred."[25] Further, approximately one out of five, or 20 percent of bluegrass numbers derived from Anglo-American folk tradition. These became part of the repertoire mainly through one of two ways: the folk background of the musicians themselves, or within the performances of non-bluegrass "hillbilly groups."[26] And nearly all bluegrass ballads derived from this same folk tradition.

The geographic roots of bluegrass can also be traced in large part to the central Appalachians. In the 1970s cultural geographer George Carney researched the hometowns or cities of bluegrass performers, relying on a catalog of 1972 musicians to identify the core bluegrass region.[27] While a small portion of musicians hailed from outside the central Appalachian region, Carney identified a clear central cluster of bluegrass musicians within the four-state mountain region of Kentucky, Virginia, North Carolina, and Tennessee—along with southern West Virginia. Indeed, Carney's map of 1972 bluegrass musicians corresponds closely to the District 12 core area discussed earlier. This alignment of a "bluegrass culture hearth" with our presumed District 12 core area only supports Collins' decision to add a Monroe-style bluegrass band to her prequel.

Into the Twenty-First Century

As the decades moved along, bluegrass music evolved and split into three distinct variations. The first generation of professional bluegrass musicians performed what historians now refer to as "traditional bluegrass." This was the standard largely set by the innovative Bill Monroe and the Blue Grass Boys. To this day, proponents of "traditional bluegrass" prefer to emulate Monroe's original, all-acoustic, unamplified instrumental mix. While some instrumental variation can be found, these groups remain steadfastly loyal to the original five instruments of guitar, banjo, mandolin, bass, and fiddle.

A second stylistic variation emerged later and remains popular to this day—known as "progressive bluegrass." These groups and their musicians are more willing to diversify their sound through electrically amplified instruments and can be found with the occasional percussion set. Their repertoire of songs might reach further outside traditional folk sources and branch into other music genres such as rock and roll.

More recently, something dubbed "neo-traditional bluegrass" has gained a following. The variation emerged in the 1980s and 90s along with neo-traditional country music. This latter movement was reacting to the general decline of popularity in country music during the 1980s, including its related sub-genre of bluegrass. Also referred to as the New Traditionalism, this music was characterized by a younger generation of up-and-coming musicians who "wrote their own material and had unique voices that sounded like nothing heard before."[28] This was basically the next generation of contemporary music that still relied on a foundation of folk traditions. The overall aim of its proponents was twofold: to bring country and bluegrass music back to its folk roots, and to provide an alternative to the growing field of pop-country music.

A related concern focused on the loss of traditional instruments—and with them the original bluegrass sound—as the country genre gave way to a more pop-rock style during the 1990s. The new traditionalists regretted this turn to country-rock. One particular song, titled "Murder on Music Row," was written in 1999 and performed by George Strait and Alan Jackson as a harsh critique of the ongoing pop influence on country music.[29] For those more curious, the neo-traditional sound can be experienced through the music of Reba McEntire, the band Alabama, George Strait, Randy Travis, and many of their contemporaries.

Given our focus on bluegrass in particular, one additional musician should not go unmentioned: Ricky Skaggs. Mostly associated with his contributions to bluegrass music, Skaggs likewise moved away from the country-to-pop crossover during the latter part of the twentieth century and "put his own stamp on the country format by infusing his bluegrass and traditional country music roots into the contemporary Nashville sound."[30] For his part, Skaggs had reached the top of the country music charts by 1981 with the release of "Waitin' for the Sun to Shine," and he remained there during most of the 1980s while compiling 12 number-one hits. The awards came fast and furious during that time, including "Entertainer of the Year" in 1985 and four Grammy Awards among numerous others. According to Skaggs' official online biography, "Renowned guitarist and producer, Chet Atkins, credited Skaggs with 'single-handedly' saving country music," referring to his prominent role in the neo-traditional movement.

With these much-deserved accolades in mind, Skaggs is important to our story primarily for his roots in—and contributions to—bluegrass music. His early career provides a story in its own right, as Ricky had intermingled early on with the bluegrass greats. Born in Cordell, Kentucky, in 1954, Ricky received his first mandolin at age five. Only two weeks after he had learned the basic G, C, and D chords expected of a beginner, his father returned home one day to shockingly find Ricky already making difficult chord changes while singing along.

One day, Bill Monroe came to perform nearby, and the crowd demanded that Ricky be invited to perform on stage with the master himself. As recalled by Skaggs' online biography, "The father of bluegrass called six-year-old Skaggs up and placed his own mandolin around his neck, adjusting the strap to fit his small frame. No one could have imagined what a defining moment that would be in the life of the young prodigy."[31]

The following year he ended up performing with Flatt and Scruggs on their own syndicated television show. Later in his teens he became an invited member of Ralph Stanley's bluegrass band, the Clinch Mountain Boys. During an interview in 2008, Stanley recalled how he met the teenagers Ricky Skaggs and Keith Whitley after Stanley had arrived late to one of his own shows: "They were about 16 or 17, and they were holding the crowd 'til we got there.... They sounded just exactly like [the Stanley Brothers]."[32] Although it meant enlarging his band from five to seven members, Stanley recognized their potential and hired the boys into the group. Skaggs performed alongside Stanley for their debut album in 1975, considered one of the most influential bluegrass albums to this day. Skaggs has tirelessly continued his impressive career, now in his mid–60s as of this writing. Among numerous bluegrass albums, his fourth was released in 2000 and titled *Big Mon: The Songs of Bill Monroe*, featuring an all-star collection of musicians including Dolly Parton, Patty Loveless, Travis Tritt, Joan Osborne, and John Fogerty.

Skaggs has further appeared in, or even led, occasional television bluegrass events, including the "All-Star Bluegrass Celebration" which aired on PBS in 2002. As with pretty much anything nowadays, this and many other live performances can be easily found on YouTube. Be prepared to turn up your volume and tap your feet! Not only do the videos provide a close-up view of the virtuosity demonstrated by these musicians, but they allow us to "put a face to the name" of these influential bluegrass and country musicians. As for the Covey—well, we will need to wait for the promised feature film to hear Lionsgate's own rendition of the traditional bluegrass sound.

15

Maude Ivory the Songbird

One of the more light-hearted debates within the Hunger Games fandom has focused on identifying possible ancestors of Katniss Everdeen. Not all of Collins' potential clues are found in her recent prequel, however, as they also spill over from the original series. In one sense, various strategic phrases and plot points virtually speak to one another between the prequel and the trilogy. Until the release of the prequel, we only had the narrative and perspective of Katniss Everdeen to glean clues about her past. Now armed with an information-rich prequel novel, many more of Katniss' stories and recollections suddenly come alive with historical detail.

As this chapter attempts to summarize—in a purely fun, interpretive way—potential connections between the Everdeen family and the Covey are abundant. And many of their stronger connections involve the role of Appalachian music. In some ways the prequel provides even more questions and loose ends than did the original series. More to the point for purposes here, which specific character(s) of the prequel might be related to the future Girl on Fire?

Possible solutions to this burning question have been wide ranging, from truly outlandish notions with little supportive evidence, to the more logical and thoughtful variety. If one's perusal of online fan sites is any indication, it would appear that Lucy Gray Baird is the number one candidate for being Katniss' ancestor. Coming in a close second might be Maude Ivory, followed then by a litany of other possibilities—few of whom can be disproven outright until Suzanne Collins decides to personally inform her readership. Still others staunchly believe that absolutely no familial connection exists at all, which could also be accurate. Like Lucy Gray in the woods—and in the ballad for which she is named—the answer may be blowing in the wind, perhaps forever.

Regardless, in a book that focuses on the music of District 12, it is difficult to remain fully separated from this ongoing conversation. I therefore make the case here for why Maude Ivory stands the best chance of being revealed as Katniss' paternal grandmother—that is, Katniss' father's mother. Before reviewing the key passages that brought me to this conclusion, it may be instructive to consider Collins' own comments regarding her intent for the prequel. In one surprisingly revealing interview for David Levithan, an editor with Scholastic, Collins discusses her intended connections between various characters. In particular, she introduces her new character of Lucy Gray Baird, though stops just short of admitting to a familial relationship:

> Focusing on the 10th Hunger Games also gave me the opportunity to tell Lucy Gray's story. In the first chapter of The Hunger Games, I make reference to a fourth District 12 victor. Katniss doesn't seem to know anything about the person worth mentioning. While her story isn't well-known, Lucy Gray lives on in a significant way through her music, helping to bring down Snow in the trilogy. Imagine his reaction when Katniss starts singing "Deep in the Meadow" to Rue in the arena. Beyond that, Lucy Gray's legacy is that she introduced entertainment to the Hunger Games.[1]

Collins therefore does admit to a planned musical connection between Lucy Gray and Katniss. She even imagines out loud what Snow must be thinking when he hears Katniss singing the very songs he had heard decades earlier.

Further, Collins all but puts to rest the popular notion that Lucy Gray is a direct ancestor of Katniss, claiming only that Lucy Gray "lives on in a significant way through her music." This seems to imply that Lucy Gray either did not survive long after the prequel, or she did not remain long in District 12 to raise a family herself. And, had Lucy Gray somehow surfaced once again back in 12 to eventually become Katniss' grandmother, why does Katniss not mention anything about these family connections, such as where her father learned all of his music?

Moreover, it is safe to presume that a distinct family history of Lucy Gray's experiences within the tenth Games would have survived as well—unless she somehow managed to keep the whole thing under wraps throughout early adulthood. But in small-town communities where most people know one another? This hardly seems likely. Finally, if Lucy Gray and Katniss were so closely related, why is Katniss so oblivious to the identity of the original District 12 victor? For all these reasons, Katniss is not likely a direct descendant of Lucy Gray.

Perhaps even more revealing was a second admission by Collins within the same interview. In a follow-up question, David Levithan asked Collins if she had known who that fourth victor might be when she wrote the first Hunger Games book, to which she replied, "Yes, but she's evolved a lot since then." With this admission, it appears that Collins had purposely intended a connection between her original series and the new prequel. This is big news. Collins did not just decide on a whim nearly a decade later to add another novel to the saga. Rather, she had already planned to write additional stories—or had at least carefully considered the possibility. Given that she provided a strategically subtle reference to the fourth District 12 victor, she likely included many other clues as well.

More to the point, Collins specifically planned for Katniss to learn the Covey's songs. What better way to have such songs handed down to her but through family kin? Given that Katniss learned her folk music skills and songs from her father, he in turn most certainly learned them from his own parents—or at least from a close family member such as an aunt or uncle (a District 12 version of Uncle Pen comes to mind). The question remains as to whether one of Katniss' father's parents was either related to the Covey or was perhaps even one of the original Covey members. As we have seen in earlier chapters, it was common practice in the mountains to orally pass down family traditions and cultural traits from one generation to the next. There is already evidence of this generational process having occurred within Katniss' own family.

Should Lucy Gray not be Katniss' direct ancestor, what of Maude Ivory herself? Let's explore why this is the most logical possibility, based on additional clues within both the original series and the prequel.

It does make mathematical sense that Maude Ivory could realistically be Katniss' paternal grandmother. First, Collins makes a point to inform readers of Maude's age. Near the beginning of the Covey's first (prequel) performance at the Hob, Coriolanus observes Maude Ivory and makes his own conclusion that she could not be more than eight or nine. Perhaps Collins was merely providing colorful background on the Covey members but revealing Maude's age could also be a clue for revelations to come. Such speculation aside, this information does allow us to calculate the timeline of possible future generations and births. As just one of numerous possibilities, let's assume that Maude is nine years old during the tenth Games. She could then conceivably be around 29 when giving birth to Katniss' father (the year of the 30th Games). This would make Katniss' father a reasonable 28 years old when his own wife gives birth to Katniss (year of the 58th Games). Katniss would then be the correct 16 years old when she is reaped for the 74th Games. Thus, both Maude and her son—Katniss' father—would be in their late 20s when they start—or continue—their own families. Even considering that average lifespans are likely shorter within the Seam, due largely to impoverished living conditions and mining hazards, this generational timeline would be realistic for Collins' contemporary readership.

The question that continues to plague us, however, is why Katniss apparently knows nothing about her grandparents. Given her sentiments for home and family explored earlier, why are her grandparents never mentioned? Would she not explain something in her narrative about the origin of her father's singing, or other aspects of her parents' younger days? Of course, one could conjure any number of reasons for her complete silence on these topics, such as Maude Ivory's untimely death, or the Covey's decision—or necessity—to leave District 12 quickly for some reason.

More likely than these far-flung scenarios is that Collins purposely omitted such information, just as she has done with respect to other aspects of her story. For instance, the unnamed fourth victor from District 12 remained a mystery until Collins revealed that individual to be none other than Lucy Gray. Given that both Katniss' father and mother remain nameless throughout the original series, this so-called absence of evidence may indicate that future books—and family backstories—still have yet to be released. None of this will be confirmed or refuted, of course, unless Collins writes a follow-up story—one that actually considers the eventual fate of the Covey and its individual members.

Despite this oddity, it is difficult to simply ignore numerous clues that may point to connections between Maude Ivory, Katniss, and her father. Those connections largely involve their shared knowledge of Appalachian music, their similar singing styles and musical abilities, and their collective familiarity with the woods and the lake. Let's focus first on Katniss' father and his own musical legacy. Katniss tells us early in The Hunger Games that her father was quite fond of mockingjays—in direct opposition to Coriolanus within the prequel. Whenever they went hunting together, she recalled, he would whistle or sing various songs, after which they always sang back. Whenever he sang, "all the birds in the area would fall silent and listen" (*THG* 43).

Katniss' father clearly commanded the attention of mockingjays, apparently more successfully than most people trying to sing. One clue here is that the birds would "fall silent and listen" because his voice was "that beautiful." Members of the Covey enjoyed similar influence over the melodic birds, singing along with them during their hikes in the woods. As established earlier, Katniss was treated with a similar respect from the mockingjays, which likewise stopped to listen as Peeta had recalled.

Speaking of the woods, it was the Covey members who knew the lake and the woods like the back of their hands. This explains how Katniss' father could effectively navigate this forested territory during their hunts. It is also logical that his inspiration for his daughter's unique name is based on his knowledge of the katniss plant. This knowledge was most certainly passed down from the Covey, whose members spend time digging up the nutritious tubers and discussing them nonchalantly in front of Coriolanus. While at the lake during one memorable passage, Clerk Carmine brings a plant to Lucy Gray that he had uprooted from the lake. To which Lucy Gray responds, "Hey, you found some katniss. Good work, CC." As was often the case, Coriolanus expressed some confusion. Lucy Gray explained that the plant will eventually grow into a decent-sized potato, which can then be roasted for eating. She continues, "Some people call them swamp potatoes, but I like katniss better. Has a nice ring to it" (*BSS* 435–36).

It follows, then, that Katniss' father would have likely gained his own affinity for mockingjays and learned about the obscure katniss plant from one of his parents. Just as Katniss gained her musical acumen from her father, it stands to reason that her father learned from the generation before him—and apparently much of it during his time at the lake.

Two additional passages within the original series only strengthen the case for a connection between Katniss, her father, and mockingjays. During the cave scene later in *The Hunger Games*, Katniss asks Peeta when his crush on her had actually begun. Peeta responds that it had been on the first day of school at age five, when his father pointed her out while waiting to line up. Clearly puzzled, Katniss asks Peeta why his father would have noticed her at all. He then explains that his father originally wanted to marry her mother, but she decided to run off with a coal miner instead—Katniss' future father. He had won over her mother with his beautiful singing, because "when he sings ... even the birds stop to listen" (*THG* 300).

According to Peeta, then, Katniss' mother fell in love with her father in part due to his singing, which had also made quite the positive impression on the local mockingjays. This is actually the second such reference to the birds' polite behavior. The third one is found within the aforementioned exchange between Katniss and Peeta within the cave scene of The Hunger Games, when Katniss sung the Valley Song in school. Peeta swears that every bird outside the windows went silent (*THG* 301).

This passage from the cave is noteworthy for several reasons. First, we now plainly see a distinct familial connection between Katniss and her father with respect to their mystical effect on mockingjays. Clearly, this unprecedented ability to stop the birds in their tracks has been handed down through the family—at least as far as Suzanne Collins was concerned.

Even more intriguing, the Covey demonstrated a similar influence over the mockingjays within the prequel. In one statement easy to overlook, Lucy Gray had just finished singing "Deep in the Meadow" to Maude Ivory out at the lake, at which point the narrator states, "Coriolanus was on the verge of dozing off when the mockingjays, who'd listened quite respectfully to Lucy Gray's rendition, began one of their own" (*BSS* 438). The birds' respectful listening behavior would have been familiar to Katniss and her father. Does "stopping and listening" run in the family?

Beyond the mockingjay connection, this same passage includes the now-famous line (for many fans, at least) vaguely referring to the "Valley

Song" discussed further in Chapter 11. It stands to reason that Collins had intentionally inserted this Easter egg to eventually point back to the prequel. This is similar to her similar clue regarding the mysterious fourth victor from District 12 discussed earlier. Collins' use of the "valley song" must have also been planned ahead of time, given the song's sizable role within the prequel.

Another song replete with generational connections is "The Hanging Tree." Just before Katniss sings it for the "propo team" in *Mockingjay*, she admits to remembering its "every word" despite not having sung it since she was around seven years old. Maude Ivory had similarly learned the ballad at a young age, claiming it had "real authority." And she was most likely the one who quietly passed it on to others. This is due to the song's having been banned in District 12, after which Lucy Gray promised not to sing it. Somehow, then, Katniss' father learns it, thus allowing Katniss to sing it much later in *Mockingjay*. During that third book, Katniss reflects back on the time she practically knew it as a household song. While home with her father one day, she had been on the floor with Prim singing "The Hanging Tree." If that weren't enough, the two girls were making necklaces from scraps of old rope just like in the song. Most important, she claims that "back then I could memorize almost anything set to music after a round or two" (*MJ* 124).

This passage provides perhaps the most significant reference to a potential connection between Maude Ivory and Katniss. Here Katniss admits that she could "memorize almost anything set to music" after only a little practice. In the prequel, Lucy Gray explains why she chose to sing her own ballad as a way to communicate with the Covey back in District 12: "One hearing's all my cousin Maude Ivory needs. That child never forgets anything with a tune." (*BSS* 173)

Why would Collins insert this information if not as an Easter egg to suggest some larger meaning? It is highly improbable that both Maude Ivory and Katniss Everdeen coincidentally enjoy the same ability, and at roughly the same young age. This does not imply, of course, that the special music skill they share is passed down genetically. Rather, this may be another literary approach to suggest a family connection between them.

As for the future of "The Hanging Tree" song in District 12, Lucy Gray essentially passes the proverbial torch to Maude Ivory while preparing to escape into the woods with Coriolanus. She assures him that the Covey will "get by" without her leading the family band, and that Maude Ivory will be able to lead the group in a few years. Lucy Gray further informs him that she is no longer allowed to sing "The Hanging Tree," per the commander's orders. She had even told the commander that he would never hear it from her lips again. After Coriolanus describes the ballad as "a strange song,"

Lucy Gray laughs and explains that "Maude Ivory likes it. She says it has real authority" (*BSS* 491).

With this exchange, Lucy Gray foreshadows her own future disappearance by supposing that Maude Ivory will become the group's lead singer. Perhaps more important, this indicates the song will most likely be passed down to future generations by Maude Ivory, not by Lucy Gray. The real question now is how the song will be taught to Katniss' father. On the surface, Maude Ivory is the most likely candidate; she is someone who not only likes "The Hanging Tree," but also has not been officially banned from singing it.

Still, we must admit to the possibility that Collins is for some reason purposely throwing her readers off track. In which case, she will someday divulge that members of the Covey taught "The Hanging Tree" and related songs to another, as yet unknown character, who in turn taught Katniss' father. Any number of scenarios could allow for this to happen. That said, given the wealth of other connections between Maude Ivory and Katniss' father, the simplest, most likely scenario is that they are related by blood in one way or another.

If this musical connection was not enough, Collins provides an untold number of additional breadcrumbs to point us in this direction. Each of these may be meaningless if taken alone, but together they seem to only strengthen the case for a family lineage from Maude to Katniss. The first may actually be rather significant, as both of these characters demonstrate classic symptoms of Post-Traumatic Stress Disorder, or PTSD.[2] One of these symptoms consists of recurring nightmares. These ongoing terrible dreams haunt Katniss to no end within the original series, to the point where she wakes up screaming at night. Likewise in the prequel, Lucy Gray explains to Coriolanus why she is helping Maude Ivory with the Herculean task of churning goat's milk into butter. She tells him that Maude hasn't slept well since she was dragged away to the Games. She may seem fine during the day, but then she "wakes up screaming at night." The butter churning process is Lucy Gray's way to "get some happy into her head" (*BSS* 394).

While it would be difficult to imagine a hereditary, or genetic transference of PTSD symptoms across two generations let alone one, this is probably yet another attempt by Collins to suggest a family relation between Maude Ivory and Katniss. Otherwise, why is this passage even included? We do not need to know that Maude Ivory wakes up screaming at night to assist with our understanding of the story. Nonetheless, there it is—essentially "screaming" at us to remember Katniss and her own persistent challenge with nightmares.

Then there are the goats. Maude Ivory has Shamus, and Prim has Lady—the latter thanks to Katniss. As discussed in a previous chapter, both families are desperately working toward independence with subsistence farming and animal husbandry, to the point where Lucy Gray envisions that the Covey will one day have its own herd. For their part, the goats play a therapeutic role for both Maude Ivory and Prim. While Maude is trying to skim enough cream from her goat's milk to churn butter (we also learn for some unknown reason that Maude loves butter), Prim's own goat provides sustenance for the family as well as something to care for.

And finally, about those snakes. Even within the book's title, *The Ballad of Songbirds and Snakes*, Collins sets up a dichotomy between those two opposing creatures. Just as the snake connotes the troublesome personality of Coriolanus Snow and the twisted mind of Dr. Gaul, we learn that Maude Ivory does not particularly care for snakes either. Rather, she prefers to remain on the "songbird" end of the personality continuum. At one point while educating Sejanus about Lucy Gray's abilities with snakes, Maude comments that she always knows where to find them, but that "they scare me" (*BSS* 433).

Lucy Gray is thus something of a snake charmer, as we learn throughout the prequel. In contrast, Maude Ivory decidedly is not. It is safe to conclude that Katniss would not be so fond of the slithering reptiles either, given that they serve as a metaphor for Snow and his treacherous ways. Similarly, the affable, upbeat Maude Ivory would likely relate more comfortably with the "songbirds" rather than the "snakes."

In all of these ways, Collins has meticulously described the characteristics and personalities of both families—that of Lucy Gray and the Covey, and that of Katniss and the Everdeens. There are simply too many parallels to merely write them off as coincidental. The only thing that seems to be missing is the metaphorical bridge to connect the two families together—and more specifically, to reveal the family connection between Maude Ivory and Katniss. Perhaps Suzanne Collins will provide that bridge in a future book that takes us beyond the prequel. In the meantime, we can continue to hope that the proverbial odds for such a thing are ever in our favor.

Chapter Notes

Introduction

1. Elizabeth Hardy, "The Ballad of Songbirds and Snakes, First Thoughts on a Sad, Familiar Song," *Hogwarts Professor: Thoughts for Serious Readers* (blog), May 22, 2020.

Chapter 1

1. Karl Raitz and Richard Ulack, *Appalachia: A Regional Geography* (Boulder: Westview Press, 1984), 32.

2. Dan Hodge, "Appalachian Coal Industry, Power Generation and Supply Chain," *Hodge Economic Consulting* (report), March 16, 2016, https://www.arc.gov/report/www-arc-gov-power/.

3. Jim Poe, "A Look at Appalachian Culture and History in 'The Hunger Games,'" *Times West Virginian*, November 15, 2015, https://www.timeswv.com/news/a-look-at-appalachian-culture-and-history-in-the-hunger-games/article_2a9f14a6-8b7c-11e5-ad77-1fe4f69156e0.html.

4. *Ibid.*

5. *Ibid.*

6. *Ibid.*

7. *Ibid.*

8. *Ibid.*

9. Sarah Baird, "Stereotypes of Appalachia Obscure a Diverse Picture," *National Public Radio*, April 6, 2014, https://www.npr.org/sections/codeswitch/2014/04/03/298892382/stereotypes-of-appalachia-obscure-a-diverse-picture.

10. David Hsiung, *Two Worlds in the Tennessee Mountains: Exploring the Origins of Appalachian Stereotypes* (Lexington: University Press of Kentucky, 1997), 1.

11. *Ibid.*, 2.

12. Poe.

13. *Ibid.*

14. Baird.

15. *Ibid.*

16. Waldo Tobler, "A Computer Movie Simulating Urban Growth in the Detroit Region," *Economic Geography* 46 (Supplement): 234–240.

17. Rick Margolis, "The Last Battle," *School Library Journal* 56, no. 8 (August 2010): 24–27.

18. V. Arrow, *The Panem Companion: An Unofficial Guide to Suzanne Collins' Hunger Games, From Mellark Bakery to Mockingjays* (Dallas: BenBella, 2012).

19. P. Kivisto, and P.R. Croll, *Race and Ethnicity: The Basics* (Taylor and Francis Group, 2012), 11.

20. Ibid.

Chapter 2

1. Patricia Cohen, "Geography Redux: Where You Live Is What You Are," *The New York Times*, March 21, 1998: B7.

2. Carole Blair, Greg Dickinson, and Brian Ott, "Introduction: Rhetoric/Memory/Place," in *Places of Public Memory: The Rhetoric of Museums and Memorials*, 1–54, edited by Greg Dickinson, Carole Blair, and Brian Ott (Tuscaloosa: University of Alabama Press, 2010), 23.

3. Irwin Altman and Setha Low, eds., *Place Attachment* (New York: Plenum Press, 1992).

4. Deidre Garriott, Elaine Jones, and Julie Tyler, "Introduction: Taking Up and Entering Critical Space," in *Space and Place in the Hunger Games: New Readings of the*

Novels, edited by Deidre Anne Evans Garriott, Whitney Elaine Jones, and Julie Elizabeth Tyler (Jefferson, NC: McFarland, 2014).

5. *Ibid.*

6. Wilfred McClay and Ted McAllister, eds., *Why Place Matters: Geography, Identity, and Civic Life in Modern America* (New York: Encounter Books, 2014).

7. *Ibid.,* 12.

8. Maria Giuliani, "Theory of Attachment and Place Attachment," in *Psychological Theories for Environmental Issues,* 137–170, edited by Mirilia Bonnes, Terence Lee, and Marino Bonaiuto (Taylor & Francis Group, 2003).

9. Altman and Low, 1992.

10. Ray Oldenburg, *The Great Good Place: Cafes, Coffee Shops, Bookstores, Bars, Hair Salons, and Other Hangouts at the Heart of a Community* (New York: Marlowe & Company, 1999).

11. Robert Riley, "Attachment to the Ordinary Landscape," in *Place Attachment,* 13–32, edited by Irwin Altman and Setha M. Low (New York: Plenum Press, 1992).

12. bell hooks, "Reclaiming Place: Making Home," in *Appalachia in Regional Context: Place Matters,* 179–188, edited by Dwight Billings and Ann Kingsolver (Lexington: University Press of Kentucky, 2018).

13. *Ibid.,* 180.

14. *Ibid.,* 181.

15. *Ibid.*

16. *Ibid.,* 180.

17. *Ibid.,* 181.

18. *Ibid.*

19. Bill Malone, "Hazel Dickens: A Brief Biography," in *Working Girl Blues: The Life and Music of Hazel Dickens,* 1–31, by Hazel Dickens and Bill C. Malone (Urbana: University of Illinois Press, 2008), 2.

20. *Ibid.*

21. *Ibid.,* 1.

22. *Ibid.,* 16.

23. *Ibid.,* 6.

24. *Ibid.*

25. *Ibid.*

26. Peter Crow, *Do, Die, or Get Along: A Tale of Two Appalachian Towns* (Athens: University of Georgia Press, 2007), 117.

27. *Ibid.,* xvi.

Chapter 3

1. Alison Blunt and Robyn Dowling, *Home: Key Ideas in Geography* (New York: Routledge, 2006).

2. *Ibid.,* 2–3.

3. Tina Hanlon, "Coal Dust and Ballads: Appalachia and District 12," in *Of Bread, Blood, and the Hunger Games: Critical Essays on the Suzanne Collins Trilogy,* 59–68, edited by Mary F. Pharr, Leisa A. Clark, Donald E. Palumbo, and C.W. Sullivan III (Jefferson, NC: McFarland, 2012).

4. *Ibid.*

5. *Ibid.,* 67.

6. Ibid.

Chapter 4

1. Tyler Blethen, "Pioneer Settlement," in *High Mountains Rising: Appalachia in Time and Place,* 17–29, edited by Richard Straw and H. Tyler Blethen (Urbana: University of Illinois Press, 2004).

2. *Ibid.,* 17.

3. Peirce Lewis, "Americanizing English Landscape Habits," in *The Making of the American Landscape,* 91–114, edited by Michael P. Conzen (Routledge, second edition, 2010).

4. Karl Raitz and Richard Ulack, *Appalachia: A Regional Geography* (Boulder: Westview Press, 1984).

5. *Ibid.*

6. *Ibid.*

7. *Ibid.*

8. Blethen.

9. C. Clifford Boyd, Jr., "Native Americans," in *High Mountains Rising: Appalachia in Time and Place,* 7–16, edited by Richard Straw and H. Tyler Blethen (Urbana: University of Illinois Press, 2004).

10. *Ibid.*

11. V. Arrow, *The Panem Companion: An Unofficial Guide to Suzanne Collins' Hunger Games, From Mellark Bakery to Mockingjays* (Dallas: BenBella, 2012).

12. Elizabeth Hardy, "Professor Sprout Goes to District 12 and the Arena: Some 'Hunger Games' Plant and Berry Thoughts," *Hogwarts Professor: Thoughts for Serious Readers* (blog), September 17, 2010.

13. Jill Olthouse, "I Will Be Your Mockingjay: The Power and Paradox of Metaphor in the Hunger Games Trilogy," in *The*

Hunger Games and Philosophy: A Critique of Pure Treason, 41–54, edited by George A. Dunn and Nicolas Michaud (New York: John Wiley & Sons, 2012), 45.

14. Gwen Watson, "The Story of the Cornucopia: The Thanksgiving Horn of Plenty," *Food for Thought* (blog), November 9, 2020.

15. Blethen, 20.

16. *Ibid.*

17. *Ibid.*

18. Boyd.

19. Blethen.

20. Stevan Jackson, "Peoples of Appalachia: Cultural Diversity within the Mountain Region," in *A Handbook to Appalachia: An Introduction to the Region*, 27–50, edited by Grace Toney Edwards, JoAnn Aust Asbury, and Ricky L. Cox (Knoxville: University of Tennessee Press, 2006).

21. Jacob Podber, "Bridging the Digital Divide in Rural Appalachia: Internet Usage in the Mountains." *Proceedings*, Informing Science + IT Education Conference (Pori, Finland, June 24–27, 2003).

22. Jackson.

23. Podber.

24. Jackson, 34.

25. Joan Schroeder, "First Union: The Melungeons Revisited," *Blue Ridge Country*, February 1, 2009.

26. Edward Price, "The Melungeons: A Mixed-Blood Strain of the Southern Appalachians," *Geographical Review* 41, no. 2 (April 1951), 256.

27. Price, 259.

28. Valerie Estelle Frankel, *Katniss the Cattail: An Unauthorized Guide to Names and Symbols in Suzanne Collins' The Hunger Games* (LitCrit Press, 2012).

29. Jackson, 34.

30. Price, 263.

31. Schroeder.

32. Price, 258.

33. Arrow, 27.

34. *Ibid.*, 28.

35. *Ibid.*

36. Jim Poe, "A Look at Appalachian Culture and History in 'The Hunger Games,'" *Times West Virginian*, November 15, 2015.

37. Jackson.

38. *Ibid.*

39. Peter Crow, *Do, Die, or Get Along: A Tale of Two Appalachian Towns* (Athens: University of Georgia Press, 2007), 24.

40. *Ibid.*

41. Crow, 25–26.

42. John Inscoe, "Slavery and African Americans in the Nineteenth Century," in *High Mountains Rising: Appalachia in Time and Place*, 30–45, edited by Richard Straw and H. Tyler Blethen (Urbana: University of Illinois Press, 2004).

43. *Ibid.*

44. Jackson, 40.

45. Crow, 24–25.

46. Karen Valby, "Team 'Hunger Games' Talks: Author Suzanne Collins and Director Gary Ross on Their Allegiance to Each Other, and Their Actors—EXCLUSIVE," *Entertainment Weekly*, April 7, 2011.

Chapter 5

1. Luke Moss, "How to Find Every Single Hunger Games Location in Real Life," *Hostelworld* (blog), August 8, 2019.

2. Lewis, 2010.

3. Spiro Kostof, *The City Shaped: Urban Patterns and Meanings Through History* (London: Thames & Hudson, 1991),145–46.

4. Peirce Lewis, "Americanizing English Landscape Habits," in *The Making of the American Landscape*, 91–114, edited by Michael P. Conzen (Routledge, second edition, 2010).

5. Kostof, 146

6. Lewis, "Americanizing," 109.

7. Kostof.

8. *Ibid.*

9. Richard Francaviglia, *Main Street Revisited: Time, Space, and Image Building in Small-Town America* (Iowa City: University of Iowa Press, 1996).

10. *Ibid.*, 80.

11. Francaviglia.

12. Lewis, "Americanizing," 112.

13. Donald Meinig, "Symbolic Landscapes: Models of American Community," in *The Interpretation of Ordinary Landscapes*, 164–192, edited by Donald W. Meinig (New York: Oxford University Press, 1978).

14. Rickie Sanders, "The Public Spaces of Urban Communities," in *Architecture Technology Culture: Public Space and the Ideology of Place in American Culture*, 263–287, edited by Miles Orvell and Jeffrey Meikle (Amsterdam: BRILL, 2009), 264.

15. *Ibid.*, 265.

16. Scott Nyerges, "Classic Five-and-Dime Stores from Yesterday and Today," *Cheapism* (blog), December 30, 2020.

17. Editors of Encyclopaedia Britannica, "Walmart," *Encyclopedia Britannica*, March 4, 2019.

Chapter 6

1. "Iconic 'Hunger Games' filming location named to National Register of Historic Places," *CBS News*. June 21, 2019.

2. Marla Milling, "How the 'Hunger Games' Henry River Mill Village is being brought back to life," *Citizen Times* (Asheville, NC), August 11, 2018.

3. "Iconic 'Hunger Games' filming location named to National Register of Historic Places."

4. *Ibid.*

5. *Ibid.*

6. Mekado Murphy, "Gary Ross Answers Reader Questions About 'The Hunger Games,'" *New York Times.*, March 30, 2012.

7. Ronald Lewis, "Industrialization," in *High Mountains Rising: Appalachia in Time and Place*, 59–73, edited by Richard Straw and H. Tyler Blethen (Urbana: University of Illinois Press, 2004).

8. *Ibid.*, 66.

9. *Ibid.*

10. *Ibid.*, 67.

11. *Ibid.*

12. Peter Crow, *Do, Die, or Get Along: A Tale of Two Appalachian Towns* (Athens: University of Georgia Press, 2007), 117.

13. *Ibid.*, xvi.

14. Ibid.

Chapter 7

1. Spiro Kostof, *The City Shaped: Urban Patterns and Meanings Through History* (London: Thames & Hudson, 1991), 215.

2. *Ibid.*

3. *Ibid.* 216.

4. Wilbur Zelinsky, "Asserting Central Authority," in *The Making of the American Landscape*, 329–356, edited by Michael P. Conzen= (Routledge, second edition, 2010), 339–340.

5. *Ibid.*

6. Kostof.

7. *Ibid.*, 209.

8. *Ibid.*

9. Kenneth Fletcher, "A Brief History of Pierre L'Enfant and Washington, D.C.," *Smithsonian Magazine,*April 30, 2008.

10. *Ibid.*

11. Zelinsky.

12. Fletcher.

13. Peirce Lewis, "Americanizing English Landscape Habits," in *The Making of the American Landscape*, 91–114, edited by Michael P. Conzen (Routledge, second edition, 2010), 109.

14. Zelinsky, 340.

15. James McGregor, *Rome: From the Ground Up* (Cambridge: Belknap Press of Harvard University Press, 2005).

16. *Ibid.*, 79.

17. *Ibid.*, 267.

18. *Ibid.*, 278–79.

19. Ross King, *Brunelleschi's Dome: How a Renaissance Genius Reinvented Architecture* (New York: Penguin Books, 2000). See also Ian Sutton, *Western Architecture* (London: Thames and Hudson, 1999).

20. Zelinsky, 342.

21. Ian Sutton, *Western Architecture* (London: Thames and Hudson, 1999), 318.

22. *Ibid.*

23. Germain Lussier, "Film Interview: Gary Ross, The Director of 'The Hunger Games,'" *Film* (blog), March 21, 2012.

24. Sarah Cunliffe, Sara Hunt, and Jean Loussier, *Architecture: A Spotter's Guide* (New York: Metro Books, 2006), 242.

25. Sutton, 344.

26. *Ibid.*

27. "The Hunger Games: Catching Fire," *Movie-Locations.com*, accessed February 23, 2021.

28. Symbols.com,. *"Capitol,"* accessed April 17, 2021.

29. Jimmy Stamp, "The Architecture of the Hunger Games' Horns of Plenty," *Smithsonian Magazine*, November 26, 2014.

30. *Ibid.*

31. *Ibid.*

32. *Ibid.*

33. Cunliffe.

34. *Ibid.*, 256.

35. David Sokol, and Nick Mafi, "31 Spectacular Buildings Designed by Frank Gehry," *Architectural Digest*, November 27, 2018.

36. Cunliffe.

Chapter 8

1. Katie Willis, *Theories and Practices of Development*, 2d ed. (Abingdon, Oxon: Routledge, 2011).
2. For an overview, see Immanuel Wallerstein, *World-Systems Analysis: An Introduction* (Durham: Duke University Press, 2004).
3. Willis.
4. *Ibid.*, 81.
5. Karl Thompson, "World Systems Theory," ReviseSociology (blog), December 5, 2015.
6. Ronald Lewis, "Industrialization," in *High Mountains Rising: Appalachia in Time and Place*, 59–73, edited by Richard Straw and H. Tyler Blethen (Urbana: University of Illinois Press, 2004), 62.
7. *Ibid.*, 63.
8. Ibid.

Chapter 9

1. "Songs," *The Hunger Games Wiki*.
2. Bill Malone, "Music," in *High Mountains Rising: Appalachia in Time and Place*, 114–134, edited by Richard Straw and H. Tyler Blethen (Urbana: University of Illinois Press, 2004).
3. John Kenrick, "What Is a Musical?" *Musicals101.com*.
4. Valerie Estelle Frankel, *Songbirds, Snakes & Sacrifice: Collins' Prequel References and Philosophies Explained* (self-published, 2020).
5. Mary Miller, "Restorying Dystopia: Exploring the Hunger Games Series Though U.S. Cultural Geographies, Identities, and Fan Response," Dissertation, The Ohio State University, 2017.
6. Debby McClatchy, "Appalachian Traditional Music: A Short History," June 27, 2000.
7. Miller.
8. Stephanie Ledgin, *Homegrown Music: Discovering Bluegrass* (Westport: ABC-CLIO, , 2004).
9. Whitney Smith, "Discovering the Roots of Appalachian Music," June 22, 2016.
10. Elizabeth Hardy, "The Ballad of Songbirds and Snakes, First Thoughts on a Sad, Familiar Song," *Hogwarts Professor: Thoughts for Serious Readers* (blog), May 22, 2020.
11. *Ibid.*

12. Amelia Mason, "The Hidden Roots of 'Hunger Games' Hit Song? Murder Ballads, Civil Rights Hymns," *National Public Radio*, December 10, 2014.
13. Hardy, "Ballad."
14. *Ibid.*
15. Mason.
16. *Ibid.*
17. V. Arrow, *The Panem Companion: An Unofficial Guide to Suzanne Collins' Hunger Games, From Mellark Bakery to Mockingjays* (Dallas: BenBella Books, 2012), 30.
18. John Granger, "Mockingjay Discussion 15: The Hanging Tree," *Hogwarts Professor: Thoughts for Serious Readers* (blog), August 25, 2010.
19. Mason.
20. Miller.
21. Granger.
22. *Ibid.*
23. McClatchy.
24. *Ibid.*
25. Frankel, *Songbirds.*
26. *Ibid.*
27. Ted Olson and Ajay Kalra, "Appalachian Music: Examining Popular Assumptions," in *A Handbook to Appalachia: An Introduction to the Region*, 163–180, edited by Grace Toney Edwards, JoAnn Aust Asbury, and Ricky L. Cox (Knoxville: University of Tennessee Press, 2006).
28. *Ibid.*
29. "The Centennial Celebration: A Brief History of These Events," *Cecil Sharp in Appalachia.*
30. Elizabeth DiSavino, *Katherine Jackson French: Kentucky's Forgotten Ballad Collector* (Lexington: University Press of Kentucky, 2020).
31. *Ibid.*
32. *Ibid.*, 2.
33. *Ibid.*, 59.
34. Daniel Walkowitz, *City Folk: English Country Dance and the Politics of the Folk in Modern America* (New York: New York University Press, 2010).
35. This popular version of "Clementine" was referenced for purposes here: https://www.nurseryrhymes.org/oh-my-darling-clementine.html.
36. Gerald Brenan, *South from Grenada* (Cambridge: Penguin, 1957), 109.
37. This popular version of "Clementine" was referenced for purposes here: https://www.nurseryrhymes.org/oh-my-darling-clementine.html.

38. Brian Hicks, *Toward the Setting Sun: John Ross, the Cherokees, and the Trail of Tears* (New York: Grove Atlantic, 2011).

39. *Ibid.*, 128.

40. Tyler Blethen, "Pioneer Settlement," in *High Mountains Rising: Appalachia in Time and Place*, 17–29, edited by Richard Straw and H. Tyler Blethen (Urbana: University of Illinois Press, 2004).

41. C. Clifford Boyd, Jr., "Native Americans," in *High Mountains Rising: Appalachia in Time and Place*, 7–16, edited by Richard Straw and H. Tyler Blethen (Urbana: University of Illinois Press, 2004).

42. *Ibid.*, 15.

43. See background and lyrics for "Fire on the Mountain": https://www.songfacts.com/facts/the-marshall-tucker-band/fire-on-the-mountain.

Chapter 10

1. Charles Perryman and West Virginia University, "Africa, Appalachia, and Acculturation: The History of Bluegrass Music," Dissertation, West Virginia University Libraries, 2013.

2. Stephanie Ledgin, *Homegrown Music: Discovering Bluegrass* (Westport: ABC-CLIO, 2004), 10.

3. Gordon Swift, "Learn the Difference Between Violin and Fiddle," *Strings Magazine*, March 31, 2021.

4. Perryman.

5. *Ibid.*

6. *Ibid.*, 27.

7. *Ibid.*, 28.

8. Cecelia Conway, "Black Banjo Songsters in Appalachia," *Black Music Research Journal* 23, no. 1–2 (March 1, 2003).

9. Ledgin.

10. Conway.

11. David Pilgrim, "The Coon Caricature," *Jim Crow Museum of Racist Memorabilia*, Ferris State University, 2000 (edited 2012).

12. Perryman.

13. Conway.

14. Allen Farmelo, "Another History of Bluegrass: The Segregation of American Popular Music, 1820–1900," *Popular Music and Society* 25, no. 1–2 (March 1, 2001), 192–93.

15. Perryman.

16. Mike Seeger, "A Brief History of the Guitar and its Travel South," *Smithsonian Music* (blog), June 2016.

17. *Ibid.*

18. Perryman.

19. *Ibid.*

20. Farmelo, 195.

21. Perryman.

22. Olly Wilson, "The Heterogeneous Sound Ideal in African-American Music," in *Signifyin(g), Sanctifyin,' & Slam Dunking*, 157–171, edited by Gena Dagel Caponi (Amherst: University of Massachusetts Press, 1999).

23. Fred Hay, "Black Musicians in Appalachia: An Introduction to Affrilachian Music," *Black Music Research Journal* 23, no. 1–2 (March 1, 2003), 13–14.

24. Ted Olson and Ajay Kalra, "Appalachian Music: Examining Popular Assumptions," in *A Handbook to Appalachia: An Introduction to the Region*, 163–180, edited by Grace Toney Edwards, JoAnn Aust Asbury, and Ricky L. Cox (Knoxville: University of Tennessee Press, 2006).

Chapter 11

1. Ted Olson and Ajay Kalra, "Appalachian Music: Examining Popular Assumptions," in *A Handbook to Appalachia: An Introduction to the Region*, 163–180, edited by Grace Toney Edwards, JoAnn Aust Asbury, and Ricky L. Cox (Knoxville: University of Tennessee Press, 2006).

2. *Ibid.*

3. Bill Malone, "Music," in *High Mountains Rising: Appalachia in Time and Place*, 114–134, edited by Richard Straw and H. Tyler Blethen (Urbana: University of Illinois Press, 2004).

4. Stephanie Ledgin, *Homegrown Music: Discovering Bluegrass* (Westport: ABC-CLIO, 2004).

5. Malone.

6. *Ibid.*

7. *Ibid.*, 118.

8. Stephanie Ledgin, *Homegrown Music: Discovering Bluegrass* (Westport: ABC-CLIO, 2004), 46.

9. *Ibid.*, 47.

10. Malone, "Music."

11. John Phillips, "The African Heritage of White America," in *Africanisms in American Culture*, 230, edited by Joseph E.

Holloway (Bloomington: Indiana University Press, 1991).

12. Ken Tate and Janice Tate, *Favorite Songs of the Good Old Days* (Berne, Indiana: House of White Birches, 2004), 29.

13. Charles Perryman and West Virginia University, "Africa, Appalachia, and Acculturation: The History of Bluegrass Music," Dissertation, West Virginia University Libraries, 2013, 41.

14. Olson and Kalra.

15. Perryman, 41.

16. Olson and Kalra.

17. Malone, "Music."

18. Allen Farmelo, "Another History of Bluegrass: The Segregation of American Popular Music, 1820–1900," *Popular Music and Society* 25, no. 1–2 (March 1, 2001), 196.

19. Olson and Kalra.

20. *Ibid.*, 168.

21. *Ibid.*

22. Rebecca Scott, *Removing Mountains: Extracting Nature and Identity in the Appalachian Coalfields* (Minneapolis: University of Minnesota Press, 2010).

23. Scott, 33.

24. *Ibid.*, 34.

25. Olson and Kalra, 169.

26. David Wylie, "National Barn Dance," *Nostalgia Digest.*

27. *Ibid.*

28. Perryman.

29. Wylie.

30. "The Grand Ole Opry Begins Broadcasting," *History*, November 16, 2009.

31. Olson and Kalra, 170.

32. *Ibid.*

33. David Hsiung, "Stereotypes," in *High Mountains Rising: Appalachia in Time and Place*, 101–113, edited by Richard Straw and H. Tyler Blethen (Urbana: University of Illinois Press, 2004).

34. *Ibid.*, 107.

35. Eugene Chadbourne, "John Lair," *AllMusic.*

36. *Ibid.*

37. Perryman.

38. *Ibid.*

39. *Ibid.*

40. *Ibid.*

41. Malone, "Music."

42. *Ibid.*

43. Tina Hanlon, "Coal Dust and Ballads: Appalachia and District 12," in *Of Bread, Blood, and the Hunger Games:* *Critical Essays on the Suzanne Collins Trilogy*, 59–68, edited by Mary F. Pharr, Leisa A. Clark, Donald E. Palumbo, and C. W. Sullivan III (Jefferson, NC: McFarland, 2012), 65.

44. Olson and Kalra, 165.

45. Scott, 38.

46. *Ibid.*, 40.

47. *Ibid.*, 39.

48. *Ibid.*, 57.

49. *Ibid.*, 58.

50. Olson and Karla.

51. Chadbourne.

52. Hanlon.

53. *Ibid.*, 67.

Chapter 12

1. Stephanie Ledgin, *Homegrown Music: Discovering Bluegrass* (Westport: ABC-CLIO, 2004).

2. "That High, Lonesome Sound: A Guide to the Instruments in Bluegrass," *zZounds Music, LLC.*

3. Neil Rosenberg, *Bluegrass: A History.* Music in American Life (Urbana: University of Illinois Press, 1985).

4. Ledgin.

5. Mayne Smith, "An Introduction to Bluegrass." *Journal of American Folklore* 78, no. 309 (July-September 1965): 245–256.

6. *Ibid.*, 246.

7. *Ibid.*

8. *Ibid.*

9. Ledgin, 3.

10. George Carney, "Western North Carolina: Culture Hearth of Bluegrass Music," *Journal of Cultural Geography* 16, no. 1 (Sept. 1996): 65–87.

11. Smith, "Introduction," 254.

12. Ledgin.

13. Smith, "Introduction," 254.

14. *Ibid.*

15. "That High, Lonesome Sound: A Guide to the Instruments in Bluegrass."

16. Ledgin, 3.

17. Smith, "Introduction," 249.

18. Charles Perryman, "Africa, Appalachia, and Acculturation: The History of Bluegrass Music," Dissertation, West Virginia University Libraries, 2013.

19. Bill Malone, "Music," in *High Mountains Rising: Appalachia in Time and Place*, 114–134, edited by Richard Straw and H.

Tyler Blethen (Urbana: University of Illinois Press, 2004), 128.

20. Perryman.

Chapter 13

1. "Bill Monroe—50th Opry Anniversary," Jan Johansson Acoustic Music, November 12, 2015, video, 21:57.

2. Charles Perryman, "Africa, Appalachia, and Acculturation: The History of Bluegrass Music," Dissertation, West Virginia University Libraries, 2013, 66–67.

3. Stephen Thomas Erlewine, "Bill Monroe," *AllMusic*.

4. Perryman.

5. Stephanie Ledgin, *Homegrown Music: Discovering Bluegrass* (Westport: ABC-CLIO, 2004), 19.

6. Perryman, 54.

7. *Ibid.*

8. *Ibid.*, 58.

9. Ledgin.

10. Perryman.

11. *Ibid.*, 18.

12. Editors of Encyclopaedia Britannica, "Bill Monroe." *Encyclopedia Britannica*, September 9, 2020.

13. Ledgin.

14. James Rooney, *Bossmen: Bill Monroe and Muddy Waters* (New York: Hayden Book Company, 1971), 41.

15. Perryman, 61.

16. Dan Beimborn, "A Brief History of the Mandolin," *Mandolin Café*, accessed November 11, 2020.

17. Perryman, 63.

18. Ledgin.

19. Perryman, 61.

20. *Ibid.*

21. *Ibid.*, 65.

22. Wayne Erbsen, "Tommy Millard—Blackfaced Musician & Bluegrass Boy," *Bluegrass Unlimited Magazine* (May 1986).

23. Perryman.

24. *Ibid.*, 65.

25. "History of the Mandolin," theMandolinPages.

26. Ledgin, 15.

27. Dan Beimborn, "A Brief History of the Mandolin," Mandolin Café, accessed April 2, 2021.

Chapter 14

1. "Bill Monroe and his Bluegrass Boys," *Rate Your Music*.

2. Mayne Smith, "An Introduction to Bluegrass." *Journal of American Folklore* 78, no. 309 (July-September 1965), 251–52.

3. George Carney, "Bluegrass Grows All Around: The Spatial Dimensions of a Country Music Style," *Journal of Geography* 73, no. 4 (1974): 34–55.

4. Paul Brown, "The Story of 'Foggy Mountain Breakdown,'" *National Public Radio*, April 1, 2000.

5. Steve Martin, "The Master from Flint Hill: Earl Scruggs," *The New Yorker Magazine*, January 13, 2012.

6. *Ibid.*

7. Charles Perryman, "Africa, Appalachia, and Acculturation: The History of Bluegrass Music," Dissertation, West Virginia University Libraries, 2013, 71.

8. *Ibid.*

9. Smith, "Introduction."

10. Perryman, 81.

11. Stephanie Ledgin, *Homegrown Music: Discovering Bluegrass* (Westport: ABC-CLIO, 2004), 6.

12. Perryman.

13. Smith, "Introduction."

14. Ledgin, 6.

15. Bill Malone, "Music," in *High Mountains Rising: Appalachia in Time and Place*, 114–134, edited by Richard Straw and H. Tyler Blethen (Urbana: University of Illinois Press, 2004), 129.

16. Ted Olson and Ajay Kalra, "Appalachian Music: Examining Popular Assumptions," in *A Handbook to Appalachia: An Introduction to the Region*, 163–180, edited by Grace Toney Edwards, JoAnn Aust Asbury, and Ricky L. Cox (Knoxville: University of Tennessee Press, 2006), 172.

17. Malone, "Music."

18. Ledgin, 23.

19. Neil Rosenberg, *Bluegrass: A History*. Music in American Life (Urbana: University of Illinois Press, 1985).

20. Malone, "Music."

21. Smith, "Introduction."

22. Perryman, 23.

23. Robert Cantwell, *Bluegrass Breakdown: The Making of the Old Southern Sound*. Music in American Life (Urbana: University of Illinois Press, 1984), 71.

24. Carney, "Bluegrass," 35.

25. Smith, "Introduction," 251.

26. *Ibid.*, 250.

27. Carney, "Bluegrass."

28. Holly Kern, MaKayla Markey, and Zane Gurwitz, "Neo-Traditionalism," Country Music Project, September 22, 2014.

29. *Ibid.*

30. *Ibid.*

31. "Ricky Skaggs: The Story," *Ricky Skaggs: A Lifetime of Music.*

32. Don Harrison, "Old-Time Man: An Interview with Mountain Music Virtuoso Ralph Stanley," *Virginia Living Magazine* (June 2008), republished September 23, 2019.

Chapter 15

1. "Scholastic Releases New Interview with Suzanne Collins, Author of the Worldwide Bestselling Hunger Games Series," *Scholastic*, May 19, 2020.

2. Vasilis K. Pozios and Praveen Kambam, "How Bad is Katniss' PTSD in The Hunger Games? We Asked the Experts," *Wired*, November 24, 2014.

Bibliography

Altman, Irwin, and Low, Setha M., eds. *Place Attachment*. New York: Plenum Press, 1992. Print.

Arrow, V. *The Panem Companion: An Unofficial Guide to Suzanne Collins' Hunger Games, From Mellark Bakery to Mockingjays*. Dallas: BenBella Books, 2012. Accessed April 3, 2021. ProQuest Ebook Central.

Baird, Sarah. "Stereotypes of Appalachia Obscure a Diverse Picture." *National Public Radio*. April 6, 2014. https://www.npr.org/sections/codeswitch/2014/04/03/298892382/stereotypes-of-appalachia-obscure-a-diverse-picture.

Beimborn, Dan. "A Brief History of the Mandolin." Mandolin Café. Accessed April 2, 2021. https://www.mandolincafe.com/archives/briefhistory.html.

"Bill Monroe and his Bluegrass Boys." *Rate Your Music*. Accessed February 23, 2020. https://ru.rateyourmusic.com/artist/bill-monroe-and-his-bluegrass-boys.

"Bill Monroe—50th Opry Anniversary." Jan Johansson Acoustic Music, November 12, 2015, video, 21:57. https://www.youtube.com/watch?v=1PBTHuHM0ew.

Blair, Carole, Dickinson, Greg, and Ott, Brian. "Introduction: Rhetoric/Memory/Place." In *Places of Public Memory: The Rhetoric of Museums and Memorials*, 1–54. Edited by Greg Dickinson, Carole Blair, and Brian Ott. Tuscaloosa: University of Alabama Press, 2010. Accessed April 3, 2021. ProQuest Ebook Central.

Blethen, H. Tyler. "Pioneer Settlement." In *High Mountains Rising: Appalachia in Time and Place*, 17–29. Edited by Richard Straw and H. Tyler Blethen. Urbana: University of Illinois Press, 2004.

Blunt, Alison, and Dowling, Robyn M. *Home*. Key Ideas in Geography. New York: Routledge, 2006. Print.

Boyd, C. Clifford, Jr. "Native Americans." In *High Mountains Rising: Appalachia in Time and Place*, 7–16. Edited by Richard Straw and H. Tyler Blethen. Urbana: University of Illinois Press, 2004.

Brenan, Gerald. *South from Grenada*. Cambridge: Penguin, 1957.

Brown, Paul. "The Story of 'Foggy Mountain Breakdown.'" *National Public Radio*. April 1, 2000. https://www.npr.org/2000/04/01/1072355/npr-100-earl-scruggs.

Cantwell, Robert. *Bluegrass Breakdown: The Making of the Old Southern Sound*. Music in American Life. Urbana: University of Illinois Press, 1984. Print.

Carney, George O. "Bluegrass Grows All Around: The Spatial Dimensions of a Country Music Style." *Journal of Geography* 73, no. 4 (1974): 34–55. https://doi-org.ezproxy.butler.edu/10.1080/00221347408980277.

_____. "Western North Carolina: Culture Hearth of Bluegrass Music." *Journal of Cultural Geography* 16, no. 1 (Sept. 1996): 65–87. http://dx.doi.org/10.1080/08873639609478347.

"The Centennial Celebration: A Brief History of These Events." *Cecil Sharp in Appalachia*. Accessed June 1, 2020. https://cecilsharpinappalachia.org/briefhistory.html.

Chadbourne, Eugene. "John Lair." *AllMusic*. Accessed April 5, 2021. https://www.allmusic.com/artist/john-lair-mn0001217348/biography.

Cohen, Patricia. "Geography Redux: Where You Live is What You Are." *New York Times*, March 21, 1998: B7. https://www.nytimes.com/1998/03/21/arts/geography-redux-where-you-live-is-what-you-are. html?searchResultPosition=1.

Collins, Suzanne. *The Ballad of Songbirds and Snakes*. New York: Scholastic, 2020. Hardcover.

_____. *Catching Fire*. New York: Scholastic, 2009. Paperback.

_____. *The Hunger Games*. New York: Scholastic, 2008. Paperback.

_____. *Mockingjay*. New York: Scholastic, 2010. Paperback.

Conway, Cecelia. "Black Banjo Songsters in Appalachia." *Black Music Research Journal* 23, no. 1–2 (March 1, 2003).

Crow, Peter. *Do, Die, or Get Along: A Tale of Two Appalachian Towns*. Athens: University of Georgia Press, 2007. Accessed April 2, 2021. ProQuest Ebook Central.

Cunliffe, Sarah, Hunt, Sara, and Loussier, Jean. *Architecture: A Spotter's Guide*. New York: Metro Books, 2006. Print.

Dickinson, Greg, Blair, Carole, and Ott, Brian L., eds. *Places of Public Memory: The Rhetoric of Museums and Memorials*. Tuscaloosa: University of Alabama Press, 2010. Accessed April 3, 2021. ProQuest Ebook Central.

DiSavino, Elizabeth. *Katherine Jackson French: Kentucky's Forgotten Ballad Collector*. Lexington: University Press of Kentucky, 2020. Accessed April 3, 2021. doi:10.2307/j.ctvl03xdnj.

Editors of Encyclopaedia Britannica. "Bill Monroe." *Encyclopedia Britannica*, September 9, 2020. https://www.britannica.com/biography/Bill-Monroe.

_____. "Walmart." *Encyclopedia Britannica*, March 4, 2019. https://www.britannica.com/topic/Walmart.

Edwards, Grace T., Asbury, JoAnn A., and Cox, Ricky L., eds. *A Handbook to Appalachia: An Introduction to the Region*. Knoxville: University of Tennessee Press, 2006.

Erbsen, Wayne. "Tommy Millard—Blackfaced Musician & Bluegrass Boy." *Bluegrass Unlimited Magazine* (May 1986). https://nativeground.com/tommy-millard-blackfaced-musician-a-bluegrass-boy-by-wayne-erbsen/.

Erlewine, Stephen Thomas. "Bill Monroe." *AllMusic*. Accessed April 4, 2021. https://www.allmusic.com/artist/bill-monroe-mn0000081083/biography.

Farmelo, Allen. "Another History of Bluegrass: The Segregation of American Popular Music, 1820–1900." *Popular Music and Society* 25, no. 1–2 (March 1, 2001): 179–203.

Fletcher, Kenneth R. "A Brief History of Pierre L'Enfant and Washington, D.C." *Smithsonian Magazine*. April 30, 2008. https://www.smithsonianmag.com/arts-culture/a-brief-history-of-pierre-lenfant-and-washington-dc-39487784/.

Francaviglia, Richard V. *Main Street Revisited: Time, Space, and Image Building in Small-Town America*. Iowa City: University of Iowa Press, 1996. Accessed April 2, 2021. ProQuest Ebook Central.

Frankel, Valerie Estelle. *Katniss the Cattail: An Unauthorized Guide to Names and Symbols in Suzanne Collins' The Hunger Games*. LitCrit Press, 2012. Print.

_____. *Songbirds, Snakes & Sacrifice: Collins' Prequel References and Philosophies Explained*. Self-published, 2020.

Garriott, Deidre Anne Evans; Jones, Whitney Elaine; and Tyler, Julie Elizabeth. "Introduction: Taking Up and Entering Critical Space." In *Space and Place in the Hunger Games: New Readings of the Novels*. Edited by Deidre Anne Evans Garriott, Whitney Elaine Jones, and Julie Elizabeth Tyler. Jefferson: McFarland, 2014.

Giuliani, Maria Vittoria. "Theory of Attachment and Place Attachment." In *Psychological Theories for Environmental Issues*, 137–170. Edited by Mirilia Bonnes, Terence Lee, and Marino Bonaiuto. Taylor & Francis Group, 2003.

"The Grand Ole Opry Begins Broadcasting." *History*. November 16, 2009. https://www.history.com/this-day-in-history/the-grand-ole-opry-begins-broadcasting.

Granger, John. "Mockingjay Discussion 15: The Hanging Tree." *Hogwarts Professor: Thoughts for Serious Readers* (blog). August 25, 2010. https://www.hogwartsprofessor.com/mockingjay-discussion-15-the-hanging-tree/.

Hanlon, Tina L. "Coal Dust and Ballads: Appalachia and District 12." In *Of Bread, Blood, and the Hunger Games: Critical Essays on the Suzanne Collins Trilogy*, 59–68. Edited by Mary F. Pharr, Leisa A. Clark, Donald E. Palumbo, and C. W. Sullivan III. Jefferson, NC: McFarland, 2012. Accessed April 3, 2021. ProQuest Ebook Central.

Hardy, Elizabeth Baird. "The Ballad of

Songbirds and Snakes, First Thoughts on a Sad, Familiar Song." *Hogwarts Professor: Thoughts for Serious Readers* (blog). May 22, 2020. https://www.hogwartsprofessor.com/the-ballad-of-songbirds-and-snakes-first-thoughts-on-a-sad-familiar-song/.

_____. "Professor Sprout Goes to District 12 and the Arena: Some 'Hunger Games' Plant and Berry Thoughts." *Hogwarts Professor: Thoughts for Serious Readers* (blog). September 17, 2010. https://www.hogwartsprofessor.com/professor-sprout-goes-to-district-12-some-hunger-games-plant-thoughts/.

Harrison, Don. "Old-Time Man: An Interview with Mountain Music Virtuoso Ralph Stanley." *Virginia Living Magazine* (June 2008). Republished September 23, 2019. http://www.virginialiving.com/culture/old-time-man/.

Hay, Fred J. "Black Musicians in Appalachia: An Introduction to Affrilachian Music." *Black Music Research Journal* 23, no. 1–2 (March 1, 2003): 1–19.

Hicks, Brian. *Toward the Setting Sun: John Ross, the Cherokees, and the Trail of Tears.* New York: Grove Atlantic, 2011. Accessed April 3, 2021. ProQuest Ebook Central.

"History of the Mandolin." theMandolin-Pages. Accessed April 2, 2021. http://banjolin.co.uk/mandolin/mandolin history.htm.

Hodge, Dan. "Appalachian Coal Industry, Power Generation and Supply Chain." *Hodge Economic Consulting* (Report), March 16, 2016. https://www.arc.gov/report/www-arc-gov-power/.

Hooks, bell. "Reclaiming Place: Making Home." In *Appalachia in Regional Context: Place Matters,* 179–188. Edited by Dwight Billings and Ann Kingsolver. Lexington: University Press of Kentucky, 2018. Accessed April 2, 2021. http://www.jstor.org/stable/j.cttlz27j0k.

Hsiung, David C. "Stereotypes." In *High Mountains Rising: Appalachia in Time and Place,* 101–113. Edited by Richard Straw and H. Tyler Blethen. Urbana: University of Illinois Press, 2004. Print.

_____. *Two Worlds in the Tennessee Mountains: Exploring the Origins of Appalachian Stereotypes.* Lexington: University Press of Kentucky, 1997.

"The Hunger Games: Catching Fire." *Movie-Locations.com.* Accessed February 23, 2021. https://www.movie-locations.com/movies/h/Hunger-Games-Catching-Fire.php.

"Iconic 'Hunger Games' filming location named to National Register of Historic Places." *CBS News.* June 21, 2019. https://www.cbsnews.com/news/hunger-games-district-12-filming-location-named-to-national-register-of-historic-places-2019-06-21/.

Inscoe, John C. "Slavery and African Americans in the Nineteenth Century." In *High Mountains Rising: Appalachia in Time and Place,* 30–45. Edited by Richard Straw and H. Tyler Blethen. Urbana: University of Illinois Press, 2004. Print.

Jackson, Stevan R. "Peoples of Appalachia: Cultural Diversity within the Mountain Region." In *A Handbook to Appalachia: An Introduction to the Region,* 27–50. Edited by Grace Toney Edwards, JoAnn Aust Asbury, and Ricky L. Cox. Knoxville: University of Tennessee Press, 2006.

Kenrick, John. "What Is a Musical?" *Musicals101.com.* https://www.musicals101.com/musical.htm.

Kern, Holly, Markey, MaKayla, and Gurwitz, Zane. "Neo-Traditionalism." Country Music Project. September 22, 2014. https://sites.dwrl.utexas.edu/country music/the-history/new-traditionalism/.

King, Ross. *Brunelleschi's Dome: How a Renaissance Genius Reinvented Architecture.* New York: Penguin Books, 2000. Print.

Kivisto, P., and Croll, P.R. *Race and Ethnicity: The Basics.* Taylor and Francis Group, 2012.

Kostof, Spiro. *The City Shaped: Urban Patterns and Meanings Through History.* London: Thames & Hudson, 1991. Print.

Lawrence, Keith. "Arnold Shultz: Godfather of Bluegrass?" *Bluegrass Unlimited* 24 (November 1989): 39–43.

Ledgin, Stephanie P. *Homegrown Music: Discovering Bluegrass.* Westport: ABC-CLIO, 2004. Accessed April 2, 2021. ProQuest Ebook Central.

Ledgin, Stephanie P. Homegrown Music: Discovering Bluegrass. Westport: ABC-CLIO, 2004. Accessed April 2, 2021. ProQuest Ebook Central.

Lewis, Peirce F. "Americanizing English Landscape Habits." In *The Making of the American Landscape,* 91–114. Edited by

Michael P. Conzen. Routledge (second edition), 2010.

Lewis, Ronald L. "Industrialization." In *High Mountains Rising: Appalachia in Time and Place,* 59–73. Edited by Richard Straw and H. Tyler Blethen. Urbana: University of Illinois Press, 2004. Print.

Lussier, Germain. "Film Interview: Gary Ross, The Director of 'The Hunger Games.'" *Film* (blog). March 21, 2012. https://www.slashfilm.com/film-interview-gary-ross-director-the-hunger-games/.

Malone, Bill C. "Hazel Dickens: A Brief Biography." In *Working Girl Blues: The Life and Music of Hazel Dickens,* 1–31. By Hazel Dickens and Bill C. Malone. Urbana: University of Illinois Press, 2008. Accessed April 3, 2021. ProQuest Ebook Central.

_____. "Music." In *High Mountains Rising: Appalachia in Time and Place,* 114–134. Edited by Richard Straw and H. Tyler Blethen. Urbana: University of Illinois Press, 2004. Print.

Margolis, Rick. "The Last Battle." *School Library Journal* 56, no. 8 (August 2010): 24–27. https://ezproxy.butler.edu/login?url=https://www-proquest-com.ezproxy.butler.edu/trade-journals/last-battle-deck-2/docview/818699864/se-2?accountid=9807.

Martin, Steve. "The Master from Flint Hill: Earl Scruggs." *The New Yorker Magazine.* January 13, 2012. https://www.newyorker.com/culture/culture-desk/the-master-from-flint-hill-earl-scruggs.

Mason, Amelia. "The Hidden Roots of 'Hunger Games' Hit Song? Murder Ballads, Civil Rights Hymns." *National Public Radio.* December 10, 2014. https://www.wbur.org/artery/2014/12/10/hunger-games-mockingjay.

McClatchy, Debby. "Appalachian Traditional Music: A Short History." June 27, 2000. https://www.mustrad.org.uk/articles/appalach.htm.

McClay, Wilfred M. "Introduction: Why Place Matters." In *Why Place Matters: Geography, Identity, and Civic Life in Modern America,* 11–16. Edited by Wilfred M. McClay and Ted V. McAllister. New York: Encounter Books, 2014. Accessed April 2, 2021. ProQuest Ebook Central.

McGregor, James H. S. *Rome: From the Ground Up.* Cambridge: The Belknap Press of Harvard University Press, 2005.

Meinig, Donald W. "Symbolic Landscapes: Models of American Community." In *The Interpretation of Ordinary Landscapes,* 164–192. Edited by Donald W. Meinig. New York : Oxford University Press, 1978. Print.

Miller, Mary C. "Restorying Dystopia: Exploring the Hunger Games Series Though U.S. Cultural Geographies, Identities, and Fan Response." Dissertation, The Ohio State University, 2017. https://etd.ohiolink.edu/apexprod/rws_etd/send_file/send?accession=osu1492434124077694&disposition=inline.

Milling, Marla H. "How the 'Hunger Games' Henry River Mill Village is being brought back to life." *Citizen Times* (Asheville, NC), August 11, 2018. https://www.citizen-times.com/story/life/2018/08/11/hunger-games-henry-river-mill-village-restore-asheville-north-carolina/884756002/.

Moss, Luke. "How to Find Every Single Hunger Games Location in Real Life." *Hostelworld* (blog), August 8, 2019, https://www.hostelworld.com/blog/how-to-find-every-single-hunger-games-location-in-real-life.

Murphy, Mekado. "Gary Ross Answers Reader Questions About 'The Hunger Games.'" *New York Times.* March 30, 2012. https://artsbeat.blogs.nytimes.com/2012/03/30/gary-ross-answers-reader-questions-about-the-hunger-games/.

Nyerges, Scott. "Classic Five-and-Dime Stores from Yesterday and Today." *Cheapism* (blog), December 30, 2020, https://blog.cheapism.com/classic-five-and-dime-stores/#slide=2.

Oldenburg, Ray. *The Great Good Place: Cafes, Coffee Shops, Bookstores, Bars, Hair Salons, and Other Hangouts at the Heart of a Community.* New York: Marlowe & Company, 1999. Print.

Olson, Ted, and Kalra, Ajay. "Appalachian Music: Examining Popular Assumptions." In *A Handbook to Appalachia: An Introduction to the Region,* 163–180. Edited by Grace Toney Edwards, JoAnn Aust Asbury, and Ricky L. Cox. Knoxville: University of Tennessee Press, 2006. Print.

Olthouse, Jill. "I Will Be Your Mockingjay: The Power and Paradox of Metaphor in the Hunger Games Trilogy." In *The Hunger Games and Philosophy: A Critique of Pure Treason,* 41–54. Edited by George A. Dunn and Nicolas Michaud. New York: John Wiley & Sons, 2012. Accessed April 3, 2021. ProQuest Ebook Central.

Paradis, Thomas W. *Theme Town: A Geography of Landscape and Community in Flagstaff, Arizona.* Lincoln: iUniverse. 2003. Print.

Perryman, Charles W. "Africa, Appalachia, and Acculturation: The History of Bluegrass Music." Dissertation, West Virginia University Libraries, 2013. https://pqdtopen-proquest-com.ezproxy.butler.edu/doc/1491167243.html?FMT=ABS .

Pharr, Mary F., Clark, Leisa A., Palumbo, Donald E., and Sullivan, C. W., III, eds. *Of Bread, Blood and the Hunger Games: Critical Essays on the Suzanne Collins Trilogy.* Jefferson, NC: McFarland, 2012.

Phillips, John Edward. "The African Heritage of White America." In *Africanisms in American Culture,* 230. Edited by Joseph E. Holloway. Bloomington: Indiana University Press, 1991.

Pilgrim, David. "The Coon Caricature." *Jim Crow Museum of Racist Memorabilia,* Ferris State University, 2000 (Edited 2012). https://www.ferris.edu/jimcrow/coon/.

Podber, Jacob J. "Bridging the Digital Divide in Rural Appalachia: Internet Usage in the Mountains." *Proceedings,* Informing Science + IT Education Conference (Pori, Finland, June 24–27, 2003). https://doi.org/10.28945/2708.

Poe, Jim. "A Look at Appalachian Culture and History in 'The Hunger Games.'" *Times West Virginian.* November 15, 2015. https://www.timeswv.com/news/a-look-at-appalachian-culture-and-history-in-the-hunger-games/article_2a9f14a6-8b7c-11e5-ad77-1fe4f69156e0.html.

Pozios, Vasilis K., and Kambam, Praveen R. "How Bad is Katniss' PTSD in The Hunger Games? We Asked the Experts." *Wired,* November 24, 2014. https://www.wired.com/2014/11/hunger-games-ptsd-analysis/.

Price, Edward T. "The Melungeons: A Mixed-Blood Strain of the Southern Appalachians." *Geographical Review* 41, no. 2 (April 1951): 256–271. http://www.jstor.org/stable/211022.

Raitz, Karl, and Ulack, Richard. *Appalachia: A Regional Geography.* Boulder: Westview Press, 1984. Print.

"Ricky Skaggs: The Story." *Ricky Skaggs: A Lifetime of Music.* Accessed October 5, 2020. https://www.rickyskaggs.com/bio.

Riley, Robert B. "Attachment to the Ordinary Landscape." In *Place Attachment,* 13–32. Edited by Irwin Altman and Setha M. Low. New York: Plenum Press, 1992. Print.

Rooney, James. *Bossmen: Bill Monroe and Muddy Waters.* New York: Hayden Book Company, 1971. Print.

Rosenberg, Neil V. *Bluegrass: A History.* Music in American Life. Urbana: University of Illinois Press, 1985. Print.

Sanders, Rickie. "The Public Spaces of Urban Communities." In *Architecture Technology Culture: Public Space and the Ideology of Place in American Culture,* 263–287. Edited by Miles Orvell and Jeffrey Meikle. Amsterdam: BRILL, 2009. Accessed April 2, 2021. ProQuest Ebook Central.

"Scholastic Releases New Interview with Suzanne Collins, Author of the Worldwide Bestselling Hunger Games Series." *Scholastic,* May 19, 2020, http://mediaroom.scholastic.com/press-release/scholastic-releases-new-interview-suzanne-collins-author-worldwide-bestselling-hunger.

Schroeder, Joan. "First Union: The Melungeons Revisited." *Blue Ridge Country,* February 1, 2009. https://blueridgecountry.com/archive/favorites/melungeons-revisited/.

Scott, Rebecca R. *Removing Mountains: Extracting Nature and Identity in the Appalachian Coalfields.* Minneapolis: University of Minnesota Press, 2010. Accessed April 2, 2021. ProQuest Ebook Central.

Seeger, Mike. "A Brief History of the Guitar and its Travel South." *Smithsonian Music* (blog). June 2016. https://music.si.edu/story/early-southern-guitar-sounds-brief-history-guitar-and-its-travel-south.

Shapiro, Henry D. *Appalachia on Our Mind: The Southern Mountains and Mountaineers in the American Consciousness, 1870–1920.* Chapel Hill: University of North Carolina Press, 1978.

Sharp, Cecil, and Karpeles, Maud, eds. *English Folk Songs from the Southern Appalachians.* London: Oxford University Press, 1932.

Smith, Mayne L. "An Introduction to

Bluegrass." *Journal of American Folklore* 78, no. 309 (July-September 1965): 245–256. Accessed June 15, 2020. https://www.jstor.org/stable/538358.

Smith, Whitney. "Discovering the Roots of Appalachian Music." June 22, 2016. https://www.ncarboretum.org/2016/06/22/discovering-roots-appalachian-music/.

Sokol, David, and Mafi, Nick. "31 Spectacular Buildings Designed by Frank Gehry." *Architectural Digest*. November 27, 2018. https://www.architecturaldigest.com/gallery/best-of-frank-gehry-slideshow.

"Songs." *The Hunger Games Wiki*. https://thehungergames.fandom.com/wiki/Songs.

Stamp, Jimmy. "The Architecture of the Hunger Games' Horns of Plenty." *Smithsonian Magazine*. November 26, 2014. https://www.smithsonianmag.com/arts-culture/architecture-hunger-games-horn-plenty-180953467/.

Straw, Richard A., and Blethen, H. Tyler, eds. *High Mountains Rising: Appalachia in Time and Place*. Urbana: University of Illinois Press, 2004.

Sutton, Ian. *Western Architecture*. London: Thames and Hudson, 1999. Print.

Swift, Gordon. "Learn the Difference Between Violin and Fiddle." *Strings Magazine*. March 31, 2021. https://stringsmagazine.com/learn-the-difference-between-violin-and-fiddle/.

Symbols.com. "*Capitol*." Accessed April 17, 2021. https://www.symbols.com/symbol/capitol.

Tate, Ken, and Tate, Janice. *Favorite Songs of the Good Old Days*. Berne, Indiana: House of White Birches, 2004. https://books.google.com/books?id=qhdUtDcSN60C&pg=PA29#v=onepage&q&f=false.

"That High, Lonesome Sound: A Guide to the Instruments in Bluegrass." zZounds Music. Accessed April 2, 2021. https://www.zzounds.com/edu—bluegrassinstruments.

Thompson, Karl. "World Systems Theory." ReviseSociology (blog). December 5, 2015. https://revisesociology.com/2015/12/05/world-systems-theory/.

Tobler, Waldo. "A Computer Movie Simulating Urban Growth in the Detroit Region." *Economic Geography* 46 (Supplement): 234–240.

Valby, Karen. "Team 'Hunger Games' Talks: Author Suzanne Collins and Director Gary Ross on Their Allegiance to Each Other, and Their Actors—EXCLUSIVE." *Entertainment Weekly*. April 7, 2011. https://ew.com/article/2011/04/07/hunger-games-suzanne-collins-gary-ross-exclusive/.

Walkowitz, Daniel J. *City Folk: English Country Dance and the Politics of the Folk in Modern America*. New York: New York University Press, 2010. Accessed April 3, 2021. ProQuest Ebook Central.

Wallerstein, Immanuel. *World-Systems Analysis: An Introduction*. Durham; London: Duke University Press, 2004. Accessed April 3, 2021. doi:10.2307/j.ctv11smzxl.

Watson, Gwen. "The Story of the Cornucopia: The Thanksgiving Horn of Plenty." *Food for Thought* (blog). November 9, 2020. https://www.gourmetgiftbaskets.com/Blog/post/cornucopia-story.aspx#:~:text=The%20modern%20cornucopia%20is%20typically, Pilgrims%20and%20the%20Native%20Americans.

Weinraub, Bernard. "UPN Show Is Called Insensitive to Amish." *New York Times* 4 Mar. 2004, late ed.: E1. Lexis Nexis. Web. 16 Sept. 2011.

Wells, Paul F. "Fiddling as an Avenue of Black-White Musical Interchange." *Black Music Research Journal* 23, no. 1–2 (March 1, 2003): 135–147.

Willis, Katie. *Theories and Practices of Development*. 2nd ed. Abingdon, Oxon: Routledge, 2011. Print.

Wilson, Olly. "The Heterogeneous Sound Ideal in African-American Music." In *Signifyin(g), Sanctifyin,' & Slam Dunking*, 157–171. Edited by Gena Dagel Caponi. Amherst: University of Massachusetts Press, 1999.

"The Work of Cecil Sharp and Maud Karpeles." *Cecil Sharp in Appalachia*. https://cecilsharpinappalachia.org/briefhistory.html.

Wylie, David. "National Barn Dance." *Nostalgia Digest*. https://www.speakingofradio.com/pdf/0494_1.pdf.

Zelinsky, Wilbur. "Asserting Central Authority." In *The Making of the American Landscape*, 329–356. Edited by Michael P. Conzen. Routledge (second edition), 2010.

Index